SNIPER
ELITE

SNIPER ELITE

The World of a Top Special Forces Marksman

ROB MAYLOR
with Robert Macklin

St. Martin's Paperbacks

Originally published in Australia and New Zealand under the title *SAS Sniper* by Hachette Australia, an imprint of Hachette Australia Pty Limited.

SNIPER ELITE

Copyright © 2010 by Rob Maylor with Robert Macklin.

For information address St. Martin's Press, 175 Fifth Avenue, New York, NY 10010.

ISBN: 978-1-250-00859-6

Printed in the United States of America

St. Martin's Press hardcover edition / December 2011
St. Martin's Griffin edition / August 2012
St. Martin's Paperbacks edition / October 2014

St. Martin's Paperbacks are published by St. Martin's Press, 175 Fifth Avenue, New York, NY 10010.

10 9 8 7 6 5 3 2 1

I dedicate this book to my wife Georgina, whose love and support has enabled me to follow my dreams, and to my girls, Lauren and Ashley, who inspire me every day and fill my life with joy.

CONTENTS

CONTENTS

FOREWORD

It gives me great pleasure to write the foreword to this riveting account of Rob Maylor's career in the Royal Marines and Australian Special Air Service.

The Royal Marines and SAS are both highly regarded elite military units, with countless battle honours earned from daring missions across the globe. Steeped in tradition, entry into their ranks is limited to the select few who are able to pass the ruthless selection and training regimes.

Royal Marines training is acknowledged as being the toughest basic training course in the world, with less than 50 per cent of those who begin completing the grueling eight month commando course to earn the coveted Green Beret. Those who succeed gain entry into a unique brotherhood. A brotherhood that live by the Commando Spirit: courage, determination, unselfishness, and cheerfulness in the face of adversity.

The SAS has a reputation for soldering excellence that is second to none. Recruited from military ranks, only a select few pass selection and complete the fourteen month 'reinforcement cycle' before joining their regiment.

Having worked alongside Rob on numerous operations it was clear that soldiering was second nature to him. He lived and breathed the profession, specialising in counterterrorism, desert and arctic warfare, covert vehicle and in particular the 'dark art' of the military sniper. Within military ranks the sniper is regarded as soldering perfection. Working in small teams snipers are trained to operate far from friendly forces, deep behind enemy lines remaining invisible to the enemy. The sniper will lie and wait for long periods of time for the opportune moment to fire a single devastating shot before moving silently onto the next target. This was Rob's speciality in both the Royal Marines and the SAS where he became a sniper team leader.

From the streets of Northern Ireland to the mountains of Afghanistan, Rob shares candid insights into his life as an elite soldier. Through rough humour Rob shares the loss of comrades on the battlefield, the sacrifices he made on the 'home front' and the shadowy world of being an SAS sniper.

Sean Chapple FRGS
(Former Royal Marine, polar explorer)

PREFACE

One of the joys of authorship – whether of fiction or non-fiction – is the way each new book propels you into a different world. The experience can be engaging, astonishing, disgusting, exciting and sometimes frightening. And occasionally – as in *SAS Sniper* – it's all of the above.

When Rob Maylor approached me with the proposal to tell his story, my first instinct was to decline. I'd had more than enough of war, not least because however one tries to avoid it, the very act of telling the stories of the battlefield legitimises and condones the obscenity of deliberate killing. I had begun with *The Battle of Brisbane* in 2000 with co-author Peter Thompson, progressing to our *Kill the Tiger* (2002), *Keep off the Skyline* (2004) and my own *Jacka VC* (2006) and *Bravest* (2008).

It was with a tremendous sense of moral relief that I turned to the political world of the then opposition leader for *Kevin Rudd: The Biography* (2008), and then – again with Peter Thompson – to the dusty mines and boardroom battles of *The Big Fella – the Rise and Rise of BHP Billiton* (2009).

However, in the interim I had been invited to meet SAS Trooper Mark Donaldson when he presented his newly minted VC to the Australian War Memorial, and I presented him with a copy of *Bravest* which tells the story of a number of our most remarkable VC winners. He was a close mate of Rob Mayor's, and he apparently enjoyed the book. So when Rob decided to retire, and wanted to tell his story, Mark suggested he get in touch.

Two things convinced me. The first was my meeting with Rob, who came to our Canberra home. I'm not sure what I had been expecting but it was not the tall, softly spoken bloke with a quiet gentility who told his tale with such unaffected honesty.

The second was the extraordinary response of the publishers to whom our agent, Pippa Masson, sent a very short outline of the story. Put 'sniper' together with 'SAS' and, it seems, a powerful reading appetite awaits. And when the opportunity arose to work again with Hachette Australia's Matthew Kelly, the last of my moral defences crumbled.

I'm glad they did. For this is a soldier's story like no other. Rob Maylor was born with khaki bones. He only ever had one goal: to be the best soldier it was possible to be. And that meant, finally, that he must aim for the peak – a sniper in the SAS – and not just any sniper, but the finest of all. I was delighted to travel with him in telling the story of that quest.

In doing so he opened for me a small window into the world of the Australian SAS – The Regiment – and I was privileged to relive with him that terrible three-hour ambush – the battle of Khaz Oruzgan – the biggest engagement of Australian forces since Long Tan in Vietnam.

That was the engagement in which Mark Donaldson won his VC when he ran back to rescue an Afghan interpreter who had been blown out the back of a fighting vehicle, and carried him 80 metres over open ground to safety. It was an action worthy of our highest award for bravery under fire, but it was not the only act of great courage that day; and some of them – including Rob Maylor's – have not been properly recognised.

He would not say so himself, but as readers will recognise, Rob's actions in protecting the American JTAC under withering fire from the enemy did more to bring the team out safely than almost any other taken on the day. It should be noted that he and other worthy recipients have yet to receive the honour that is their due.

It is my hope and belief that his remarkable story, as told in these pages, will go some way toward compensating for that failure, at least among the reading public. Rob gave himself willingly to the soldier's life; it was only when the mutual love between himself and his family took a proper precedence that he laid down his arms. But it would be fitting if his efforts on Australia's behalf were sealed with the reward he so richly deserves.

Robert Macklin 2010

robert@robertmacklin.com

PROLOGUE

Afghanistan, 2 September 2008:

The Taliban had caught us in a classic ambush. Somewhere between 100 and 150 fighters were pounding us from three sides – down in the green, up in the high ground and to the front of us. Two of my closest mates were badly wounded. Then a rocket-propelled grenade (RPG) exploded a metre behind me and tore into my legs and back.

Hoady and I ran for the American Humvee about 40 metres in front of us and we were getting absolutely hammered by fire. I got clocked on the elbow. Luckily I was running; that meant the elbow was bent and the bullet from the Taliban fighter skimmed off. Had it been straight it would have gone right through and I'd probably have lost my lower arm.

I could see rounds striking the hard ground in

front of me and as we raced for the car I could see bullets hitting its armoured flanks. All of a sudden it too was a target, a magnet. An American who was watching said later, 'Man, that was awesome. The bullets were chasing you everywhere; we thought you were history.' The car was getting absolutely smashed.

Hoady grabbed the door handle and yanked it open. There were six members of the Afghan National Army inside. I kept on going. I saw a ditch, a washout, about 30 metres in front of the car, slightly off to the left flank, right beside the road. I ran down towards it and threw myself into it. It was close to half a metre deep, just enough for my body to move around without showing over the edge. I still had my sniper rifle so I got down behind it and started to observe for any targets.

I was hurting. As I was running between the cars I could really feel my wounds. The shrapnel had cut into my foot, my calf, my thigh, my arse and my lower back. I was in a lot of pain and covered in blood.

Suddenly I was taking fire from 360 degrees. I could tell that I'd been targeted. There were rounds hitting the edge of the washout from every side. It was at that point that I looked down at the ground, the hard, flinty ground of Oruzgan. I shook my head and said, 'Are we ever going to fuckin' get out of this?'

1

THE HUNTER

I was born to be a soldier. I have no idea where it came from. Certainly no-one in my immediate family was that way inclined. My father had no time for the military life at all. Maybe he lost a relative in World War II, I really don't know, but he was dead against it and still is. But from my earliest memories I was attracted to soldiering.

I have always thought I had a pretty normal childhood. But one Christmas when I was very young my parents gave me some little plastic toy soldiers as a present and it wasn't long before I had hundreds of them, plus Action Man, a British-made boy's doll that came with a range of military uniforms and plastic hardware – the best toy in the world – ever! I used to make parachutes for him out of plastic bags and throw him off the roof of the garage. When I wasn't playing war with the other kids around the area, I was living a military fantasy through Action Man, my toy soldiers or watching war films that starred the likes of David Niven, Anthony Quayle, Roger Moore, John Wayne and Michael Caine. Come to think of it, maybe that's not normal after all.

Both my parents are from Anglo-Saxon stock. My father Bob and mother Sara migrated from Cheshire to New Zealand in 1964. He's retired now and living in Perth. He was a toolmaker and she was a receptionist when they married. They've lived a quiet life, not much socialising and much less now that she suffers from multiple sclerosis.

Mum seems to be handling it okay. They go to the MS society in Perth, do what exercises she can and stay in touch with the new drugs as they come onto the market. But we've never been particularly close and that's mostly my fault, I suspect. I never had a strong relationship with my father as a kid. He couldn't really talk to me. We don't argue or anything, but we just didn't talk much and over the years nothing's changed. I was happy living in my own world pursuing my own interests.

I was the eldest; my sister Louise is three years younger than me and it was the same with her – we have never really been close. She's been in Canada for about 15 years and I haven't spoken to her in that time. Even as a kid I didn't get on with her either. I just liked different people.

We grew up in Manurewa which is in South Auckland, New Zealand; a quiet, respectable area at the time. Our school backed onto farmers' fields and it wasn't uncommon to see a group of children laughing and shouting as they chased a frightened rabbit or hare from one side of the school to the other.

I never particularly liked school and always resisted learning, something I regret now. I can't put my finger on why; I just didn't like it and spent most of my time daydreaming about the Rhodesian bush war or being on patrol with the Americans in Vietnam. They tell me I'm bright enough and whenever I did a military course I always produced good results. I find something has to really interest me before I'll put my mind to it and somehow school just didn't cut it. We had a class of about 20 and I had one really good mate, Craig Sharpe, a real champion of a bloke. In fact we're still the best of mates today. Generally we'd hide up the back to muck around.

We both loved the outdoors – sport and hunting ranked right at the top. Of course, my father hated me shooting, so I had to ease him into the idea and started off with the old spud guns, which were great. But it took a lot of convincing for my father to get me a slug gun. It didn't help when I was shooting birds through my bedroom window with a friend from school, when this bloke didn't check his muzzle clearance and shot the wooden sill, putting a nasty-looking hole in it. Because I knew what was going to happen when my old man came home, I began to panic. I couldn't patch the hole up because there was too much damage. I just had to take this one on the chin. My old man went mad and I copped a few wallops for that one. I reckon I deserved it. It wasn't abuse, it was general discipline; pretty much the way he was brought up.

It didn't stop me shooting. Next I bought a .22 BSA Meteor Super.

The father of one of my mates from high school was the principal of a nearby girls' borstal – a low-to-medium security prison for juveniles – and it was surrounded by acres of land on an estuary. So we used to go down there with a shotgun, .22s and slug guns and shoot birds, rabbits and ducks and seagulls; anything that moved really. We'd take light bulbs down there and throw them in the estuary – they'd float in and out with the tide and we'd shoot them too.

Craig and I both left school at 15. I really wanted to join the New Zealand Army but my father wouldn't wear it at any price. And he's never changed.

In 2003 after selection for the Special Air Service (SAS) and a number of courses into the cycle you are awarded your beret. There's a ceremonial parade. The family comes along and it's a day when you really feel you've made it into the top level of your chosen profession. The captain who was running the reinforcement cycle at the time said to my father, 'You must be proud of your son.'

'No, not really,' he said, 'He's too old – shouldn't even be here.'

That's why we don't get on – we're just totally different. He has never asked me about the work I do, and that's okay. But I think it's sad if there isn't a bond between the generations, and that was part of my reason for leaving the SAS while still relatively young – to make my own family bonds stronger.

Anyway, since the army wasn't an option, both Craig and I did apprenticeships. This meant I left school without any educational qualifications at all, but I was unlikely to pass any of the exams anyway, so at 15 I got my driver's licence and became part of the New Zealand workforce.

Craig became a horticulturalist and I signed on for a mechanical apprenticeship in a small work-shop in Manurewa with a bloke called Roger Ber-tram. Roger was about 40 at the time, a short fellow, very wiry, no fat on him at all, and he occasionally sported a goatee. His claim to fame was that he was the New Zealand speedway champion 10 or 11 years in a row. No doubt this attracted a bit of busi-ness. Speedway fans would bring in their cars to be fixed and he'd charge them for the privilege of meeting him. Some would return, but most felt that they were over-charged and wouldn't come back.

I got on with him very well. He was very profes-sional, very down-to-earth, and wasn't afraid to tell people the truth, even about their cars. He was a brilliant mechanic, especially when it came to the big V8s. I was never going to be a top mechanic but Roger was patient with me and I crewed for him a few times at Waikaraka Park, one of two speedway venues in Auckland. These cars were built with a few modifications. The alloy and titanium space frame cradled a heavily worked V8 that was normally aspirated, which means the fuel was fed into the engine through a carburettor and not fuel injected like the sprint cars at Western Springs, the other Auckland venue.

I was too inexperienced to do any mechanical repairs on the car between races so I just ended up being the gofer and pushing the car on and off the race track with a few of the others. There was a fair bit of posing to be done as well – after all, I was working for the New Zealand champ. There was a lot of competition and testosterone being thrown around the pits area, and most people loved to hate Roger because he was such a serious competitor.

Coincidentally, Roger did his mechanical apprenticeship while in the New Zealand Army. I remember his stories at lunch time of fixing heavy machinery in the pine forests while on exercises. Generally they had to make or repair broken items, as there were no spares. Little did I know at the time that mechanics would play such a big part in our battles against the Taliban.

He was also a boxer as a young bloke, and one night while watching him race things got a little out of hand and tempers boiled over. A few of our crew ended up in fisticuffs with the crew of another driver. I stood back and watched as it was all rather pathetic. It was all over in seconds and no-one was hurt, only the odd bruised ego, but our team got a few good shots in.

Unfortunately Roger sold Speedway Automotive to a bloke named Bob Homewood, another race car driver, whose passion was rally and circuit cars. Bob was an older man with a very clever mechanical mind. He had a strange air about him and always seemed very on edge, as though he was about to explode.

It was okay for the first 12 months, but morale took a big dive when one of the other lads, John Kelly, was fired in front of me after a heated argument. I felt bad for him as he was a good worker and friend. I should have stuck up for John that day but didn't and I still carry that burden today.

Throughout my apprenticeship, Craig and I continued to knock around together even though we had separate careers. One day he invited me on a pig-hunting trip with a mountain of a man called Jim Hales. He had a tattoo of a star in the web of each hand and slicked-back hair. He had a very tough looking exterior but he turned out to be a lovely bloke.

He too had a New Zealand Army and boxing background and was as strong as an ox. In his pig-hunting prime around Tokoroa, he was reported to have carried two pigs out of the bush at a time. I'm guessing he would wear one like a backpack by tying its legs together and then drape the other over the top – quite a feat considering the pigs weighed from 30 to 70 kilos each.

Our first hunt took us to a private property just outside of Kaiaua, on the eastern flats of the Hunua ranges not far from South Auckland. Jim had two working dogs for tracking and bailing up the quarry – Adam, a bloody nut case, and a labrador/pit bull cross which resembled a fit looking lab with a large head. I can't remember what her name was but I eventually ended up with Sid, one of her pups.

Anyway, off we went and soon, legs pounding and lungs burning, Craig, Jim and I were nearing the crest of a steep and heavily vegetated hill when in the distance we heard, 'Yap! Yap! Yap!'

Feral pigs are very strong and are as hard as nails; they can carve a dog up with their razor-sharp tusks quite easily. They use them to gore and cut like a pair of scissors. The dogs hang onto the pig's ears to hold its head down, which stops it from running off, but either way it's a little too close to their adversary's weapons. We had to get there quick.

Over the crest and running down the steep hill, it wasn't long before my body started to travel faster than my legs. I could see where the ground dropped away in the distance and tried to stop. I was kidding myself! I tried to grab a Ponga trunk (a tall native fern) to stop me, but on impact the rotten trunk exploded into dust and I kept on going, straight off the small cliff landing face first in the soft undergrowth.

Craig who was behind me, fell over with laughter. Jim just kept on running towards the commotion. I picked myself up, quickly threw a few obscenities at Craig and continued with the chase. The barking became louder, and suddenly through the thick green foliage we could see the two dogs had a nice looking Captain Cooker bailed up in the creek line. It was a sow, 40 odd kilos. 'Good eatin' size,' Jim said as he burst through undergrowth and crashed the 2 metres into the trickling creek.

He rapidly closed onto the rear of the black feral animal; with the dogs at the front, he grabbed its back legs with huge hands that looked like a bunch of bananas and twisted the sow so she fell on her back; knife in hand and with a swift movement Jim had severed the carotid artery and cut into the trachea. Brightly coloured blood pumped by a rapidly beating heart gushed and bubbled from the throat. We watched on as her movements became gradually less aggressive until she lay still.

It took Jim only seconds to show us how to dress the animal and prepare it for carriage out of the bush. He tied the trotters of each side together with baling twine and turned it into a very heavy and uncomfortable pack. Craig was first up to start the extraction of our Sunday roast and it wasn't long before Craig's back, bum and the tops of his legs were covered in blood from the carcass. He did extremely well to carry it as far as he did, then with great relief Craig handed over the 'backpack' to me. 'Fuckin' hell, this is heavy!' I muttered under my breath. It wasn't long before I was in the hurt locker but I wasn't going to show the other two that I was struggling. It was about 3.5 kilometres to Jim's home-made VW ute but the terrain for the first 2.5 kilometres was through pristine native rainforest as thick as jungle. There were times when I would walk 3 metres uphill, but then slip back five; I'd pick myself up and give it another crack.

Downhill presented different challenges as it was quite treacherous under foot and I took a few bruises to the back of my head where the pig's jaw cracked me every time I fell backwards. All the time both front trotters were putting direct pressure on each clavicle, and my legs started to tire by the minute. 'Surely we aren't far from the car by now!'

When we broke out of the bush and onto the rolling cleared pastures I could see how far away Jim's ute was. 1 kilometre to be exact, but it seemed bloody miles away! Jim let me struggle for about another 500 metres before he took the pig off me. I did say, 'Nah, it's okay mate, I'll take it.' But Jim insisted; he was probably concerned about the painful look on my face. But I reckon it was a personal test of his to see if I was tough enough to be invited back.

Jim threw the pig onto the wooden tray at the back of the ute and strapped it down with more bailing twine. Even though it had gone four in the afternoon, we sat on the grass next to the VW and ate our cut lunches. Jim asked me where should we hunt next weekend. I had passed the test!

I continued to hunt with Craig and Jim as often as I could until I travelled to England. Jim was an absolutely magic bloke and very down-to-earth; he called a spade a spade and if he said he was going to do something he would. One time he got sold a dud from a dodgy car yard; they told him that if he wasn't satisfied with it over the weekend to return it and they'd give him his money back.

When he did they welshed on the deal. Jim said, 'If you don't give me my money back I'm going to drive the car through your showroom window.' The salesman didn't take him seriously. He should have. Jim drove the ute through the huge glass window, hitting a couple of cars before he stopped. The mechanics from out the back heard the crash and came out to investigate then started to fight with Jim. Bad idea. He knocked most of them out.

The court found Jim guilty and ordered him to pay $10,000 in damages, but he was an absolute champion. He died while he was out hunting. He was in his late 70s. He just keeled over and died out in the bush; active to the end – he wouldn't have had it any other way.

* * *

After John was sacked the atmosphere in the small workshop steadily got worse. I approached Bob's competitor, Frank Malia, who had a similar workshop down the road. He was keen to take me on and tried to transfer my apprenticeship to him. Bob was far from impressed by this and slowed the process down so that I actually finished my apprenticeship with him.

During this time I had made some good friends through the Manakau Technical Institute, which we had to attend every Thursday night as part of the apprenticeship. We all shared something in common: an enjoyment of alcohol. We smoked a bit of pot on the odd occasion but never really got into it; beer was the drug of the day and we loved it! It did have its side effects like any other drug and turned me into an obnoxious slob. But every weekend was a big one. We'd all get together after work on the Friday whether it was at a party, pub or at someone's house, then proceed to get as drunk as possible.

We would talk a lot of shit and spent hours crapping on about which chicks we fancied, and how other blokes we knew were fuckwits, and the way we would bash them if we ever saw them again. Of course it was all talk and just for show, but in reality, I had become that 'fuckwit' we were all talking about!

We would do stupid things like spend all afternoon in the Thoroughbred Tavern in Takanini, and then, heavily pissed, drive somewhere else for a beer. One Saturday afternoon at the tavern we found out that Billy Idol was playing at Mount Smart stadium. 'Let's go!' one of the lads said. 'We don't have any tickets,' replied another. 'Fuck it, we'll jump the fence!'

We were all in our work clothes. I was wearing a blue and white chequered work shirt, jeans covered in grime and black oil, and dirty steel-toe-capped boots. Paddy drove there in his old Holden ute. Jase, Gaz and myself were topping up with DB draught, a local beer, while getting buffeted by the cold wind in the open tray. Those days we used to drink from the 745 ml bottle and it was not uncommon to easily polish off a dozen by yourself. It was also cheaper than the cans and stubbies; you got more beer for your buck.

As soon as we parked the car at Mount Smart, and after a welcome piss against the side of the ute, we conducted a quick reconnaissance of how to get in. The perimeter fence was wire mesh and of poor design; it stood 2 metres tall and ran straight past a large row of bushes. 'Perfect!' We then watched the security guards to quickly identify their habits and routines. Once happy we'd figured out their patrol route, the plan was to scale the fence from the bushes and run straight into the crowd inside the big tent.

Next thing I knew, two of the lads were on top of the wire and just about to drop onto the other side. I didn't waste any time and started to scale the fence. John Martin dropped onto the opposite side right in front of me. It was then I knew I had a problem; my boot was caught. I knew the security guards would arrive any second and started to panic. 'John! John!' I screamed. He stopped and turned. 'My fuckin' boot's stuck. Push it out!'

Part of the wire had wedged itself under the steel cap as my boot parted the mesh and pushed through. John ran back and to my relief freed my foot after a brief struggle. In a flash I was hot on his heels heading for the tent opening. Inside we found ourselves under the steel frame of the terraced seating and began to work our way to the front of the concert. Unbeknown to us we'd been seen and the security guards were in pursuit. We did get to watch some of the concert before being thrown out though.

About then I started to realise what an idiot I was becoming and decided to start changing the lifestyle I'd slipped into. I thought about it long and hard and came to the conclusion that although you personally have a good time, and don't see anything wrong with it, you don't see what effect it has on your character and performance and on the people close to you. I reckoned I was probably on the verge of alcoholism. I enjoyed it but wasn't dependent on it. I still enjoy a beer to this day, and sometimes do drink to excess, but I don't let it 'consume' me!

Anyway, it was time to make a change.

2

MARCHING OUT

Some of my mates – John Martin, Willie and Clive – were planning to go to the UK. Their idea was to base themselves in or around London then find temporary work and when they'd saved a few bob travel to Europe. This sounded like a good opportunity for me to get away from Auckland and start fresh. The thought of travel also excited me.

So I spoke to the lads and we agreed that I'd meet them in England after visiting relatives in Cheshire. I also needed to shed some unwanted kilos that seemed to have appeared out of nowhere. 'How did I get that bad?' I thought. Suddenly it was just like I'd woken from a bad dream, and I decided to clean up my act.

I sold my two-door MK1 Cortina and started riding my bicycle to work. I bought a punching bag and started a routine of press-ups and sit-ups. I'd previously been a member of a martial arts club before I became pisspot, so I incorporated that into my fitness routine in the garage of my parents' house.

The fitness program took a while to get up to speed and by the time I was in full swing my apprenticeship had finished and I was a free man staring at the tarmac through a window of an Air New Zealand 747 awaiting its departure from Auckland airport.

I sat next to a couple of German blokes who were keen to tell me all about their adventures in New Zealand. I was 21 by now but they had seen more of the country than I had. I was quietly jealous and listened intently. All their stories intrigued me and I wanted to get out there and experience it all for myself. We got absolutely blind drunk on Steinlager and their English deteriorated into a gibbering mash. At Singapore we shook hands and parted to find the gates of our respective flights. I think I slept the rest of the way to Heathrow.

It was good to meet all my relatives in Cheshire and experience their way of life – and their pubs. I stayed with my grandmother, 'Nan' Maylor. The pubs in the UK are the centre of their social lives and you end up spending a lot of time in them while physical exercise takes a back seat. All my good intentions fell by the wayside. I quickly put on a bit of weight – a winter coat – without realising it.

Soon after Christmas I met up with the Kiwi lads in Banbury, Oxfordshire. They were renting a tiny, damp, two-bedroom flat above a hairdresser's shop. I slept on the floor. The boys were in and out of poorly paid jobs and working all sorts of silly hours, so it wasn't long before we decided to head off to the Continent. I had a little bit of cash I had saved up but was rapidly drinking through it. The others were in the same boat. John Martin and I decided we had to get ourselves back into a bit of shape and started doing exercises and running before we went away.

We had paid for a train ticket valid for a couple of months, anywhere in Europe. After a bout of bad weather John, Willie and I decided to head south leaving Clive behind. We initially travelled from Banbury to London then across on the underground to another station that would take us to Dover, where we would catch the ferry across the English Channel. But first we had to exit this station and take a short walk to the underground.

Out of the train station the air was cold and it was raining again. The roads were incredibly busy, and also quite narrow for a major city. The footpaths were also busy so we had to watch where we were walking as it was easy to catch someone with your pack as they zoomed past. I was starting to get annoyed at their lack of manners. This was the first time I had been on foot in London and I had a lot to learn. We finally entered the staircase that led down into the underground. Fortunately Willie had been in London before because he was the only one who could understand the coloured diagrams of the different train lines.

Once on the right platform I looked around and wondered just how the hell everyone was going to fit on the one train. I knew it was near as there was a cool rush of air caused by the train as it charged through the tunnel system. When it arrived it was everyone for themselves and there was a mad rush to the open doors, which created lot of pushing and shoving to secure a place, but we all managed to squeeze on.

There was a lot of tutting and shaking of heads as we took up valuable space with our packs. I wasn't used to all this city madness and felt well out of my depth. I was starting to get very angry and anxious to get as far away from the place as possible. We passed through several stops before getting to ours and it was a relief to get off that bloody train. So, wearing my woollen black and red checked Swandri bush shirt that I brought over from New Zealand and carrying the cheap and nasty backpack I'd bought from a camping shop in Chester, I stepped onto the wooden escalator to take us to another platform.

We had been on it just a matter of seconds when this bloke wearing a dark suit started shouting and swearing at me. That was it, I cracked. I swung around and said quite nastily, 'What's your fuckin' problem!' He quickly ducked into the gap I had created when I turned around muttering something I couldn't understand, and then ran up the rest of the staircase. If I hadn't been tilted off balance by my pack I would've grabbed this bloke and asked him why he was being such a wanker.

John realised what was going on and said to me, 'You need to stay to one side mate, so people can get past.' I quickly looked around and realised I was the only one standing on the right side of the escalator. It would have been handy if the boys had given me a heads up on the unwritten rules of the underground, and even London for that matter, as I was now quite pissed off, but also embarrassed as I was the centre of a bit of a scene. The steep learning curve had begun.

The train ride to Dover didn't take too long and before we knew it we were boarding the ferry bound for Calais in Northern France. When we arrived we decided to push on while the travel bug was still fresh and active inside us. From Calais we took a two-hour train ride to Lille and got there at dusk. One of the boys had a Lonely Planet travel book that suggested certain backpacking hostels to stay in so we played safe and followed the prompts from the book. Right now, being able to speak French would've been a huge help. I shouldn't have been such a dickhead at school and actually taken the opportunity to learn while I could. But we quickly picked up some of the essentials like *pommes frites* and *bière* (French fries and beer).

Shortly after we settled into the backpackers' hostel we all went for a bit of a look around the town for something to eat. Funnily enough we found ourselves in a little bar sampling the local beers. Conscious of our lack of funds, we downed several each and then turned in for the night ready for the four-hour journey to Paris.

The train ride was very picturesque but we had to change to a city line on the outskirts. When we got off we were met by some 'street people' who make their living by fleecing strangers any way they can. They prey on the young and unsuspecting and we stood out like dog's balls. Fortunately we were fore-warned. We had heard stories of tourists having the bottom of their packs slashed causing most of their possessions to fall to the ground. The thieves then had a brief chance to sort through the gear and take what they could before you'd realised what was hap-pening. So we kept a close eye on them and got through unscathed. But this was the way it was go-ing to be until we returned to England.

Our first stop in Paris was McDonald's, which wasn't too far from the Arc de Triomphe and on the perimeter of a large roundabout called Place de la Concorde. There wasn't much concord hap-pening. I can't remember how many accidents we saw but it seemed like just as the two parties from one prang stopped arguing with each other, there was another.

We found a hostel and dropped off our packs then headed for the Eiffel Tower and a truly amazing view of the city. After that we walked to Trocadero, which is to the north-west and is a large museum-type building where we admired the sights in awe. We noticed several black North African fellas selling trinkets on a small blanket, when all of a sudden they all hurriedly wrapped up their wares and ran off with the police hot on their heels. I'm guessing they were either illegal immigrants or selling their gear without a licence, or both. But they must have had someone out to act as early warning.

The darkness quickly descended upon us and Paris was transformed into the city of lights. As we walked the streets we were approached numerous times by street peddlers trying to sell us hashish, cocaine and marijuana. One even covertly produced a small sample. We weren't interested but every time we said 'No!' the bloke dramatically reduced his prices. In the end he was practically giving it away.

We decided to check out the sights in one of the red-light districts close to our hostel. There was no way I was prepared for the bombardment from pimps and bar owners trying to get our business, in some cases pleading with us! The novelty wore thin very quickly so we headed out of the area and found a bar for a few beers.

A day later we caught what we thought was an overnight train to Andorra, but the trip took two days. There were a few unexpected stops that weren't on the timetable and one train terminated in the middle of nowhere. We couldn't get through the language barrier at all at the station, and shortly after we had arrived it closed. We ended up staying the night there on the freezing tiled floor. We must have gained some altitude during the journey because it was really cold and the air was a lot thinner.

Our connecting train rolled in at 6 a.m. and, feeling like a camel's armpit and looking like I'd been dragged through a hedge backwards, I double-checked I hadn't left anything behind and climbed aboard. After another epic journey we came to a stop in the snow-covered mountainous region of Andorra, a small tax-free country on the border between France and Spain, almost totally reliant on international finance and tourism.

This suited us down to the ground as our finance wasn't that great. We were after a cheap skiing holiday, and this was definitely the place. We found some inexpensive accommodation, ditched the packs and headed for the high street to check out what was on offer.

We ran into several backpackers from New Zealand and Australia, who pointed us in the right direction for ski hire, bars and nightclubs – all the essentials. We found the little side street they described and got fitted up for a set of skis and boots each. As soon as they waxed the skis we took them back to where we were staying ready for the following day on the slopes. And after a good feed of paella we went off in search of the bars.

It wasn't long before we stumbled upon one and took a look inside. It was pretty quiet but the alcohol was cheap and flowed freely. They also provided bar snacks, which we quickly devoured. After a few beers we started on the spirits as we found they were cheaper. And no measures – they'd just pour it in. 'Is that enough? Nup! Okay, here's more.' We came up with a few cunning plans on how to save money and one was to take full advantage of the free bar snacks. Typical tightarse Kiwis you might be saying, but we were on a shoestring budget and had to make the most of our limited funds. We ate very little throughout the whole trip. In fact we sometimes sacrificed food for alcohol. 'Eating is cheating!' became the catchcry.

We met a few locals along with several backpackers who all pointed us towards the best nightclub on the mountain so, half cut, we decided to make our way up the steep road in the freezing conditions to check it out. As we got closer we could hear the music pumping and the dull roar from what sounded like hundreds of people inside trying to talk to each other over the volume of the music. This place was going off!

John stopped for a leak and Willie and I went in and parked ourselves at the bar a few metres from the door. The DJ was doing a great job of working his magic and keeping the patrons fired up. As John approached the club the DJ focused everyone's attention on the glass door he was just about to enter. John didn't see the smooth patch of wet ice right on the doorstep, and as he stepped on it his feet shot out from underneath him and he became horizontal about a metre in the air. Bang! John landed flat on his arse.

There was an instant cheer and roar of laughter, us included. John arrived at the bar with a dented ego and a sore arse and looked slightly embarrassed as he hobbled over and ordered a beer. I was falling about all over the place with laughter and unable to talk. The club quickly returned to normal and people began to dance on the tables and even the bar.

The barmen lined up a load of shot glasses along the bar and topped them all up with vodka; the DJ started a countdown and everyone at the bar helped themselves to a shot or two. We knocked back several each before they all disappeared. This went on several times throughout the evening. We were absolutely baggaged by the end of the night, and same as always, went home empty handed. Trying to chat up women while absolutely blind drunk has never worked for me. Funny that. Even my wife Georgina knocked me back when we first met some years later!

It was a bit of a struggle to get up next morning

to head up to the ski lift, but after a bit of breakfast things started to look a bit clearer. I'd learned to ski in New Zealand and these slopes were fantastic. There were several different routes to select and they varied in difficulty. By the end of the day we were cruising the toughest of them.

We took it a little easier on the alcohol that night – we were also knackered from a full day on the slopes – but the next night we over-indulged as we were leaving the following day for Barcelona. This journey took us through thousands of acres of cork trees and as we got closer to the coast we started to see olive groves. On reaching Barcelona we slipped into a similar routine as before and found a cheap backpacker hostel, ditched the packs and headed out to see the sights.

It was now mid-afternoon and everything was closed. We'd forgotten that the Spanish love an early arvo siesta, but we managed to find a bar that was open and ordered a few Bacardis; then did our Andorra trick and got stuck into the bar snacks. The following day we made our way south with a couple of Australian blokes and Anna, a Swedish girl, stopping off at a small coastal village. The backpacker hostel we found was closed, but the woman inside said we could leave our packs there until we came back that evening before we had to get the overnight train to Grenada.

We caught a taxi into the main part of the town to get something to eat, but ended up in a bar having a liquid lunch. When it was time to leave we were well away. I bought a carton of San Miguel for the trip to Grenada and the world was looking pretty good. Trouble is, when we arrived at the hostel to get our luggage the woman had locked it all up and gone home.

We could see our packs through the glass of the front doors and we were running out of time to get to the station to catch our ride, so Willie climbed up on the roof and broke in through a flimsy door. After jogging down the stairs he opened the front door and let us in. Then it was flat out to the station before someone saw us.

Safely on the train we cracked a relaxing San Miguel and looked around for the sleeping space. They told us when we bought the Eurail tickets that everything was included, even sleeper cabins, but apparently not in Spain! I decided to have a few more beers with John before I got my head down, but a few became most of the carton. So when I did decide to get some sleep the only room available was on the parcel shelf above the seats. Somehow I managed to get up there all right, but it wasn't long before the rocking motion made me feel sick. I had to get out of that cabin quick, but missed my footing getting down and ended up in hcap on the cabin floor. I did manage to get to the toilet in time, but had to stick my head out of a window to suck in some fresh air.

Grenada was truly a magnificent place. It is at

the base of the Sierra Nevada mountains and I wish we had spent more time there. The Aussie boys went their separate ways in Grenada, but Anna the Swedish girl was heading to Morocco too and decided to travel with us.

When we arrived in Algeciras early in the afternoon it was too late for the ferry across to Tangier, Morocco, so we ended up staying the night. This gave us time to look around and conduct a recce on where we were to get the ferry in the morning. It wasn't long before we attracted a few drug peddlers trying to sell their goods – hash, cocaine and marijuana – once again dramatically dropping their prices every time we knocked them back. I know these blokes were trying to make a living, but their persistence quickly became a pain in the arse.

The ferry crossing took a few hours and all went quite smoothly until we reached Tangier customs at the other end. Finally through the organised chaos, we discovered that our rail passes were no good in Africa so we had to get around by bus. So early the following morning we headed for Marrakesh, past the Atlas Mountains and through some very steep and nerve-racking terrain. The bus looked and felt like it was built about 70 years ago using the cheapest materials available. It was painted dark red with a thick yellow racing stripe along the side. I reckoned it had probably never had a roadworthy inspection in its hard life, and as a mechanic this did worry me slightly. It was an accident waiting to happen.

The seats were wood covered with red vinyl on a steel frame and seemed to have been built for pygmies. We were packed in like sardines but the locals must have been used to it; all we heard from them was a frustrated tut and a sigh. On the roof were hessian coal sacks full of chickens. There were also push bikes, and even 100cc motorbikes tied down with an assortment of twine and rope. This was going to be a long and painful trip.

We did stop a couple of times on the way, mostly so the driver could get out to a have a piss and a smoke, and we all took advantage of that. There were no public toilets, so a private space along a wall or several metres away from the bus was good enough, females included! I was shattered by the time we arrived in Marrakesh, mostly mentally knackered as I had subconsciously driven the whole route for the driver hoping we would get there in one piece.

It was just before dusk, which meant the food stalls were starting to fire up for the evening's activities. We accepted the fact that we would probably come down with some gastro complaint, but I was starving. I went for the barbecued chicken and cous cous, probably not a wise choice in meat but it was cooked over a flame and cooked well, so I took the challenge. I did end up with the shits – we all did – but it could've been anything: in those conditions an unwashed glass would've done the job.

The souks, or markets, were absolutely amazing –

probably unchanged for hundreds of years. It did get a little frustrating at times with nearly all the stallholders trying to get us into their shop to part with our money, especially since we didn't have any. But if you could push past all the hassle, it was a great experience.

We left three days later for a coastal city called Agadir, and another lengthy and arse-numbing bus ride. Agadir looked like it relied on tourism, as there were plenty of huge hotel complexes, most of which had bars and nightclubs built into them and nearly all were whitewashed. We did gain entry into a couple of the hotel clubs, but though the music was loud they were nearly all empty. The alcohol was too expensive for us so we opted for a smaller local bar.

The following day we decided to head up the coast to Anchor Point, a favourite spot for surfers. Once there we quickly made friends with other backpackers and some of the surfers and we were invited to a house that some of them were renting. They had cooked up a huge feed in the tagine using a large freshly caught tuna.

We hooked in. If it hadn't been rude we would've licked the tagine bowls clean we were so hungry. Then they passed around the hash. They handed the joint to me first and I thought it would've been very unfriendly of me to decline the offer, so I pinched the joint between my forefinger and thumb and took a couple of good tokes. We left our newfound friends' house a little worse for wear that evening and I reckon I had the best night's sleep of the whole trip.

By this stage Anna was starting to look pretty good, and when she went topless with us on the beach one afternoon Willie decided to put the hard word on her. He put in some very hard yards that night and left her room very frustrated and disappointed. She even told him to tell John and me that we weren't getting anything either, which kind of pissed on our fire somewhat.

It was a bit of a shame to leave that small fishing village to start the tedious journey back to England and Banbury. The journey was almost identical to our trip south; we did a few more overnight train stops in slightly different towns. A Canadian bloke who was travelling by himself joined us in Tangier and stayed with us until we got to Madrid.

We were sitting in a square in the middle of the city and he produced a block of Moroccan hash the size of a tobacco tin from his backpack. I couldn't believe he got it through customs in Spain as I had my bags pretty thoroughly searched. 'Better make sure I haven't been ripped off,' he said as he prepped a small block for his cigarette. He put it to his lips and sparked it up, after a big drag he passed it around and we all spent the rest of the afternoon in a state of splendid relaxation.

We stopped off in Paris for a couple of nights and I remembered a book I'd read a few years previously about an Englishman who joined the French Foreign Legion in the 50s. Even though this bloke had a bit of a rough time, it intrigued me. I began to talk to John about it and finally said to him, 'Let's not go back to England; let's join the legion.' Boy, am I glad now he told me to pull my head in. If he had said yes I'd definitely have gone through with it.

When we reached Calais we caught the hovercraft across the Channel to Dover, taking 45 minutes instead of the usual two hours. By this stage we had run out of cash; we couldn't even afford the duty-free alcohol. That's what you call 'broke' in any language.

Once back in old Blighty we needed to find work so we called into a temp agency, which turned out to be owned by a Kiwi woman. She organised an interview for John and me at a chocolate factory and we got the job there and then. It entailed packing endless bars of chocolate into cardboard boxes – mind numbing stuff, 12 hours of 24 golden foil-wrapped bars per box. We took the money at the end of the shift and never went back. I did slip a bar into my pocket at the end of the day just to see what this choccy I'd been packing tasted like. It was bloody disgusting! It must have been some cheap and nasty cooking chocolate but we were so hungry on the walk home, we both held our breath and ate half each.

As we still needed some sort of cash flow John and I joined the other two lads on a nearby American

Air Force base. This place resembled a small city. I'd never seen anything like it. I met the supervisor, who quickly directed us to the kitchens. 'Great,' I thought, 'there'll be bugger all to do as I'm on the night shift.' How wrong I was. Not only was this place huge, it was alive 24/7. Servicemen and women seemed to come and go at the dining hall all night.

Some of the major timings were the midnight feed and the 5 a.m. chow down. I whisked 2,000 eggs for the morning meal, two eggs per bowl, 1,000 serves of bloody scrambled eggs, which vanished within minutes of the dining hall opening its doors.

We didn't return to that job either, but we needed decent full-time work, something interesting and enjoyable. Two days later John and I borrowed a friend's car and made a rather desperate and uninvited trip to Silverstone raceway, a famous race track where there were permanent workshops owned by former race car drivers and enthusiasts who built, repaired and designed race cars.

After several knock-backs we got lucky and both secured mechanical jobs in a small but very professional workshop. John was put to work to rebuild a V6 Ford Sierra engine previously owned by a famous Swedish rally driver, and I began to help one of the other mechanics repair the front suspension of a Ford Escort rally car, which I was more than comfortable with as I'd had a lot of experience on them as an apprentice.

It wasn't long before I became bored with this and decided to make my way north back to Cheshire. There was also an ulterior motive behind my decision. I had met a girl – Carla – just before Christmas and wanted to see her again. She was working behind the bar at the Coach and Horses in a little place called Neston. During the day she was a hairdresser and she used to do some dancing in clubs as well. A romance blossomed. She was a good sort, very fiery, like her mother.

We became very close over the next few months and I found a job at a mechanical workshop. But I soon realised being a mechanic didn't really suit me and I lost interest in it quite quickly. In a way I was marking time – I really wanted to join the forces but timing was always against me and I kept getting sidetracked.

I'd had enough of the UK and Carla was more than happy when I asked her to move to New Zealand with me. That was a mistake. Once back in New Zealand things really didn't go according to plan. We found out Carla was pregnant and so decided to get married, which I thought was the right thing to do. Our son Lee was born in Middlemore Hospital, South Auckland, and I was at the birth.

Carla became very homesick during that time and four months after Lee was born we made the long return journey back to England. Back in the small Cheshire village we lived with her mother and her sister in a council house. Not much fun there. We started to fight and argue and things just got worse and worse, even when we moved into our own rented council house.

I was working with my uncle fitting double-glazed windows, doors and conservatories, which wasn't what I was put on this planet to do either. It was okay in the summer but once the winter came it was more like a punishment than a job. More often than not my hands were numb with cold and difficult to use – not good when you're working with glass. It wasn't long before I sliced through the end of one of my fingers and had to have it stitched back into place. The company we were working for did a lot of tele-marketing and posting of leaflets to drum up busi-ness. So it had its peaks and troughs – sometimes there would be just a couple of days work a week and then my uncle would do the odd job on the side. That was where we fell out. One of his relatives wanted the windows replaced in his house and my uncle said, 'Come and do it with me and we'll share the profits.' I had an idea of what he stood to make on the job and said, 'Oh yeah, no worries, sounds good.' So I did a full day's work for him and at the end of the day he only gave me 20 quid, I wasn't happy! At first I thought he was joking around. I took the money expecting him to call me back and tell me he was only messing around, but his van slowly disappeared down the road. That was it for me, everything went downhill from there.

My marriage was going from bad to worse; we

began to fight a lot and were slowly drifting apart. Finally I thought, 'I'm getting out of here.' I caught the bus to Liverpool where I walked into the army, navy and air force recruiting office and straight up to the army desk. The staff sergeant asked if I needed any help. A few unrelated thoughts did cross my mind when he said that, but I came back with, 'I want to join the Parachute Regiment.'

3

MARCHING IN

I chose the Parachute Regiment based totally on a documentary I'd seen in New Zealand in the early 80s that followed a platoon through their recruit training. I'd loved it. But in Liverpool the overweight, lazy-looking staff sergeant was from the King's Own Regiment – a local regiment from Manchester and Liverpool – and not quite what I'd imagined a soldier to look like. He gave me a few brochures then booked me in for testing.

I was still living with Carla, even though it was a very rocky time. She came to the recruiting office with me to get a family perspective of military life as we thought getting out of Neston might help our relationship. Neston is such a small place where everyone knows your business – it's rumoursville – and certain elements take great pleasure in talking about people and then throwing in their own twisted fantasies, so by the time a rumour gets back to you it's 10 times worse. This can really test a weak relationship.

A couple of weeks later I returned to the recruiting office and was shown to a classroom with some other candidates. We were given a pencil, an eraser and finally the entrance test. Once completed you had to undergo an interview to decide what corps or trade you were considered suitable for. Because I didn't have any school qualifications at all it was quite a nerve-racking time for me. My feelings soon turned from apprehension to relief as I was told I was eligible for the Parachute Regiment. There were a number of other units and regiments included in that list, the Royal Marines among them.

As I sat in the cold corridor waiting for another interview, a Navy chief petty officer who was working from the recruiting office started to chat to me. He asked me what I was looking at joining and then proceeded to poach me to join the Royal Marines. He showed me into a room and played a video of the marines that went for about 20 minutes. It started by saying the Royal Marines were the navy's amphibious infantry, which sort of put me off as it wasn't the navy I wanted to join. But by the end of the recruiting video I had eyes the size of dinner plates. I had never seen anything like it before.

I quickly realised that while the marines were

part of the navy, they were a separate entity within that organisation. The video showed marines fast roping from helicopters, patrolling in the Falklands and Northern Ireland, in the jungle and skiing on exercise in Norway. They were riding on rigid raiders, which are small, fast-moving watercraft with a flat hull, to tactically insert marines onto a beach or a rocky coastline. Then it showed the marines conducting sniper training and parachuting. These were also my first real images of sniping. In that instant I pushed the idea of joining the paras aside. It was exactly what I saw myself doing. I was totally sold on becoming a Royal Marines commando.

The chief petty officer then saw the army sergeant who was processing me and told him I'd changed my mind. The tubby sergeant wasn't too happy. 'What are you doing?' he said. 'I'm joining the marines,' I replied rather proudly. He asked me why and I told him there was more opportunity in the marines. The real difference is that the Royal Marines are a corps that is self-contained. Whether you're a clerk, a driver or a landing craft operator you all go through the same course. But right then I didn't realise just how tough that commando course would be. I walked out with a train ticket for 4 March 1992 to attend a three-day potential recruits course (PRC) at Lympstone, the Commando Training Centre (CTC) in Devon.

Lympstone had three training wings covering recruit training, officer training and infantry support training, plus command courses for noncommissioned officers (NCOs) and other specialist courses. The potential recruits course (PRC) was a series of mental and physical tests followed by several interviews from various staff. I had been keeping myself fit but when I was given the date to start the PRC I increased the intensity of my training and also followed a fitness guide from the recruiting office.

At CTC the testing phase started in the gym at 0600 hours. It was a huge complex that housed a large pool, squash courts, weights and cardio gym, and a large wooden-floored open area approximately 45 metres long and 20 metres wide. It was a place I came to fear over the following months.

The experience was quite a shock to the system, the physical training instructors (PTIs) were very overbearing and oozing with confidence, which made us all very nervous. The first test was the US Marine Corps (USMC) test that consisted of 60 press-ups in 2 minutes, 100 sit-ups in 2 minutes, 18 pull-ups and 40 burpees (full body exercises). A few of the lads had to vacate the gym to vomit after the burpees.

At the end of each of these tests we stood to attention and when our names were called we had to shout out our score. 'Maylor!', 'Seventy, staff!' I shouted. 'Fuckin' listen in Lofty, you were told to do 60!' I was proud of my 70, but I had finished my press-ups well before the 2 minutes was up and kept going.

Almost immediately after the USMC, and still breathing hard, we were lined up outside the gym with a physical training instructor (PTI) barking instructions in his well-practised and high-pitched PTI voice for a timed run. Three miles (4.8 kilometres) in total, we ran the first half as a squad, then the second half as a timed individual best effort around the ring road of the camp.

After getting cleaned up we proceeded to a classroom where we were given a maths and English test. This worried me more than the physical side. The rest of the day consisted of interviews with staff from various branches, such as the medical staff from the sick bay and career advisers. That evening we familiarised ourselves with the rest of the potential recruits, asking questions about backgrounds and family.

Suddenly I was awoken by a strange buzzing noise, then *plink, plink, plink* the fluorescent bulbs in our room began to warm up. I still hate that sound today. It took me a second or two to realise what was going on as I peeked through my barely open eyes. 'Get up, you lot, you've got a big day today, and it starts by cleaning the heads!' the duty directing staff (DS) asserted. I peered at my watch. 'Fuckin' hell! It's only 5.30 a.m.,' I whispered. At first I thought my watch was wrong, but then I heard other moans and groans that suggested otherwise. As I got into the combat trousers and jacket that were issued to me the day before I could hear the squeak of footsteps from combat boots as the DS made his way back down the tiled corridor 'Hurry up, get moving!' he shouted. 'Best you start moving your fingers, Lofty, if you want to get to the galley for scran [marine slang for food]! You lads can't afford to fuck around if you want to join the corps!' Other motivational one-liners and naval terminology echoed through the concrete building.

At the rush we gathered cleaning stores and began washing down the urinals, toilets and floors of the hoods (ablutions). Once that was complete there were mirrors to clean and copper pipes and taps to polish. This was all inspected by the DS when we were finished. We did this every day we were in barracks.

We all knew how much energy we expended the previous day so we tucked into the scran that was on offer in the galley. Not a good idea! Soon after we had eaten we were herded into the back of a Bedford 4-tonne truck that was bitterly cold and driven up to Woodbury Common where we were met by the PTIs. They took us through a few warm-ups which resembled a physical training (PT) session in itself, and then ran us around the endurance course through bogs, tunnels and streams. It wasn't long before I passed several lads who were bent over on an uphill stage staring at their breakfasts for the second time. The physical challenges continued throughout the day and the following morning, but by this stage some of the lads were starting to doubt their performance and were looking quite weary.

The PRC was hard going but I was quietly confident that I had performed well. And when the news came, some lads weren't so lucky, they were either told to improve in certain areas and to retry in three to six months, or were just bluntly told they were unsuitable. I was rewarded with a date to start training at the end of that month along with a handful of others from the same PRC. We couldn't stop talking about what we were going to do once in the marines and what commando unit we wanted to go to.

It seemed an age before 30 March came around, but nervously I met some of the other lads once again at Liverpool Lime Street station. Once on the train heading south reality hit home and we all began to feel very apprehensive about what was to come. Of course no-one would let on, but the tone of the conversation and the way we were all fidgeting made it very noticeable.

The Royal Marines' basic training is the longest of any NATO combat troops – 30 weeks – so we had a right to be nervous. In fact, some say it's the toughest in the world. It now takes 32 weeks to become a Royal Marine commando as they include Viking armoured vehicle training in preparation for operations in Afghanistan.

We were met at Lympstone station by one of the induction corporals in uniform, who instantly got stuck into us about being 'civvy twats' and to hurry up and get into 'fuckin' single file'. 'What the hell is single file?' I thought, then some more of the switched on 'civvy twats' started to form a line. I followed suit feeling rather disorientated and wondering what I had got myself into.

We were marched up the hill past the bottom field where the 30-foot (9-metre) rope tower, regain ropes and assault course were situated. It made me feel sick in the gut as it had pain written all over it; we'd already had a taste during the PRC. Then up the gentle slope of the main street of the camp were accommodation blocks, or 'grots', as they were called, offices, shops and the induction training wing, our home for the next two weeks.

First impression of the camp was of a low-security prison. It was surrounded by a tall wire fence curved at the top away from the camp with three to four strands of barbed wire running horizontally along the top of it. I wasn't sure at that stage whether it was to keep us in or unwanted guests out.

The camp was orientated east–west and the railway line ran north–south at the back of the camp. On the opposite side of the track was an estuary that was tidal from the English Channel and also fed from the River Exe to the north. We became very familiar with the thick, deep sludge they called mud in the coming months.

During the following couple of days they assembled us into our training troop, which was designated

637 Troop. We were 28 strong. However, over the course of the next seven months the troop numbers changed significantly, mostly due to injuries. During the first few days we were issued uniforms and field equipment and given lessons on how to prepare and care for this kit. Some very late nights ensued – cleaning gear, washing clothes by hand and then ironing them to a very high standard. The creases on your trousers, shirts and PT shorts had to be razor sharp. This at first seemed impossible to achieve, as I had never touched an iron in my life before. But there and then the standard was set; if your kit wasn't up to scratch then you could stand by for an absolute physical beasting – an extra physical training activity used as punishment to instil discipline and team building. So I struggled with the iron for ages, only to produce 'tramlines' instead of the single crease. But after a while I mastered it. Working together and helping each other out was very high on the marine's ethical list; failure to do so resulted in another beasting for the whole troop. Emphasis was also placed on personal hygiene to avoid passing on sickness, to keep fit and healthy in the field and removing some of the nasty smells a body can develop after physical exercise or living in the field.

We wore bright orange tabs on our epaulettes to indicate to the Lympstone staff what stage we were at in training. This was something of a lifeline against military discipline, since it was accepted that recruits in those early stages would make small mistakes. For example: forgetting to march around the area, leaving your beret in your pocket after leaving a building, and of course the most common offence of all, forgetting to salute an officer. We were called 'lumi nods': 'lumi' due to the orange tabs and 'nods' because recruits nodded off to sleep during lessons, particularly after lunch, due to the long hours and strenuous physical activities. The learning curve was steep and friendships were forged.

At the end of the two weeks our fitness training was in full swing: we had started with basic circuit training in the open gym concentrating on cardio and coordination. We were becoming more familiar with the corps and its history and discipline, how to launder our uniforms correctly to that all-important standard, how to march, and most importantly, who and how to salute. Not saluting an officer resulted in a horrific 'face ripping', which is a total invasion of one's facial space by the offended officer who 'inadvertently' spat all over you amid his outpouring of verbal abuse. He would then report you to your training staff, who also spat all over you during their verbal barrage.

I have never been keen on soldiers saluting officers. I think many of them use it as a tool to fuel egos and to make them feel superior to the rest of the human race. I definitely think there is a time and a place for it but it shouldn't be abused. Traditionally, to salute an officer was to show that the soldier was not carrying a weapon, it was also an acknowledgement of the commission they carry from their respective commanders-in-chief, not the officer themselves; in practice, I always felt it was respect for the individual, and that respect had to be earned.

After the two-week induction phase we moved into our new troop accommodation where we were to spend the next 28 weeks. We met our new troop DS or staff as they were called. Some were Falklands War vets and more recently had seen active service in the first Gulf War. All had completed tours of Northern Ireland, some more than others. I had great respect for these guys.

We all felt as proud as punch when they told us to take those ridiculous lumi tabs off and start acting like soldiers. We were now just called 'nods' and now the hard work really began.

We started to learn about the various weapons the corps had and how to use them. Our personal weapon was the SA80 rifle made by Enfield, which we kept throughout our time at Lympstone. I thought it was an unusual design but very capable of carrying out what it was built for. It is a gas-operated 5.56 mm semi-automatic assault rifle. The size of its barrel bore is 5.56 mm; the projectile is slightly larger than the size of the bore in order to form a gas-tight seal. When a round is fired it produces a lot of gas due to rapid combustion of the propellant inside the cartridge case. This gas forces the pro-

jectile down and out of the barrel; some of the gas
is diverted within the rifle back towards the bolt and
internal working parts. This gas then forces these
internal organs rearwards, which re-cocks the trigger mechanism. A return spring that has been compressed then pushes these parts forward to pick up
another round from the magazine and guide it into
the chamber. The bolt is locked in place and the
weapon is ready to be fired again. Just pull the trigger,
and the process starts again.

Gruesome Twosome, our second field exercise,
came around all too quickly. This was conducted
on Woodbury Common, the marines' 2,500-acre
field training area. Woodbury Common is rolling
countryside mostly covered in gorse bush, a spiny
shrub that can grow up to 2–3 metres tall. It also
has plenty of vegetated areas and open ground that
is shared by the general public. All cuts and scratches
had to be disinfected at the earliest opportunity as the
'Woodbury rash' would lead to infection. Apparently
there was a chemical in the ground left over from
World War II. Once there, the DS took off their usual
angry heads and replaced them with even angrier
ones, and over the following four days we got absolutely hammered.

Gruesome Twosome served several purposes: it
gave the DS a good idea of what we were all made
of, and it gave the blokes who really didn't want to
be there the opportunity to part from the corps and
go back to civilian life. They physically challenged

us at every opportunity. They would conduct spot kit inspections for the whole troop and throw dirty items into the bushes while giving some poor sod a face ripping. Individuals were never punished, it was always the whole troop that would suffer a random physical exercise. If the DS couldn't think of a new one, off-hand press-ups was always a favourite. Everything we had learnt so far was driven home by exhausting physical exercise incorporating a particular activity.

One night they led the troop into a false sense of security, and told us to get some rest as we would need it for the following day. This exercise was the first time many had slept out in the open for more than one night, and was the first step in teaching the marine to look after himself and his equipment in the field. The training team also hammered home the importance of personal admin and the 'buddy-buddy' system of working together. We all slept – we had just fucked up! We forgot to place sentries on our night harbour position, and very early that morning we were woken by a torrent of pyrotechnics to simulate being mortared, followed by the deafening crack of blank small arms ammunition. During the pauses the instructors were shouting orders and dragging recruits out of their sleeping bags.

As we bugged out from our compromised harbour position, some of us realised that in the confusion a few blokes had left items lying on the ground, like sleeping bags and webbing, which contained important items like ammunition and water. Unfortunately, no-one saw the rifle that was left behind by a stunned recruit.

We all suffered immensely for the next four hours. They made us sprint up and down hills with packs on and packs off; we leopard crawled everywhere once again with packs on and packs off; we practised fire and movement, packs on, packs off; all pretty hard for the lad who didn't have a weapon.

It was light when that punishment finished and they ran us back to our 'compromised harbour position' to look for items left behind. The lad without the rifle was in a state of panic. We searched the area for a good 20 minutes. We found tent pegs, a roll mat (a thin foam sleeping mat used to insulate you from the ground), a poncho, and other small items, but no SA80.

The training team moved us from that area to a gravel track and lined us up along it. They knew who this poor bugger was but gave him the opportunity to confess to the crime, which he did. He had no choice; he was the only one standing there with hands empty. I can't remember what they said to this bloke but it scared the shit out of me; my rifle was one item I was never going to forget. His punishment wasn't over; he was told to sprint back to the harbour position and collect the Elson.

The Elson is a steel toilet. It has a half decent toilet seat but the inside is really nothing more than a steel bucket. Every troop takes one onto Woodbury Common. You have to – a new recruit troop is inducted into the marines every two to four weeks, so if the Elson isn't used then you can imagine just how much human waste would be covering the common.

He returned minutes later with the steel dunny. The DS got him to hold it above his head while dressing him down once again. The poor bloke then dropped it, which spilled its contents onto the gravel. He panicked and in a flash dropped to his knees and began to scoop the shit and sweet corn back into the steel bucket. The training team were stunned! We were all stunned. They stopped him and told him to take the dunny to an admin area and wash his hands. This bloke did stay on with the troop and to his credit marched out with the rest of us at the end of training.

We continued to get punished for various infringements throughout the day and were all glad to hear that we were to speed march back to Lympstone once the field stores had been packed up and put on the Bedford 4-tonne trucks. Speed march is a run/walk activity based on a 10 minute per mile pace designed to get soldiers from A to B carrying equipment with a sense of urgency but without injury or totally flogging themselves and unable to fight at the end. The shortest distance back was 4 miles (6.4 kilometres) but we hardly ever took that route. At that moment we didn't care how far it was – we were heading home!

Unfortunately we didn't anticipate just how physically knackered we were; none of us had been pushed this hard before. This resulted in us dragging our feet on the speed march back, probably delaying the training team from getting home at a reasonable hour. The troop sergeant took offence at our sluggishness and when we reached base marched us straight down to the mudflats of the River Exe. Once lined out on the edge of the mud flats in full combat uniform, belt webbing, weapon and helmet, we began to leopard crawl through the mud towards the outgoing tide 20 metres away. It was quite a struggle battling through the gluey mud. It stank too.

When we reached the watermark we were told to conduct a series of low-profile movements until we were chest deep in the freezing murky water of the estuary. We were then to hold our breath and submerge ourselves underwater for the count of 10, which was very difficult due to the freezing water. If someone surfaced before the end of the DS's count we all went under again. This happened several times and I was really starting to get pissed off. Finally the main culprit drew on his last energy reserve and passed the 10-second test.

At last it was over. With water still draining from our clothes and equipment we made our way back across the bottom field to the accommodation totally exhausted and feeling very sorry for ourselves. But every man knew there was still work to be done before we could knock off for the day – weapons as well as stores had to be cleaned and returned; weapons and webbing had to be completely free of mud and grime, as these items would be inspected and no-one wanted a repeat of that day's treatment. We ended up taking our gear into the showers with us – probably not the best thing for the drainage system especially after you've squashed the build-up of mud and grass down the drain with your toes, but that was the most efficient way to get our kit cleaned.

Finally, work done, we got to knock off; I can't remember what we did that weekend; probably slept for 48 hours straight, a great way to spend my 25th birthday.

On Monday there were a few empty places in the ranks and we were left with the guys who really wanted to be there. The DS reshuffled our three eight-man sections and appointed recruits as section commanders and 2ICs. Each section was then broken into two fire teams of four men, nominated Charlie and Delta fire teams. I was chosen to be a section commander – a daunting thought as I had never been put in such a position of responsibility before. However, I remained in that position throughout our time at the training centre. It was now week five and we were looking at more weapons training, harder physical training sessions and longer field exercises over the coming weeks.

Week 10 saw the exercise Hunter's Moon, a survival exercise that started with a 14-kilometre pack walk (yomp) into the training area on Dartmoor. The weather was dismal for the yomp in and everyone got soaked to the skin, but it cleared up in the following days. Early that morning we were searched and stripped of any luxuries then instructed how to make shelters from the natural material found in the surrounding environment and from the contents of our survival gear.

Once they were convinced we had taken all this in, they divided us up into fire teams and showed us to an area where we could begin building our own rudimentary shelters. We organised work parties to gather materials for the construction, and every hour or so stopped work for more lessons on finding and purifying water, making and preserving fire, signalling for help, hunting and trapping, and celestial navigation.

They showed us what we could eat and how to prepare it. To call it 'food' was a bit of a stretch. There were dried worms to be crushed and made into a soup, nettle tea and boiled snails. If Napoleon was right and an army marches on its stomach, you wouldn't get far on that menu. It might have been appetising back in the Dark Ages (if you were starving) but I prefer to forage for my tucker in a supermarket. However, we all had to take part in finding this 'survival food', make a fire to cook it, and then eat it.

Then came the rabbit. One of the corporals from the Mountain and Arctic Warfare training wing gave a demo on how to prepare a freshly caught rabbit. He showed us a very quick and clean way to kill the animal as humanely as possible but half the troop still managed to fuck it up. Some had three or four goes at it; some couldn't do it at all.

After a good feed of rabbit washed down with nettle tea, we got our gear ready for the night's activities, but first we checked the snares we had strategically placed to catch an unsuspecting rabbit as it ran under a fence or into some bushes. Empty! At night we conducted navigation to a rendezvous (RV), where we were met by one of the training team who gave us coordinates (map grid references) to another point, small amounts of food or information to be taken back to our shelter area.

The rabbits must have sensed we were in the area because night after night the snares were empty and the worm soup was no substitute. Then one morning to our surprise and delight one of the snares had caught a rabbit. This was great for morale, but one rabbit didn't go far between four. Our bodies were now starting to break down through lack of nutrition and we were getting lethargic. A small bowl of worm soup and a morsel of rabbit just wasn't enough fuel to cover the energy we were expending.

As the final task of the exercise, they gave us the scenario that we had been compromised and a large enemy force was on its way. With no time to waste we had to dismantle our shelters and cover up signs of our presence as best we could, once again not leaving anything behind. Everything in training was done with a sense of urgency, so when we were organised we got together as sections again and were quickly led with packs onto the base of a very large and very steep hill. Quick instructions followed and we were off racing the others to the top of the hill. During the ascent everyone dug deep and managed to find an energy reserve from somewhere, God knows where, but we found it. With arms pumping diagonally across our bodies trying to aid with momentum, and snot and saliva tracking horizontally along the sides of our faces like a crusty snail trail, we encouraged each member on and helped the lads who found it more of a struggle.

There was no time to rest once we reached the top. A very vocal and fit staff member who ran with us was urging us to keep going. It was a welcome relief to be on the descent, but we still had to watch our footing; a twisted or broken ankle would result in removal from the troop and weeks or even months of rehab to become fully fit again. At the base of the hill we refilled our water bottles from our webbing, sucked in as much oxygen as possible and prepared ourselves for the walk out. We all struggled over the following hours but we put mind over matter and made it to the finish line.

Our bodies were going through a radical change. Not only were we looking different, but we were also becoming fitter and stronger by the day. The physical training was relentless and the PTIs always pushed us to the limit. We had all reached a similar level of fitness, but as human nature dictates, you will always get people who are naturally stronger than others, and some who will always struggle. The training program at Lympstone has been purposely designed over many years of experience not only to give you the best chance of success to finish training, but to turn you into a very strong willed and physically fit Royal Marine capable of great feats of endurance.

It didn't seem like it at the time; it felt more like a physical beasting, and I remember feeling quite nauseous before every phys session, as the PTIs just seemed to punish your body lesson by lesson. We feared the PTIs, as they were beholders of mega amounts of pain that could be forced upon you at the drop of a hat. And if you were a 'slug', you got extra treatment!

Unbeknown to us, this was a great team-building tool, and slowly we began to work together more efficiently by helping each other and conducting our own mini-inspections, also rechecking the training program to see if there was any extra kit we needed for the next lesson. God help you if you turned up to the lesson unprepared.

In the minutes before we had to be formed up in three ranks outside the grots, fear and anxiety began to creep in and there was a mad rush to the heads that resembled more like blind panic to evacuate the bowels. This became the norm before every session, and some of the noises and grunting that echoed the concrete and tiled ablutions will haunt me forever. Arguments sometimes developed as some poor sod desperate to drop his load was waiting to get into an overused cubical. Time was critical!

Week 15 was Baptist Run, yet another test exercise, but this was more like an exam on what the recruit had learnt up to that mark – testing all the basic skills but with special emphasis on field craft and the ability to live in the field. These included skills like stalking, giving target indications, and navigation. All recruits had to pass Baptist Run before they could advance onto the next stage.

An award called the Craig Medal was given at the end of this testing phase in acknowledgement of a recruit's all-round performance during this exercise. I was surprised – and pleased – to be the recipient of this award. That was the first of a number of awards I would be presented with during my time at Lympstone.

That weekend they granted us a well-earned

long weekend leave, so a handful of us took the short train ride to Torquay on the southern coast and let our hair down for the couple of days.

I also tried to patch things up with Carla over the next few months but it just didn't work out, and the divorce went through without any fuss as we mutually agreed that the relationship was not working.

4

OUT IN THE COLD

Now that we had the basics, it was time to really step up to the specialised areas of our trade. We conducted more advanced live fire activities, worked with Sea King helicopters and conducted amphibious operations. This meant we were ready to conduct ship boarding parties from either the sea or air.

A core section of the UK's Joint Rapid Reaction Force are the Royal Marines of 3 Commando Brigade. They are on permanent readiness to deploy across the globe. Royal Marines are experts at mounting amphibious operations from either helicopters or boats. This is a unique capability amongst the British armed services.

Our training included time at the Royal Naval Air Station (RNAS) Yeovilton in a mock helicopter simulating a crash into water. We were strapped inside a basic helicopter frame that plunged into a swimming pool. In the first step a crane lowered the frame into the pool slowly and when fully submerged we did the drills to exit the helicopter and swim to the surface. Once the instructors deemed us competent the final simulation was done in complete darkness and the frame turned upside down when it plunged into the pool. Divers were circling the frame in case anyone had a panic attack or had difficulty getting out. These skills would be put the test by me years later in a life-or-death situation off the coast of Fiji.

We trained with the Royal Marines Assault Squadron at RM Poole and learnt how to conduct night operations using Rigid Raiders. These are small boats powered by an outboard engine that can travel up to 40 knots in all sea conditions and carry eight lightly equipped troops or five fully equipped. Using the 'raiders' we were taught how to infiltrate enemy lines from the sea and conduct clandestine night raids on key installations such as communications centres. Since the Royal Marines were also the UK's mountain troops we had to learn climbing and abseiling, including how to get marines off a cliff top quickly after completing a raid. To do this you abseil facing downwards and literally run down the cliff face.

We also learnt fighting in built-up areas (FIBUA) as it was called then, and as far as I could tell it didn't seem like tactics had changed much at all since World War II. But I guess as the old saying goes, 'If it's not broken, don't fix it.' As always, we were constantly being tested through every physically demanding exercise.

At this stage we had to pass a 6-mile speed march to enter the commando phase of training; if successful we replaced our navy blue training berets for the khaki caps originally worn by World War II commandos. While wearing the cap we weren't allowed to walk and had to run everywhere while in the training centre, but to conserve energy and reduce the risk of injury we reduced the run to a shuffle.

Exercise Holdfast came around all too quickly for us. We had heard through the 'Nod' grapevine, or 'Gen buzz' that this was extremely hard going. It is a defensive exercise that places a lot of emphasis on nuclear, biological and chemical warfare (NBC) and the threat from air attack.

Each section needed to carry a very heavy load of stores into the field to help in the construction of the position: shovels, picks, materials for construction of the overhead protection (OHP) and as many sandbags as you could carry. We split the stores up within the section and packed them into our already overweight bergens (large back packs).

The contents of a bergen for this particular exercise included seven days rations, warm and wet-weather clothing, a dry set of combat trousers and jacket, spare socks, undies and T-shirt, gloves, spare water, spare 5.56 mm and 7.62 mm ammunition, binoculars, poncho, radio equipment, spare batteries, sleeping gear, helmet, foot powder, toothbrush and toothpaste, baby wipes for personal hygiene and to conserve water, shaving kit, first aid kit, and full NBC gear, which consisted of rubber overboots, NBC suit, gas mask, inner and outer gloves and the testing kit.

Each section also had to carry a general purpose machine gun (GPMG), which weighed 25 pounds and the sustained fire (SF) kit which included tripod, C2 sight and other ancillaries. I am unsure of the total weight, but believe me, it was bloody heavy! So after a rather painful and exhausting 12-mile (19-kilometre) yomp to Woodbury Common we stopped short of our proposed defensive location late that afternoon.

It was raining, as usual. We positioned ourselves into all-round defence, which gave us 360-degree security in case we were unexpectedly attacked from any direction. In the prone position, weapons pointing forward, we loosened both shoulder straps and rolled the bergens off our backs, leaving the master arm through one strap. This was to expedite any extraction from the hasty harbour we had just developed. A four-man recce was designated with the aid of the DS. They left their bergens with us and patrolled the five hundred metres or so forward to get eyes on the area before giving the all clear for the proposed site.

The recce team led us in and placed us into the positions where the trenches were to be dug. Once secure, we placed sentries and began our work routine. With blister upon blister, and pins and needles in the wrists and elbows, we jarred our way through the rocky topsoil. It had stopped raining for the night so sparks flew up from the flint as we struck it with shovel and pick. Soon we hit extremely hard clay, which almost brought the digging to a halt, and after a day and night of hard work removing it lump by lump through the intermittent downpours, we reached a silt layer. What a relief.

Things started to move a lot quicker from that point, and we were able to complete the OHP and concealment by day three. We still had the outer defences to finish off, which were the razor wire fences, minefields and trip flares. We also linked each pit with D10 wire and a dynamo-powered field phone, and heavily sandbagged our machine-gun positions.

The rain was starting to get heavier now and one of the lads had noticed the floor of the trench was starting to look like a shallow flowing stream. We had dug in some rudimentary drainage, but obviously not enough to get rid of the rainwater that was finding its way through the silt layer and into our pit.

Every defensive exercise I have done throughout my career it has pissed down with rain. We were now pretty knackered, and trying to sleep in freezing cold water and mud in the bottom of the sleeping pits at the end of the trench didn't help matters. So when the sun finally did break through the gloom, lethargy began to sweep through the troop and you found yourself nodding off in the direct sunlight.

It wasn't long before the training staff noticed this and decided to do something about it. As soon as I saw these bastards storming over and shouting at everyone to stop what they were doing I felt sick in the stomach. I could tell by their demeanour that we were going to get hammered again. I was warm for the first time in days and just starting to dry off nicely. I was quite comfortable with the routine we had slipped into. So I was less than impressed as we set off at a blistering pace down a nearby track to look for a steep yet open hill – open so the DS could watch everyone complete their punishment and could pick on the stragglers.

It was on such hills we usually conducted a fireman's carry or sprints. We eventually found a hill that fitted the requirement, but suffered a few punishments in between like press-ups and burpees. Once there, we played an all-time favourite of the training team: 'Pays to be a winner!' On a signal we'd sprint up the hill and, depending how charitable the DS were feeling, either the first two or four to reach the summit would be excused the next climb, or until told to rejoin the punishing routine.

Totally alert now and wet again thanks to 'Peter's pool', which is a waist-deep stagnant pond on the nearby endurance course, we belted our way back to our trenches. There we were reminded to 'look after' each other, which meant keeping everyone awake. By now it was week 23 and everyone had hit a low point in training. Morale was on the verge of becoming an issue and blokes looked unmotivated. I'm guessing this was the case for every troop at that stage in training. You could see the light at the end of the tunnel, but you still had a very long way to go.

The attack started the next night with a simulated artillery or mortar strike, then, 'Here they come,' whispered one of the lads with the common weapons sight (CWS). With the naked eye I could just make out several black shapes that resembled human figures emerging from the grey background and advancing to contact. The tension was building by the minute as we waited for the order to open fire. Weapons at the ready, I could feel myself becoming quite nervous.

The enemy were moving in a tactical formation called arrowhead, and they were coming for a fight! We could now see that their scout had diverted past the simulated mine field and was leading them straight towards us. Within seconds we heard the 'pop', of the first trip flare and could see the dull yellow glow begin to brighten as the dark silhouettes of the enemy dashed for cover. Instantly, using the direct method of target indication, one of the lads shouted at the top of his voice, 'Eighty metres . . .

slight left . . . enemy in open . . . Rapid fire!' Then all hell broke loose!

Little did I know that 16 years later, I would be on the receiving end of a very similar weight of fire that lasted for three hours, be wounded twice, and left wondering if we were ever going to get out of it alive.

At 0600 hours on the crisp Monday morning, dressed in combat boots, denims, webbing weighing 30 pounds (14 kilos) and rifle, we formed up in three ranks outside the gym nervously awaiting our troop PTI to brief us on the morning's activity: the introduction to the endurance course. In our sections the PTI would lead us on the 4-mile (6.4-kilometre) run to Woodbury Common and to the start of the course.

The troop gathered round, then the PTI spoke about the cross-country course and ran us around it, stopping at the various stages, and demonstrating and briefing us in detail on what was required at each obstacle. It consisted of several muddy bogs; tunnels which varied in length, difficulty and also water levels; steep hills; Peter's pool; the sheep dip; and the smarty tubes. The water tunnels, which were two pipes completely submerged in muddy water, took three people to complete the exercise, and were about halfway round. The first person ducked into the pipe and the second pushed him as far as he could, often submerging himself in the process. The third person at the opposite end reached down the pipe, cheek resting on the water's surface to grab hold of the first bloke and pull him out. All three members rotated through the obstacle.

This three-man drill was done for a very good reason: the pipe diameter was quite small and some of the larger blokes had trouble getting through in webbing. There was also a point in the pipe where we were on our own; neither of our mates were able to help, and we just had to hope we had enough momentum to cover those crucial centimetres.

Once we reached our mate's fingertips he could grab hold of our clothing or webbing yoke to give us a welcoming hand. It did become quite nerve-racking if the drill went a split second longer than we'd hoped. There was also the feeling of anxiety before we entered the pipe. We were already struggling to suck in as much oxygen as possible; then all of a sudden the icy cold water took away what little breath we still had.

On completion of the course, it was an individual 4-mile effort back to Lympstone and straight down to the 25-metre range, where we were given 10 rounds. The minimum standard was six hits on a very small target that replicated being set out at a range of 200 metres within a short time. For some, completing the course wasn't too difficult; however, reaching that minimum standard on the range was. If the course was completed well within the time but too many shots were dropped on the range, you would have to endure the whole course again until you passed.

Introduction to the endurance course over, we got cleaned up and ready for the next lesson, which ran for several hours. But after a massive lunch in an attempt to put back some of the nutrients we had burnt up that morning, we all became very tired and started to nod off during the painfully boring signals lesson. The signals sergeant cracked the shits and then proceeded to run us all down to the bottom field where he made us crawl halfway along the regain ropes and then drop into the icy cold water of the tank beneath. We then did some shuttle sprints just to dry off a little before we went back into the classroom.

If that gonk monster gets a firm hold of you, you will never be able to resist the temptation to close your eyes, not even for that split second when you think the instructor is not looking. I now know after instructing on courses that it is painfully obvious when someone has been struck by the gonk monster. Their facial muscles relax and droop and their eyes become very heavy. Soon after they're away with the fairies until subconsciously they wake themselves, but only to return to that semi-conscious state soon after – or they get a very rude awakening from a third party.

A rude awakening or some physical exercise to

introduce more oxygen to the body is generally the best solution, but continuing the lesson when there are people nodding off is a waste of the instructor's time.

The following day we conducted a complete timed run through the endurance course. We had 72 minutes to complete the 6-mile (10-kilometre) circuit. But first we had to run 4 miles (6.4 kilometres) from Lympstone in boots, denims, combat jacket, 30 pounds (14 kilos) of webbing and a weapon to get to the start of the course. Once there we set off in syndicates of three at two-minute intervals down a winding gravel track; not a good place to roll an ankle.

The first obstacles were the dry tunnels. They were constructed using corrugated iron and star pickets and were wide enough to crawl through on hands and knees. However, the floor had many knee-smashing rocks inside. Once out, there was a short run to Peter's pool, and its depth depended on the time of the year – as a rule it was about waist deep. There was a rope secured at both ends to help pull yourself through, but now we were wet and we had a hard slog ahead. All the time there was a DS running beside us, mostly encouraging us, but from time to time they slipped in a 'Hurry up, you fuckin' dickhead, you're letting the team down', or a very angry 'Get that weapon out of the dirt, you knob!' 'You better make sure you clean that properly before you fire it!' The DS would always make sure we pulled the barrel through before we fired our rifles at the end of the endurance course.

A short run from the water tunnels brought us to the sheep dip. 'Great – more water!' Then up a muddy embankment where your boots sank into the sticky mud. Now we started to trip over ourselves because in that very short time our energy levels had been sapped by the physical exertion and the undulating muddy trail.

We then hit the smarty tube, a small but long tunnel that was angled uphill, which snagged your belt kit, slowing your progress. Generally this tube was half full of water, making crawling very difficult, because with every forward motion we made a small wave thick with mud that slapped our faces and got in our mouths and eyes.

There was one tunnel left after the smarty tubes, and on completion of that we had to cock the working parts of our weapon to the rear and the DS would inspect it. If the working parts or barrel were fouled in any way by mud, gravel or a small twig, we would have to go through that tunnel again.

Having completed all the obstacles there was now the individual 4-mile (6.4-kilometre) run back to camp and onto the range. After an initial short uphill run the road back to camp was mainly downhill from there so we could make up a lot of time until we hit 'Heatbreak Lane', and passed the sign on the right: 'It's only pain, 500 m to go'. It was hard going on the knees but well worth the effort. All that was left was the range shoot. We quickly checked over our rifles and pulled the barrel through with some cloth threaded through a lanyard to remove any small foreign objects that would interfere with the 5.56 mm projectile. Almost immediately we were given the instructions: 'Load, action, instant.'* It was then up to the individual to take control of his breathing and apply all the marksmanship principles to put all 10 rounds into the target (or not). As soon as we applied 'safe' on our rifles the time stopped. My time was 67 minutes, and I knew I could cut it down after a couple more run-throughs. Once our rifles had been inspected and cleared from the range by the DS, we had to strip the weapons down and thoroughly clean them before handing them back to the armoury. Cleaning included removing all carbon residue from the ignited propellant, scrubbing the bore with a bronze brush to remove carbon and copper fouling from the projectile, and a detailed wipe-down to remove any dirt. Once done the rifle was oiled and returned.

We also had the bottom field or the 'battle fitness' test, to contend with. This included climbing ropes, the assault course and a fireman's carry for 200

---

* *Load:* Safety catch is checked it is on SAFE and then a magazine is placed into the weapon.

    Action: Safety catch is rechecked and the cocking handle is pulled back then released. The bolt will guide a round into the chamber and lock it in place. Sights are checked or adjusted.

    Instant: Safety catch is switched from SAFE to FIRE.

metres that had to be completed in less than 90 seconds, all with kit and rifle. Then our focus shifted to the final exercise that was rapidly approaching. We were both excited and apprehensive about it – excited because it was the last big hurdle we had to get over, and apprehensive as we knew it was going to hurt. This final exercise tested us in everything we had learnt throughout our time in training. It started with a huge yomp into the Dartmoor training area in appalling weather, which remained with us for the entire exercise. To make things worse I badly hurt my foot on the walk in, but continued on as I didn't want to get back-trooped at such a late stage. We lived in the field for the 10 days and were always on the move. We conducted troop attack after troop attack until it became second nature and everyone was completely exhausted. The exercise finished with a deliberate attack on Scraesden Fort near Plymouth. The fort was built in the mid-1800s. It was heavily overgrown, making it relatively easy to conduct our reconnaissance to plan the attack.

On completion of final exercise we were all inspected by a couple of medics. Some lads had large, bright red sores on their lower backs and shoulders where the skin had been worn off by the constant rubbing of the issue personal load carrying equipment (PLCE) bergens, and nearly all of us had painful chafing between the thighs. A few lads had huge blisters to contend with and some had worn all the skin off the soles of their feet.

Back at Lympstone the training team sent me to the sick bay to get my foot looked at, and an X-ray revealed that I had a cracked metatarsal. I was absolutely gutted, as this could mean months of rehab and the end of a long journey with 637 Troop. The training team advised that rehab was the best thing to do, but I was adamant that I was going to march out of training with the rest of 637 the following month.

To get me over the line I had to strap my foot heavily and live on painkillers when we started the commando tests that haven't changed since the original commandos of World War II. They are run over four consecutive days and are all completed with a minimum of 30 pounds (nearly 14 kilos) of webbing (when dry!) and a weapon. They began with a 9-mile speed march on roads and tracks, which had to be completed as a troop in less than 90 minutes, followed by a full troop attack on Woodbury Common.

We conducted the troop attack on football fields across the road from CTC. This emphasised the importance of speed marching as a means of delivering a body of men fit for battle when they arrived. Once we had completed the 9 miler it was traditional for every troop to march into CTC led by a ceremonial drummer from the Royal Marines Band Service.

Then came the combined Tarzan and Assault courses. The Tarzan course is an aerial confidence test of rope and wood obstacles up to 8 metres above the ground and beginning with the 'death slide'. Once completed this leads straight into a circuit of the bottom field assault course and finishes at the top of a 10-metre wall. All of this has to be completed in less than 13 minutes.

Next came the endurance course pass out, which had to be completed in 72 minutes; and finally the 30-mile speed march south across Dartmoor from Oakhampton Camp to Shipley Bridge completed as a section and carrying additional emergency equipment. I finished all the tests, but ended up on crutches and couldn't participate in the easiest activity of all: the King's Squad Pass Out Parade. Only 14 orginals finished with the troop. The average 'pass out' rate is less than 50 per cent.

I had made some good mates at Lympstone but you don't necessarily get drafted or posted to the same unit. Three of us from training went to 40 Commando: Daz and Jacko went to Bravo Company and I went to Charlie Company. We lost touch shortly after. Most of the other lads from 637 went to 45 Commando based in Scotland.

5

AND IF YOU THOUGHT THAT WAS COLD

Like many a new marine, Norway was my first real exercise abroad. At 0400 hours on a cold Monday morning in early January 1993 dressed in ski march boots, denims, Norwegian army shirt, olive green 'woolly pulley' and green beret, we boarded the coaches that were to take us to the docks in Plymouth. It was drizzling (naturally) and you couldn't see anything out of the windows because of the condensation on the inside. I was quite excited by the fact that I had only been out of training several weeks and was already heading overseas on a major exercise.

As we reached Plymouth it was starting to get light and the condensation on the windows was nearly dry, which allowed us to see part of this historic city. This was the port that farewelled the

Pilgrim Fathers in 1620 as they set off on the *May-fair* to establish a colony in the New World that turned out to be America. I felt I was heading for a new world too, and it couldn't come quickly enough.

We pulled into the ferry terminal where we got a glimpse of the ship we were to travel on: Royal Fleet Auxiliary Landing Ship (RFA) *Sir Galahad*, the replacement for the vessel that was sunk in the Falklands in 1982. I was disappointed by the size of it, as I had imagined it to be a lot bigger. It was still drizzling. Suddenly the doors opened and cold air blew into the warmth of the coach. With it came the company sergeant major (CSM) who advanced past the first two rows of seats. Everything went quiet, 'Okay lads, hopefully this will run smoovly, but remember we're dealing wiv fuckin' matelots [navy personnel] so be patient,' he said in his thick cockney accent.

He explained what was going to happen over the next few hours, and then moved to the next Charlie Company coach to brief them. The majority of 40 Commando were waiting on the dock to board. It was all laughter and piss-taking as we boarded via the back ramp and into the smell of diesel and carbon monoxide inside the tank deck. We carried on our large brown kit bags over a shoulder and dropped them into troop lots. Inside the tank deck amid the hive of activity most of our vehicles were already parked with precision – Bedford 4-tonne trucks, Land Rovers and the Hagglund BV 206D tracked snowmobile, which looked like a box on rubber tank tracks.

There wasn't much accommodation, which meant we were all tightly packed into the ship and literally living on top of each other in bunks. I imagined this partly resembled the living conditions of marines on board ships for the last several hundred years.

After finding a bunk space it wasn't long before we set sail out of the Sound and turned left into the English Channel and a rising sea. For the first two days we were hammered by stormy weather and very rough seas. I didn't mind it too much but 90 per cent of the blokes were extremely ill during that time. Things started to settle down once we sailed into the shelter of the fjords of southern Norway. I couldn't believe the difference in conditions, and in no time at all the lads started to appear out of the woodwork to walk around the ship, get some fresh air and to do physical training on the deck.

The fjords were amazing, steep-sided hills that ran straight into the freezing deep water. I expected to see more snow on the hills but it was still drizzling, which didn't give the snow chance to settle. We began to see more snow the further north we travelled and also noticed we had more hours of darkness, until there was only one hour of light a day – or so they said; it seemed dark all the time. As we disembarked one of the lads suddenly pointed out the northern lights: a slow, swirling reflection of light. I'm unsure what causes it, but it looks very similar to an eerie thin cloud. The journey had taken four days and when we reached our company location we were split up: the 'sproggs' (marine slang for new or young), me included, and the 'old hands'. The old hands had been to Norway before so they stayed in location, and the novices moved to Malsevfossen, which was just north-east of Ose where we would complete the Novice Ski and Survival Course. This consisted of learning to cross-country ski with emphasis on safety and survival in the Arctic.

One of the first things we learnt was an acronym called HAVERSACKS: **H**ave a map, compass and first aid kit; **A**lways wear the correct clothes and carry spares; **V**ictuals in case of emergencies; **E**nsure you have the proper equipment; **R**emember international distress signal; **S**eek local advice; **A**lways leave a route card; **C**onserve your energy; **K**now your limitations; and **S**afety in numbers. All pretty obvious to me now, but as a young marine who hadn't done anything like that before it was very important advice, so I listened intently.

The mountain leaders (MLs) instructing on the course gave us a list of items we needed to carry in the pockets of our windproof smocks, which they regularly policed over the following two weeks by conducting spot checks. This was generally followed by a bit of PT in the snow if items were missing. Now I was confused; I thought I'd left this kind of punishment or 'corrective training' back at Lympstone!

I enjoyed the skiing and was grateful that I'd learnt my way down the slopes of New Zealand. But cross-country skiing is difficult, and even more difficult when you are carrying weight. To lighten our person load and to take more stores into the field we used a fiberglass sled called a pull, which is pulled from the front, or is pushed from behind by inserting the steel spike of the ski pole into a bracket at the rear. This is extremely hard work and very difficult for novice skiers like us. As the ski tuition continued and the days grew longer, we learnt ways of identifying avalanche areas and techniques to give you the best possible chance of surviving one. We even conducted an ice-breaking activity: the MLs took us out onto a frozen lake and chainsawed a rectangular hole in the ice, exposing the freezing water. The ice was about 30 centimetres thick, and the hole the MLs carved was about 2 metres by 3 metres. We novices looked at each other. Surely not. Soon our worst fears were confirmed. We were going in!

Before we entered the water we had to prepare our kit by removing one arm from the shoulder strap of our packs so we could get rid of it if we were in trouble. We had to take our hands out of the straps of our ski poles and hold them in one hand, then slacken off the ski bindings from the back of our boots so we could jettison them without too much trouble. The drill was to ski into the hole and swim to the other end, then climb out of the water using the spiked ends of the ski poles to stab the ice like ice picks, hand over hand dragging your body out of the water.

When I hit the water the instant cold forced the breath out of me. They told me to keep my face out of the water so when I gasped I wouldn't take in a mouthful. The cold shock would place enough of a strain on the heart without that. In fact, we were told, the cold water would suck out the body's heat 32 times faster than cold air, our extremities would quickly become numb and the deadly effects of hypothermia begin after the loss of only a couple of degrees of body heat. So every effort should be made to exit the water as soon as possible.

No argument from me on that one. I was in and out just as quickly as humanly possible. Once out of the hole you rolled in the snow which acted like a giant sponge and sucked most of the moisture from your wet clothing. After changing into a fresh and dry set of clothing the MLs supplied a tot of navy rum. I've always begrudged having just one drink, or just one tot; to me it's more of a tease than a gesture of goodwill, but as a gesture of goodwill, I drank it.

The course culminated in a long cross-country ski and survival exercise. They split us into groups of five and showed us how to build a snow cave and soon after we had to do it ourselves. Our cave was pretty simple; we just dug into the side of an extremely compact wall of snow. We started low, which was to be our entrance, and gradually worked our way inside the wall. Once we had a decent-sized cavity we went to work inside on the sleeping benches and 'cold trench'.

Cold air is slightly heavier than warm and will flow to the lowest point of the cave, so the cold trench kept this air off our sleeping benches. But we also needed an escape route, so off the end of the cold trench we dug a small tunnel that led to the outside. This was just big enough to slide down face first. Once the MLs checked it out and gave us the thumbs up for safety they took most of our food and warm gear then cleared out leaving us with just the basics.

It was a very long night indeed. We had a roster up and running so we had at least one person awake all the time. The man on duty also had to keep an eye on the candle that we kept burning inside the cave because if it went out it was from a lack of oxygen, and in that case we'd have to quickly check the ventilation or get out. The ventilation was a ski pole stuck through the roof of the cave.

It was so cold that night none of us got much sleep. I watched that candle for hours. It was about 5 centimetres in diameter but because it was so cold the wax on the outside didn't melt except when the flame flickered and touched the sides causing a honeycomb effect all the way down to the base.

Exercise over, we shared our experiences with the lads from the other groups. Some stories were not so good. Some of the others had one of the three junior officers in who generally wanted to take charge of the whole situation and practise their skills of delegation. This pissed off the blokes immensely. One even argued that he should light a fire inside the snow cave to keep warm. Fortunately for me, the group I was in were all junior NCOs and below, and we worked well together.

We had an end-of-course piss-up in the township of Malselvfossen where we all had a skinful and enjoyed ourselves. A 4-tonne truck turned up to take us back to the accommodation. We were all so pissed that we didn't feel the bitter cold of the minus 15 to minus 20 degree Celsius night temperature as we sat in the back of the truck wearing only jeans and a T-shirt.

Back in Ose we met up with the other lads and settled into the company routine. Our accommodation was log cabins specifically built for the summer season, but they served our purpose. About 1 kilometre to the rear of our cabins was a civilian ski field that provided us with extremely cheap lift passes. We put them to good use on our days off.

Our work routine consisted of section drills, troop drills and then building up to a company-sized activity. We practised the fire and movement skills on skis that we had learnt on NSSC and gradually reached the point where we successfully conducted section attacks without constantly falling over. Fighting on skis is extremely hard, slow work and requires a lot of practice. If you just had to concentrate on staying upright on your skis you could master that without too much trouble. But keeping up with others, wearing equipment, using your rifle, changing magazines, etc and it all becomes quite difficult to keep your balance. Even the kneeling firing position can become a challenge. Once you have fallen over, the momentum of the attack is slowed down, and generally the bigger the stack, the longer it takes you to get sorted again, and more often than not a foot has slipped out of the bindings. It can be quite comical at times.

When on the move and leading the section, troop or company in thick snow, you had to 'trail break', and we all took turns at this as it was quite hard work (very good for the quads and triceps), especially when there was a fresh dumping of knee-deep snow. We had to wax the base of our skis for certain snow conditions. The ski wax we used came in two categories: grip and glide. Klister was the grip wax we used for new snow and icy conditions, and Glide wax was used for normal or slightly slushy conditions. If you screw this up you'll either find it very difficult to ascend or end up with clumps of snow stuck to the base of your ski. We would carry these two waxes with us everywhere.

Some other bits of kit we used to make life a little easier in those conditions were Gore-Tex gaiters that slipped over our boots to provide a certain amount of protection from the wet snow to help keep your feet dry, absolutely essential in those conditions. Snowshoes were good for walking on soft and deep snow. However, walking in snowshoes wasn't the easiest thing to do and required plenty of practice and expended a lot of energy. We carried these everywhere as a backup for skis. Our packs were always very heavy, generally about 40 kilos, and contained warm clothing, sleeping bag and Gore-Tex bivvy bag, rations, safety equipment, snow shovel, radio equipment, as many batteries as we could pack and shared section stores. It wasn't uncommon for a pack to get up around the 60-kilo mark, especially if you were the bloke carrying the four-man tent. I was unfortunate enough to carry one of the tents for our section for the whole deployment. And because the thing was so heavy it changed your whole movement dynamics completely.

The rations were a mix of dehydrated scran and 'boil in the bags'. The dehydes were the best as you got a more substantial meal from them; we also used to thicken them up by crushing the crackers into the mix. If our logistical chain was working properly we would sometimes get supplemented with fresh rations usually handed out by Chris, the CSM. Most blokes, me included, would take a selection of spices out into the field and add them to the ration pack meal. Curry was the favourite.

Sometimes I used to take garlic or a fresh onion to add a little more tang.

Our clothes needed to be worn in layers and not too tight or blood flow could be restricted, which would invite cold-weather injuries. Wearing loose layers would trap air, increasing insulation to keep the body warm. Several layers of lightweight clothing are more effective than wearing one article of equivalent thickness; and you could always remove a layer to prevent excessive perspiration. If you sweat too much your clothes will become wet, thereby decreasing insulation, and when the sweat evaporates your body will cool. This is very noticeable when you stop and remove your day sack or pack. The sweat on your back rapidly cools down and so too does the sweat that has been transferred onto your pack. When it comes time to move and you throw your pack on, it's like strapping a block of ice to your back – not a nice feeling.

You were constantly trying to keep one step ahead of the elements, but the one thing I found a real challenge was the wind chill factor. Minus 4 to minus 28 degrees Celsius was the average temperature range we experienced, and wind dramatically amplifies the effects of these freezing temperatures. Frostbite was a constant threat and we often had frost nip in the cheeks, which was recognisable by small white dots appearing on the skin – this is the tissue starting to freeze.

'Creamed in' was slang for having an accident which had the potential for injury. Many a time I 'creamed in' face first. We also called it a 'Yeti' because that was what we resembled afterwards. Thankfully I avoided injury this time. If the snow is soft and deep your arms will disappear up to the armpits and your bergen will slide forward, pinning your head down and causing you to suffocate. It may take a while for your mates to get to you because generally they will have fallen over too – from laughing. But once the boys get to you it generally takes two to help you back onto your feet.

Our first company-sized activity was on a day when the weather was pretty bad. The wind was very strong and it was snowing heavily. In fact, the wind was so strong that when I stretched my arms out to the side parallel to the ground, the wind blew me up a small gradient. Admittedly we were on skis, but when travelling with it we could really get some speed up.

It was this wind that was partly responsible for 'Mac' McDonald falling into a small ravine on our way back to the accommodation. We had decided to take a different route back to Ose, one that led us on a very tight path past a deep creek line. Mac was hit by a strong gust of wind which unbalanced him. He slipped and fell into the ravine. Two lads quickly removed their skis and climbed down to him. He had the stuffing knocked out him but was otherwise okay.

Sadly, Mac was later killed in Iraq when working as a security contractor. He was quite a comedian. Back on home turf, someone at 40 Commando organised some strippers and a comedian to do a show. After the strippers finished their first routine, the comedian took the stage and started his show; it wasn't long before he was really struggling; military personnel are the toughest audience to please. Mac, seeing this as an opportunity to demonstrate his own talent as a comedian, bounded onto the stage, snatched the microphone and pushed the comedian out of the way. The crowd roared with laughter and he was extremely funny, but even he couldn't compete with the strippers and it wasn't long before the audience told him to shut up and get the girls back on. However, in Norway his accident was a reminder to treat the environment with caution; a momentary lapse in concentration could be fatal.

Another company exercise took us towards a mountain about 3 kilometres south-east of Ose where we split up into sections. Mike, my section commander, was very experienced in Arctic warfare and an experienced civilian and military ski instructor. We were dressed in our camouflage whites, a white silk jacket and trousers that allowed the snow to slip off the surface instead of melting and soaking the fabric. Underneath we wore a windproof smock and trousers. We also wore our belt webbing, rifle and day sack, which contained a few essentials like extra warm kit, a thermos flask of hot coffee and some safety equipment.

Mike led us off into our night exercise and we entered a narrow valley. He reminded us all about the dangers and signs of avalanche, especially 'booming'. This is the sound made by tonnes of snow collapsing onto a lower, unstable layer of crystallised snow formed very early on in the season. It's not a good sound to hear when in a steep-sided valley. And it wasn't long before we experienced the booming of snow slabs becoming very unstable. Slab avalanches are extremely dangerous, but any avalanche can be bad.

We continued to ski carefully up the valley until we got to the base of a small mountain. We had previously applied plenty of fresh wax onto the underside of our skis, which gave us the traction we needed. However, it was a hard climb to the top. Once there we cracked open the flasks of hot coffee and admired the view and the lights of Bjerkvik. Suddenly the cloud cover came in and the wind picked up. We quickly put our flasks away and moved to the leeward side of a huge rock. The snow began to fall and became heavier by the minute. Mike made a decision to get off the mountain before we were forced to stay there overnight, but by this stage we were minutes from getting caught in a whiteout.

Just before we set off Mike issued a few instructions about staying together and avoiding injury. As we slowly and carefully skied down the side of the mountain the snow got heavier and the wind picked up even more. Because the majority of our eight-man section was relatively inexperienced in Norway, we struggled to keep visual on the person in front; and it was damn near impossible if you creamed in. But even (or especially) in times of trouble we still managed to have a laugh at each other – the more spectacular the crash the funnier we found it.

It soon reached the point where I didn't have a clue where we were going. I was heading downhill, which was good enough for me. Hopefully there were no obstacles in the way. All of a sudden I heard a worried call: 'Aarrgh, Rob, Rob, wait, wait!' It was Simmo who was about 6 ft 5 in (196 cm) and not too good on skis. He was sliding on his back and floundering around like a flipped-over turtle. This image I found extremely funny, even when he knocked me off my feet. Still in hysterics, we picked ourselves up and tried to catch up with the others by following their fading tracks. When we reached the base of the mountain we all crashed into each other because one of the lads in front had fallen over.

The weather was still poor, so Mike continued to navigate using his map and compass and led us back to the company location. 'Thank fuck for that,' I said as I loosened the bindings on my skis and stepped out of them. Navigation is difficult in snow-covered regions because when the landscape is covered by a white blanket it looks completely different to what is shown on the map.

We had earlier erected a 10-man tent for our section, so as Mike went to check in with the boss, we all got inside and got the wets (naval term for any kind of drink) on. To pitch a tent, you first had to dig down into the snow deep enough to provide shelter from high wind and to also give cover from enemy fire and view. To aid in concealment we generally arranged a white net over the green tent. A few feet down, the snow had been compressed and become quite hard so it could be dug out in large blocks. We used this to build the side walls. Once they were up we shovelled the loose snow back on to take away the unnatural shapes of the man-made block wall.

Sometimes we would also dig a trench system that connected all the tents and sentry positions, particularly if we were going to be in the location for more than 12 hours. Weapons and skis were kept outside – the skis wouldn't fit in the tent and it would be a nightmare getting out in a hurry with them. We always left our weapons outside so they wouldn't be subjected to condensation; if that occurred the rifles would freeze and be inoperable.

In the snow pit we also designated a pisser, usually marked with a stick and surrounded by orange or yellow urine-stained snow – orange because the work routine in Norway was quite fierce and dehydration was a common problem. It took a few wets to get the body back to a reasonable state of hydration. To make a wet in the field we had to melt snow in a pot over the peak burner (fuel cooker), but keep an eye out for yellow/orange snow, definitely a trap for young players.

I made that mistake once. Several days into an exercise and after a long cross-country ski journey we stopped for the night. By dark all the tents were in and admin finished. I was absolutely knackered by this stage but it was my turn to collect the snow for cooking. We started our night routine and got stuck into cooking up some hot scran. Mine barely touched the sides. I needed more warm water to wash out my mess tin, so before long I was digging back into the bag of snow I had collected. 'Aarh, for fuck's sake' – it was mostly yellow.

It turned out that while digging in the tent, one of the blokes took a swamp (piss) right where I had collected my snow. Bugger all I could do about it now. I just made sure next time I had a better search of the ground before thinking of my stomach. Funny thing was, I'd cooked for two as usual and shared the scran and wets. I can't exactly remember who my 'oppo' was that night, but I do remember he reckoned it was top scran. I said nothing.

The peak cookers worked from pressure-fed fuel, usually naphtha, which burnt extremely hot and clean. The standard operating procedure (SOP) to start your cooker was to release the pressure, pump it six to eight times, open the valve and attempt to ignite the gas. If you followed that procedure, more often than not you would be successful. But sometimes problems did arise like the jet becoming blocked, which caused blokes to gorilla fist it and force more pressure into the canister than usual. All this did was leak highly flammable fuel everywhere, but because the fuel was so light and thin you didn't realise it had leaked. On one particular night when I was moving between tents, I heard this muffled thump and an excited commotion coming from a tent. As I turned I saw an orange glow from inside Yorkie's tent, all of a sudden the flap was thrown open and a huge fireball shot out. The cooker landed with a 'thump' about 2 metres from the door of the tent and momentarily turned into a small cloud of fire. The commotion and swearing continued so I rushed over to see what was going on and just caught the tail end of Yorkie rolling around in panic and a couple blokes trying to lie on top of him to extinguish the flames.

When he emerged from under the human sandbags, I couldn't help but crack up with laughter. He'd singed both eyebrows, fringe and moustache. But because he had jet-black hair the singed parts were a light tan colour: he looked like he'd just stepped out of the hairdresser's with highlights done to his face. A bloke shouldn't laugh, I know. The poor bugger was probably in pain but the snow soon cooled him off and he was pretty bloody ugly to start with anyway.

Between exercises we conducted several range shoots and this is where I first experienced the radical effects on ballistics of extremely cold weather. The cold didn't allow the propellant of a round to burn completely or as rapidly as it should, so the correct muzzle velocity was never achieved. This meant the effective range was shortened, as the projectile was travelling slower. To compensate for this we had to aim slightly higher than normal. I also encountered other problems such as fitting a gloved finger into the small SA80 trigger guard. One of the lads thought he'd trial his SA80 on an exercise with the trigger guard removed, which worked well until he creamed in and had a negligent discharge (ND). Lucky for him we were using blanks. We also had to become familiar with alternative firing positions, such as crossing your ski poles at the handles to use them as a makeshift bipod. The lads who carried the light support weapons (LSW) fixed spare circular ski pole 'baskets' to the bottom of the bipods to stop them from sinking into the snow.

Back at Ose the wild nights in the bar resumed. We organised several 'silly rig' nights – fancy dress, usually with an outlandish theme – that generally got out of hand. The barmen came from volunteers within the company and generally didn't get too much hassle from the blokes, until Billy the 'pongo' (marine slang for army personnel) was the barman. Billy was a champion of a bloke despite his parent unit; he had passed the Royal Marines' all-arms commando course and was seconded to us for a couple of years, but this night he called last orders at the bar way too early. He was instantly verbally abused and this was followed by a volley of bottles.

The boys thought this was a great laugh and a good way to clear the tables of empty bottles, so poor old Billy had to duck and dive out of the way of wave after wave of these tumbling projectiles. One did actually catch him on an elbow, which cut it quite deeply. 'You fuckin' dickheads!' Billy shouted, and returned fire. Now I was ducking for cover. The fire fight died a natural death, probably because all the ammo was broken, and a couple of lads made sure Billy was okay. We then continued to act like animals – after all it was a Viking run! Nevertheless, we always managed to clean the place up pretty well after a good night – maybe we were just removing the evidence.

The weather in northern Norway is very unpredictable – conditions can be perfect one minute, deadly the next. We got caught in a whiteout towards the end of a two-day company exercise; fortunately we had some very experienced MLs amongst us and were only about 8 kilometres from Ose when the weather closed in. I thought we were just going to harbour up and see the blizzard out, but Al, one of the MLs, decided to lead the company back to Ose. I have no idea how he did it as I couldn't see 20 metres in front of me.

After that little experience a 20-kilometre cross-country ski and navigation exercise (navex) was organised. We went clean skin but still carried our safety stores. By 'clean skin' I mean we were still in windproofs with cam (camouflage) whites over the top, but didn't carry any webbing or a rifle. They broke us up into sections and we set off at different timings, each member navigating and leading the section through a nominated leg.

The wind had been quite strong over the previous week and we were in the middle of a cold snap, which meant most of the snow had turned to sharp ice, making it very difficult to ski on. At the end of the navex, we all met up at the top of a freshly graded forestry track. This was just too good a track to ski down sensibly. I don't know who started it, but in an instant we were off racing each other down this winding track. It was wide enough for a large truck; on the right was the high ground and to the left was a reasonably steep gradient where some of the lads ended up after creaming in then finding themselves in amongst the birch trees. Christ knows how no-one wiped themselves out.

I was racing with a couple of lads who were just as keen as me to get to the bottom of the track as fast as they could. One lad took a tumble and disappeared from view, and it wasn't long before I did the same. One of my skis caught an edge on the hard packed snow and the skis crossed over each other. I hit face down and winded myself. As I slid to a halt one of the lads stopped to make sure I was okay. I dusted myself down and refitted the ski that had come off, then continued the race.

At the bottom we conducted a head count to see if we had lost anyone as it was quite a mad dash. Happily we were all present and (more or less) correct.

There was a big contingent of US marines on deployment to Norway at the same time and, being Americans, they had brought everything: ships, landing craft, tanks, Bradley troop carriers, Humvees; you name it, they brought it. A small element stayed with us at Ose. There wasn't any spare accommodation for them so they erected their 10-man tents on the snow-covered football fields. The weather was bad but by that stage at least we had about four hours of daylight. The Americans were struggling to put these tents up in the weather so we all went out there and gave them a hand.

Some of our blokes were wearing just windproof trousers and a Norwegian army shirt for warmth. The Americans thought these blokes were not right in the head. They were probably right. The US marines were wearing white boots that they called Mickey Mouse boots. They looked like gumboots on steroids. But they had insulation on the inside and looked very warm indeed – totally different from our pussers (anything supplied by the corps or navy) ski march boots; they even had a valve in the side to relieve pressure build-up caused by altitude.

Our boots were pretty primitive, especially compared with what was on the civilian market. You really had to look after them and apply copious amounts of nik wax to keep the leather supple to stop them from cracking when they dried out. The wax added a token layer of waterproofing that just washed off or wore off with hours of use. We had to wear Gore-Tex gaiters as well to keep our feet dry. Anyway, these Mickey Mouse boots fascinated me – not very practical for soldiering in the field, but perfect for the rear echelon areas.

We participated in a two-week exercise with the rather large American force acting as the enemy, which I found to be very unfair odds. What I didn't appreciate at first was that these guys didn't like the cold, and whenever possible they would remain in the warmth of their vehicles or tents, giving us a lot of freedom of movement during the exercise. Our section came across a lot of fresh vehicle tracks during a reconnaissance, so we thought we'd follow them up to see where they led. We had a frozen lake to our left and undulating ground on our right that paralleled the base of a long feature. We used the undulating ground to conceal our movement as we tactically skied towards a set of powerlines that ran from left to right in front of us.

As we reached the powerlines that paralleled a road we looked left and saw an American Humvee about 100 metres away parked in the middle of a T-junction. The rear of the vehicle was facing us and we could see mist emitting from the exhaust as the hot fumes met the freezing air. There was also a tube-launched, optically tracked, wire command, data link, guided (TOW) missile launcher mounted on the roof and facing across the frozen lake.

Mike gave us his plan on how he wanted us to approach this vehicle. Once happy with the plan we removed our skis and the eight-man section split in half leaving a team to secure our lay-up position (LUP). The rest of us pepper-potted forward in the dead ground towards the Humvee. (To pepper-pot is to fire and move, although at this time you're not actually firing. You still provide security to the moving elements by covering the threat area as you tactically advance. It is similar to leapfrogging without actually jumping over someone's back.) Once there, Mike and I covered each other's movements to the left rear of the vehicle, rifles in the shoulder and at the ready.

The best approach to a vehicle is by using its blind spots, as the occupants are likely to be preoccupied with what they can see through the windscreen. We peered in through the rear window and could see three US marines, all asleep. Mike knocked on the driver's window. The driver opened the door with a

nod and a 'Hey, man'. Mike replied, 'We're the enemy, mate, and you are now dead.'

'Okay, man, that's cool' was the reply, and the
door closed.

When we got back to the LUP one of the lads told
us that he had noticed some smoke coming from
about 30 metres away across the road. On closer inspection we could make out a well-used side track
and we decided to investigate. As we got closer we
could see an American 10-man tent. There was no
movement in the immediate vicinity, which allowed
us to move freely to the tent. Mike opened the door
and walked in. I followed with one other. 'Damn,
where'd you guys come from?' one marine said.
'Hey, guys,' said another.

Mike said the same thing to these blokes: 'You're
dead.'

'That's cool, man. You guys want a coffee?'

We declined the offer, exchanged pleasantries
and then left to marry up with the troop boss. This
exercise was not going to be the most satisfying.
The US marines had totally given up on the idea of
working in those freezing conditions. We encountered the marines a few more times during the
course of the exercise, but their performance didn't
improve.

6

HEATING UP

We were to work alongside the US marines again on a training exercise in Kuwait after the first Gulf War. Our operational area was a town that had once housed 60,000 Kuwaitis before being blasted and ransacked by the Iraqis. The houses and other buildings were made from cheap concrete blocks and plastered on the outside. Most had four rooms inside; the front of each house had its own little walled courtyard with entry through a tin door hastily fixed into the plaster.

We conducted a lot of urban combat training there and helped train the Amiri Guard who were responsible for the safety of the Amir. These guys saw action against the Iraqis but were swiftly overwhelmed by huge enemy numbers. The massive aircraft carrier USS *Nimitz* was in dock and some of their boys joined us as we took the Kuwaiti soldiers into the field. The Americans had fitted them out in brand-new uniforms and camouflage gear complete with M16 carbines. But what we didn't realise was that there were a couple of boxes of live ammunition in this kit that they had started to load into their magazines. We were using blanks while conducting this training as a few civilians still lived in the area. Luckily someone noticed and put a stop to it before anyone was shot. The Kuwait experience was good and showed me how diverse the Royal Marines were. Seven weeks earlier we were enduring frozen conditions in Norway, and now we were sweltering in the desert heat.

Summer leave in August couldn't come soon enough. We'd had a busy year so far and it was only going to get worse. When we returned we would start our build-up training for a six-month operational deployment to Northern Ireland. The IRA hated us with a passion, and the feeling was mutual but the truth is we were the blokes in the middle with fanatics on both sides. But the Protestants were on board with the English and patrolling into a Protestant area was a welcome relief on the nerves.

Before we deployed to Northern Ireland we completed an intensive three-month counter-insurgency training course. The training camp had its own mock-up town complete with shops and other servicemen and women playing the role of local inhabitants.

On one occasion I was on guard duty at the main gate of the mock Security Forces base when a car pulled up about 4 metres away. The drill was to check any vehicle and occupants before allowing them access but when I approached I noticed that the driver was looking and acting very distressed; he was playing the part well!

My immediate thought was that the car could be booby trapped with an improvised explosive device (IED) and the driver had been ordered to drive the car into the base before the IED was detonated. I had to get him out quickly. I tried to open the driver's door but it was jammed shut. Jumping on the bonnet of the orange Hillman Avenger I stamped on the windscreen which to my surprise (and the driver's) shattered. I dragged the driver out and quickly pulled him inside the safety of the base.

All the training is captured by CCTV spread all over the mock town so that the instructors can play back videos to discuss the training with everyone. That evening they played my 'improvised technique' which got roars of laughter from everyone.

Training included riot control, day and night patrolling, covert surveillance and lots of time spent learning about the area we would working in, or 'our patch'.

The six-month tour was from November 1993 to April 1994, and our area of operations was West Belfast at the foot of Black Mountain. We were based in Fort Whiterock, which was regularly targeted by the IRA and the 10-metre-high galvanised iron perimeter fence had hundreds of bullet holes in it. In fact we stopped counting at 270 and every now and then a fresh one would appear.

The first significant incident happened while I was on security duties at the camp. I was on the upper level of the main gate sanger (a fortified base or tower allowing movement and observation from inside that will withstand multiple strikes from small arms fire and small explosions like grenades) as 8 Troop were about to start their night patrolling program. After checking their equipment and actioning their rifles, the first brick (a four-man patrol) started to hard target (hard target is running and zigzagging or even constantly moving and changing position and body profile to make yourself less of a target) down the 150-metre access route to Springfield Road and into the notoriously dangerous Turf Lodge area. Ten minutes later I saw a flash that for a split second I thought was lightning. Actually it was an IED attack on one of the four bricks that had just left Whiterock.

The blast destroyed a gate and blew two members of that brick across the road and into a front garden. I actioned my weapon and reported the blast. Fortunately no-one was badly hurt and after some medical care and a couple of weeks off the guys returned to work.

There were countless incidents while patrolling the streets of West Belfast. We were spat on and pelted with bricks, bottles, broken glass, rocks, wood and anything else they could get their hands on. On one occasion while night patrolling in a lightly armoured Land Rover I narrowly missed being hit in the face by a bottle that was thrown from a group looking for trouble. As we drove past them we copped mega amounts of abuse, so I turned to change my arcs to cover their movements. 'Bang!' The bottle smashed right in front of my face on the spring-loaded Perspex shield that I was just about to push down. There wasn't a lot we could do in that situation and the locals knew it. We were there to support the Royal Ulster Constabulary (RUC), and that was more of a police issue.

While the Catholics were supposed to be the bad guys it was a Protestant that caused us the most grief – one John Adair, the head of the so-called Ulster Freedom Fighters (UFF). He had strong links with Del, one of the lads from 8 Troop. Del was a Protestant originally from Northern Ireland, and for him the conflict was personal. And it wasn't long before he put himself in a very compromising situation. Unbeknown to the rest of us, Adair had approached him and the two had come to an agreement. Soon Del was tipping him off about our movements. Adair would then organise to attack the IRA or a Sinn Fein office shortly after we patrolled past it.

The first attack was a drive-by shooting on a

known 'player' (IRA member) at a bus stop. A large number of rounds hit the shelter but no-one was injured. Then they launched two attacks on the Sinn Fein office on Andersonstown Road. On the first occasion, shortly after we had patrolled past it, a vehicle stopped and a UFF member exited and rigged up an old grenade on trip to the main gate of the office. The grenade fuse was set on instant and would have immediately detonated when the gate was opened and pin pulled. Luckily, it was found before it caused any damage. The second time they attacked that office they waited for us to get a fair way away. The UFF then drove up to the front of the office and fired an AK47 at one of the players who was on a ladder doing some repairs to the outside of the building. He was hit several times in the legs.

We reacted to the incident but once again got there too late. Suspicions were aroused and Del was placed under surveillance after he spent his leave with John Adair. He was arrested when he returned to Fort Whiterock, and spent the next five years in prison. Del was a well-liked bloke in Charlie Company and we were all shocked to hear of his arrest and the details why. As a whole we didn't condemn his actions; in fact, he gained even more respect from us even though it was the wrong thing to do.

Adair and his Protestant mates were pretty hopeless. They were the only ones who could fire 30 rounds into a crowded bar and not hit anyone! They fired an RPG at a pub on the Falls Road and the grenade hit the roof. We did find this quite funny though.

We reacted to an incident in our area of operations involving the parachute regiment. One of their vehicles was targeted by a MK16 mortar. These mortars were home-made and laid horizontally on a milk crate or some other platform that could support it to get it on target, and could be detonated from as far as 400 metres away. We provided some support and cordoned off the area to provide security and preserve the scene for forensics.

During these cordons we searched areas and people, set up vehicle checkpoints and did our best to provide security. An incident like this generally lasted a minimum of four hours, although we provided one cordon that lasted 12 hours and we had to be replaced by the other troop. They were tough on the nerves because at any time you could become a target.

In another incident a 16-year-old boy had been 'kneecapped' in both knees with a .22-calibre rifle for stealing the wrong car. He was lured to a park then given the good news. We arrived on the scene as he was crawling backwards towards his house.

A house invasion took place while we were patrolling on foot in a particular area. They bound and gagged the occupants and then set up a firing position in a room on the second storey of the house where the window faced Kennedy Way, an uphill road. They planned to carry out a 'sniper' shoot onto one of our patrols; in fact the patrol happened to be the one I was in.

As soon as we entered Kennedy Way and started to walk up the hill the hairs on the back of my neck stood on end. I was one of the two rear men in that four-man brick. The other was Grenville 'Wadders' Waddington, who later said he also felt something unusual. This wasn't the first time I'd had this feeling so I became extra vigilant. Maybe I'd developed a soldier's instinct. But we covered each other by pepper-potting, rifles at the ready as we moved up Kennedy Way and out of view from the window of that house.

Back at Fort Whiterock it wasn't long before they told us what had happened. The occupants of the house were held under guard but near enough to the shooters to hear what they were saying. Apparently they were too scared to initiate a contact on either of us as we were covering each other too well. They could have compromised their position and got caught, or more likely, shot.

On another occasion while our four bricks were patrolling along Glen Road at night, one of the section commanders, Paul Ashcroft, found a freshly placed MK16 mortar sitting on a milk crate at the top of Ramoan Gardens orientated towards Glen Road. It was placed to hit either military or RUC vehicles that were in the area. We set up a quick cordon and two bricks aggressively followed up the command wire that was part of the firing device. All the signs were fresh, but the bad guys had disappeared.

That morning we finished our patrolling program and were picked up by the quick reaction force (QRF) using a Saxon four-wheel-drive armoured vehicle. These guys were on constant standby at Fort Whiterock. They would deploy if there was an incident and a multiple required their help. (A multiple consisted of four bricks usually with two RUC constables.) We could also use the QRF for pick-up and drop-off. This particular morning after being picked up, shattered by the intense patrolling program, we were travelling uphill in the back of the Saxon on the Monagh Bypass towards Fort Whiterock. The Mike Echoes – the military escort for the RUC – were travelling downhill in their Land Rovers at the same time. As we passed each other a MK16 mortar was fired from the side of the road and narrowly missed the rear of our vehicle but it glanced off the windscreen of the lead Land Rover. The windscreen was cracked and the mortar landed somewhere in the vacant land opposite.

I didn't realise we had been targeted until I heard the troop boss shout, 'Contact!' We debussed and contained the area the best we could. The boys traced the command wire back to a well-known player's address. I felt extremely lucky after that as

I'd been sitting on the right side of the vehicle with my back to the incoming mortar.

For us in the middle of the Troubles it was a test of nerves. It was so volatile – you could incite a crowd with just the wrong eye contact and suddenly you'd have an angry mob advancing at you throwing bricks, bottles and stones. They worked on the fact that if they didn't have a firearm we couldn't shoot them, and they knew our hands were tied by a set of very tight rules of engagement. So we had to be extremely careful how we treated a violent situation.

If one of the lads did slightly overstep the mark through sheer frustration, the mob would retaliate by becoming even more violent. If a civilian was hurt in any way it would give them licence to twist the truth and to extract maximum amount of compensation from the British Government, and of course there were always plenty of witnesses.

Most of the time we were ordered to cautiously move away from a mob and let it die a natural death without ruining public relations. But a few times we had to call on the RUC to assist in dispersing a persistent crowd. This was extremely frustrating for us, because as soldiers we didn't want to be seen to be weak and walking away from trouble. It is very understandable to me why soldiers serving in Northern Ireland or even veterans crack every once in a while. It was, however, very satisfying to catch one of these serial troublemakers out when he found himself in the wrong spot at the wrong time. I was glad to see the back end of that tour as it was very busy and wearing very thin towards the end.

I made some extremely good mates at 40 Commando. 'Chappy' was one of them. He was in 9 Troop, Charlie Company, and is now a well-known polar explorer. He asked me to do an expedition with him that he called the Icelandic 500 – the first ever ski crossing of Iceland towing sledges weighing up to 90 kilos, which carried the necessary equipment and rations to survive the harsh winter crossing. I said I was more interested in soldiering, but Chappy went on to complete the first military expeditions to the north and south poles. In 1993 Chappy and I went to Kenya and stayed with George Aggett, an ex-bootneck (slang for marine) and good friend of Chappy, on his farm that looks at Mount Kenya on the horizon, a truly magnificent view. George took us hunting a few times and fishing at their huge dam. At night there was no TV and they very rarely listened to the radio. So we mostly drank Tusker beer and spun a few yarns. While there Chappy and I took advantage of our location and travelled to Uganda and Zaire. We also saw the gorillas in the mountains before they were butchered by rebels coming through from Rwanda.

Chappy is quite a character and extremely confident in his soldiering ability. He is also a terrific leader. In our bar one night in Norway it was young AJ Smith's 21st birthday. As 9 Troop's senior corporal, Chappy decided to make him a 'death wet' – a pint glass filled with an assortment of spirits. There was a little ceremony that accompanied the death wet and everyone shouting, 'Scull, scull, scull!'

AJ knocked back the concoction in one hit and it wasn't long before he started to turn green and was handed a bucket. The death wet resurfaced along with his dinner into the blue plastic bucket. Chappy, being the tightarse he is, decided not to waste the pint of spirits they'd paid for and encouraged the 9 Troop lads to drink the contents of the bucket. In fact, Chappy went first and knocked back a decent mouthful. Some of the contents stuck to his moustache, which made him look like a kid after drinking a glass of milk. He then proceeded to lick his moustache and then chew on the piece of tomato skin that was stuck in it.

I watched from another table and physically had to stop myself from being sick. Once the bucket had gone around, Chappy had another crack at it, and then offered it to the rest of the lads in the bar. He got no takers. 'Stick it up ya fuckin' arse, Chappy!' And 'You're sick mate!' is all he got.

Chappy was like me. We both lived by the Royal Marines' ethos of 'work hard, play hard'. Later in Chappy's career in the marines he became an officer.

In Norway, we had a company dining-in night – 'top table' as it was called – and the theme was 'formal suit'. Of course we didn't have any formal clobber, as we were deployed on a three-month exercise. So the blokes decided to raid the Q store of all their large black plastic bin liners and make dinner suits from them. Some put tremendous amounts of thought into making these, and some didn't. But it didn't matter; everyone had a suit.

One of the rules for a top table is that you cannot leave the table until you either have permission from the OC, or until all the formalities are completed. So the lads stocked up on beer and got stuck into it well before the event. Within minutes of sitting down at the table a bucket was being passed around underneath it so blokes could relieve themselves. Some couldn't wait and just went where they sat. One of the blokes used an empty wine bottle that was promptly passed up to the OC. We all urged him to have a swig, which to my disbelief he did. He then spat the contents back into the bottle and gave us a look of horror and disgust while wagging his finger.

I thought, 'You dickhead.' If someone hands you a very warm wine bottle and tries to get you to drink it, there's obviously something wrong with it; all the combat indicators were present to suggest it wasn't wine, but something else. This was the same dickhead who jumped off a wharf during that trip to get out of a major field exercise – he made it look like he fell! Being wet in Norway can be extremely life threatening, so the OC was whisked away to a nearby hotel for a warm bath and change of clothes.

Another mate was Big Thomo; I can't remember

his first name as it was never used but he was a hard man to handle when roused with the drink. I remember walking out of Kingstons night club near the base in Taunton, Somerset, one night when we had returned from Norway, and seeing Thomo sitting on this civvy's chest pounding him in the face. The shots he was delivering were rather pathetic so we just had a giggle and carried on to Lotus Flower, a Thai takeaway.

Alcohol in Norway was ridiculously priced and being underpaid British soldiers we couldn't afford the crazy £5 a pint it used to cost. So we would buy one or two and then conduct an exercise called 'mine sweeping'. This involved identifying a reasonably full pint that was unattended or not being closely guarded by a local Norwegian, and then swiping it for our own consumption.

One night in a bar in Bjerkvik, Big Thomo got caught. (C Company had two Thomos, so we called one Big Thomo and the other Little Thomo.) The bar erupted. I remember Thomo planting one on this bloke and then it was all in since naturally we had to support him. Next thing I felt a big bang on my face and I was dragged out of the bar and thrown into the back of a Land Rover, Thomo followed a few seconds later. There were four of us in the back of that freezing Land Rover all the way back to Ose. The vehicle commander was one of our own from another unit. He was on what the corps called 'shore patrol' making sure we kept out of trouble.

He wasn't happy with our performance but did the right thing and got us out of there as the local police had been called. I'll never forget that 30-minute drive back to Ose; the temperature was below minus 10 and all that was separating us from the elements was the canvas tarp.

Before Thomo joined the corps he used to work as an entertainer: he played the guitar and sang. One weekend during summer leave 12 of us, 'the orphans' as we called ourselves, decided to spend some time at the Butlins holiday camp in Minehead. This was about 45 minutes drive from Taunton. We all arrived together and were actually turned away at the gate by security. However, one of the guards did the right thing and said if we were to come back in twos and threes they would give us a pass until midnight.

Once inside we had a few beers while watching a cabaret show, then Thomo decided he was going to get up on stage and do a rendition of Frank Sinatra's 'New York, New York'. To my surprise he was very good. However, 2 a.m. came around all too quickly and we'd had a skinful. A big fight started and all 12 of us got stuck in. At one stage Big Thomo went to headbutt this bloke, but because Thomo really is quite 'unco' he telegraphed his intentions that told this bloke what he was about to do. So the bloke moved out of the way and Thomo became unbalanced. His front foot slipped forward on the wet floor and he somehow ended up on his back. His opponent then jumped on his chest and made a pathetic attempt to strangle him. Thomo looked over at Little Thomo and me and said rather calmly, 'Would someone get this fuckin' lemon off me?' We obliged.

The police arrived shortly after and all 12 of us made a run for it. Pete and I ran towards the beach, crossing the road and jumped off the wall and into the sand. We heard a police officer shouting behind us. Fortunately the tide was out so we were able to lie in the night shadows cast by the rocks at the low-tide mark. The police officer stood on the wall and shone his torch along the beach but soon gave up. Big Thomo lost his wallet and military ID card during the fight and sheepishly had to return the following day to retrieve it.

Friday mornings at 1100 hours we always had 'rounds' – an inspection of the accommodation by the CSM and the OC – before we knocked off for the weekend. As rounds were being conducted we had to stand at ease by our beds in uniform until brought to attention by a senior corporal who then reported the accommodation ready to inspect. This time the CSM and OC were accompanied by the regimental sergeant major (RSM) and the commanding officer (CO) of 40 Commando, known as 'the Moose'. Thomo always ran his own routine, and on this particular morning he got caught out. We were all standing at ease when we heard the door burst open followed by a loud 'Oi, fat arse!' Thomo had just finished in the shower and met the inspection team head on. His only escape route was through our grots. He sprinted straight towards the fire escape at the far end of our room completely naked with towel in hand. As he ran through with the RSM hot on his heels his thongs flew off, making the RSM stumble momentarily. Thomo got through the fire escape and was gone. The RSM was wild. He turned to us furiously shaking and pointing his pace stick randomly. 'Who was that fat cunt?' he shouted. We denied everything and struggled immensely to stop ourselves from laughing.

But while we played hard, we prided ourselves on our professionalism in the field. On the whole, the Royal Marines are good hard soldiers and cheeky bastards who were always up for a laugh. In fact, one of them, Matt Howley – or H as he is called – did me the greatest favour of my life.

I first met H when I marched in to Charlie Company at 40 Commando. I instantly liked him as he had a 'no bullshit' attitude and was a quiet but very professional soldier. H played a lot of rugby for the marines and his local club. And, being a Kiwi, it's in my nature so I was happy to join him in the team. A few times when we were ashore (marine slang for off base), usually at Kingstons night club I had noticed his sister Georgina. By that stage I was usually blind drunk and making a fool of myself. I was really attracted to her – she was beautiful, blonde and very bright – but she must have thought I was a drunken idiot.

I returned to New Zealand in 1994 on leave and suddenly found myself in a different world. It was like getting my freedom back. I realised what a lovely place it was and for the first time in ages I didn't feel constricted. I'm not a fan of crowds or heavily populated areas. I love the open spaces and going back to New Zealand made me realise what I was missing. While there I spent most of my time hunting and fishing and got part of my life back. It was like two separate worlds. But there was one thing missing: Georgina.

Soon after I returned to England I was placed on restriction of privileges (RPs), a form of punishment given to soldiers designed to screw you around from 6 a.m. until 10 p.m. on each day of your sentence. I'd received five days RPs after a drunken scuffle in the accommodation at Norton Manor and caused £150 damage to a door after kicking it open when a bloke locked it in my face.

Charlie Company was on guard duty at the time so I didn't get too much grief from the guard commanders especially when H was the guard 2IC. I was up at the guard room in full combat equipment with him and I asked if he'd fix me up a date with his sister. He said, 'Come and play rugby on Saturday and I'll make sure she's there.' That was it. We hit it off from there.

'George' was a nurse but her family was all military. Even her mum was in the services for a short spell – the Women's Royal Army Corps. George's brother Karl was also in the marines, and the youngest, Boris, was an officer in the Royal Corps of Signals. Her father was in the Royal Corps of Signals for 23 years and during that time was posted to Rinteln, Germany, where George was born. When I met George her father was working in Oman; he'd retired from the army but had a civilian contract over there. When he got back in late 1994 I got on really well with him. He was an old-school career soldier.

Shortly after we met, George went to Cyprus on a two-week holiday that she had organised months before. We could hardly believe how much we missed each other and from then on we were pretty much inseparable; that is, until I had to deploy on exercise to Norway again. Just before George and I got together I had passed selection for Brigade Patrol Troop (BPT) – 3 Commando Brigade's reconnaissance troop. It is run by the Mountain & Arctic Warfare Cadre so naturally Norway was the perfect training ground for the troop. I had opted for BPT, as some of the lads from 40 had started to get drafted to units and jobs that they didn't want to go to. Commachio Group in Scotland guarding the submarines was where a large proportion of the lads went. I didn't want to go there. I wanted action.

Once settled into the Norway routine again we

decided to head to one of the civvy ski slopes to upgrade our skills. However, we were on 'pusser's planks', the wide-based cross-country skis that were standard marine issue. Cross-country or tele-mark skiing is a different style to downhill skiing – to turn you slide one leg forward of the other into what looks like an awkward, half-squat kneeling position. Your knees are crossed and leaning the way you want to go.

I was struggling to get this right and became more and more frustrated as I was creaming in all the time while others gracefully skied past me. So I decided to head down the slope as fast as I could to have a break and a coffee. A couple of the lads whipped past as soon as I started my descent, so I crouched over and tucked in my ski poles under my arms to pick up the pace. Towards the bottom of the slope I saw the lads catch some air from a bump in the snow and land safely. I thought I'd do the same as they made it look so easy, but as I got closer to the jump the light faded and a big soft shadow cov-ered the slope making it all look smooth. I lost sight of the jump. Suddenly I hit the bloody thing totally unaware and in a split second was looking down on the town and remember seeing all the house and street lights, then *bang!* I'd hit the deck.

I landed on my right shoulder breaking and dis-locating it. As I slid face first to a stop I was think-ing, 'I'm really hurt this time.' Luckily a Norwegian nurse was on hand and helped me out. I felt like a real goose as this happened about only 50 metres from the front of the cafe. Some of the boys were drinking coffee and watching me as I hit the jump. They skied over in fits of laughter. I wanted to laugh as well but the pain was too bad. They took me to a doctor's surgery where he reduced the pain with the help of some very good painkillers and muscle relaxants.

However, the doctor didn't have an X-ray machine there so I had to wait until I got back to England to have the injury examined properly. But even then they missed the break at the top of my shoulder. It wasn't until three weeks later when I saw a surgeon at the naval hospital in Plymouth that he realised something was wrong, as my range of movement wasn't what it should have been at that stage of recovery. My shoulder took a long time to get back to full strength and it was 12 months before I could do a full-arm stretched pull-up.

It didn't help my recovery either when the troop had returned from Norway and decided to do a day's parachuting on Woodbury Common. I landed very heavily on my shoulder, which made it impossible to use. I couldn't pull on the risers to deflate the canopy. This led to me being dragged 20 metres through the dry gorse bushes. I looked like a bloody hedgehog when I finally stopped.

In April that year they flew my patrol from BPT out to Brunei for a five-week, long-range reconnaissance course in jungle warfare. 'Fozzy' was the patrol commander, a Falklands War vet and more than capable of handling the task. We flew to Hong Kong for a two-day stopover at Osborne Barracks to conduct a bit of admin and to catch a connecting flight. There was plenty of time to visit all the famous bars in the city, which we did. An American aircraft carrier was in port at the time, so there were a lot of US naval personnel in town. We joined in with their banter, took the piss and generally had a good time with them. By the time my mate 'Pea' and I headed back to Osborne Barracks on the underground it was getting light. At the station in Kowloon outside the barracks, we saw a familiar sight: Tom McPherson, another member of our patrol, a big bloke with ginger hair. He was sprawled out over one of the benches fast asleep. When we woke him he was suffering badly from the effects of dehydration caused by alcohol and the humidity of the tropical climate. He looked terrible. Mind you, I was no pretty picture either. My eyes felt like they were full of sand and I was desperate for sleep.

On arrival in Brunei we had a three-hour drive in the back of a truck to Training Team Brunei (TTB) and our accommodation. It was pouring with rain and I got soaked. I didn't mind as it kept me cool and replaced some much needed fluid in my system. The senior instructors were from Britain's 22 SAS and there was also a New Zealand

SAS instructor. This was the first time I had encountered anyone from the SAS and I was quite impressed.

The course started with health and medical issues in a tropical environment, then went on to signals training and survival followed by the tactical package, which included patrolling, ambushing, tracking, live fire break contacts and field craft. Our work on the range was quite demanding. One of the 22 SAS instructors took our patrol through this phase and I got a lot out of it. He was very demanding of our performance. If he didn't like something about the drill we would have to do it again until it was perfected. He gave us tips such as 'Drake shooting', an SOP used in jungle warfare. Due to the lack of visual distance in the jungle it is inevitable that you will encounter the enemy at very close range, and may not see them at all. So to 'Drake shoot' is the practice of rapidly shooting at multiple locations where you think the enemy could be situated.

While the training was excellent, the heat became unbearable at times. After working the range we spent a couple of nights in the jungle (J for short), to get used to living under the thick canopy. It can be a little bit cooler in the jungle because you are out of the direct sunlight, but the humidity is twice as bad. You are constantly wet due to perspiration and the afternoon downpours, which can be a welcome relief. We slept in hammocks to protect our bodies from the crawling jungle floor, as the last thing you want is to become a liability to the patrol from infected insect bites. This is just one of many problems for soldiers in a tropical environment.

After a few days training back at the lines we prepared for a block of 23 days in the jungle. We were joined by a six-man patrol from the American Army Special Forces, the Green Berets. These blokes were based at Okinawa, and we got on well with them. There was also a pathfinder patrol from 5 Airborne Brigade, US Army Rangers and a patrol of Gurkhas. We deployed into the area by Huey helicopter and rappelled into the jungle onto a small landing site. Because the fuselage of the aircraft was small we had to tie off our abseil ropes and stand outside on the skids with two men on each side. I imagined this is what it was like for some Special Forces groups being inserted into Vietnam. Once on the ground we pulled the excess rope through the figure 8 descender (a descending device that the abseil rope runs through to give you a controlled descent) and disappeared into the jungle.

The sound of the living jungle was brilliant but the things that lived there could be a worry. It wasn't long before leeches had attached themselves to our legs looking for a warm feed. During stand-to timings, early morning and evening just on dark, a particular insect would arc up, producing quite a loud cicada kind of noise; we nicknamed it 'the stand-to bug', as it only made its noise during those times.

Towards the end of the exercise we met the rest of the course in preparation for the final six-day exercise culminating in leading a company of Gurkhas into an area to attack an enemy camp. First we had to clean, test and adjust our equipment, replenish rations and water, re-bomb with ammunition and stock up on new radio batteries. Once again we were inserted by rappelling from a Huey and slipping quietly away deep into the jungle. The going was tough to start with, as we had to 'cross-grain' through some very steep terrain and the patrolling speed was slow. 'Cross-graining' is a term used for patrolling off tracks. Tracks are never used, as you run the risk of compromise; also the locals would notice instantly if there were foreign marks or footprints, as they know every inch of their backyard so well. Once we were in the approximate area of the enemy camp the patrolling was cut to a minimum and we conducted a couple of recces to locate the camp.

The live fire camp attack was extremely good and I got a lot of personal satisfaction from it, even though Pea had trouble understanding my hand signals, which momentarily forced him towards another firer. But Fozzy had good control over us and all ran smoothly. In fact I enjoyed the whole course. I thrived on the jungle environment. The jungle can be as difficult as working in the cold of Norway. Both have their dangers and both are uncomfortable, but it's really all in the mind. If you let these environments get to you, it will tear you apart, but if you stay focused on the job you'll come through with flying colours.

At the end of the course there was the usual de-servicing of equipment, debriefs, signing of course reports, etc. And once all the work was done a rugby match was organised for Saturday afternoon between the course members and the expats who worked in the area. I couldn't play as I was still getting over the dislocated shoulder, so I got stuck into the beer instead with a couple of others and cheered our side on. I can't remember who won, but I do remember looking at my watch the following morning at 0400 hours and thinking, 'Fuck, I've got to get up in two hours.' We were to catch the coach to the airport around 0630 to fly back to Hong Kong. I was feeling rather sorry for myself as were most of the other blokes. Just before I boarded the coach one of the pathfinder lads casually 'parked his custard' at the door. That did not help.

The journey to back to Osborne Barracks in Hong Kong was very painful, although the trip didn't take too long, and we were in the pub by 1900 hours. We spent five days in Hong Kong, which meant we could have a pretty good look around and relax during the day on the beach at Repulse Bay.

When I returned to the UK and the barracks routine I felt very unsettled. The Brunei experience had been interesting and I had learned a lot about jungle warfare, but I couldn't toss that memory of my leave in New Zealand. And by now George and I were very close. In fact, I'd bought her an engagement ring in Hong Kong and asked her to marry me.

7

HOT SHOTS

I did my first sniper course in July 1995. This was – and still is – a world renowned course. The British SAS use it and one of their members was on my course. There was also a guest instructor from the US Marine Corps Scout Sniper School who had some good ideas and was very proficient in pistol shooting.

One idea he advocated that I didn't agree with – and still don't – was the use of a drag bag. You place your sniper rifle in it and drag it behind you when you need to crawl. I think it is tactically unsound, because immediately there's the need to carry two weapons: one in the bag and the other in your hands, since otherwise you're defenceless. Also, the drag bag causes too much 'sign'. Snipers crawling through grass or undergrowth cause enough damage to the foliage by themselves; add another object a metre or so behind your horizontal profile and you leave even more sign, not to mention the frustration of it snagging on obstacles.

The course ran for six weeks covering ballistics, marksmanship and field craft. This included developing observation skills through binoculars and spotting scopes, judging distance without any aids, interpreting aerial photography, navigating by day and night, camouflage and concealment to blend in with the surrounding area, and the art of stalking.

Back then we used the 7.62mm Accuracy International L96 rifle with a Leupold fixed 8-power magnification scope. The rifle had been developed by Malcolm Cooper, who was a British sport shooter. Cooper was the founder of Accuracy International and the holder of two Olympic gold medals in the 50-metre shooting event. The rifle itself was very accurate, producing good hits out to 800 metres. Its predecessor, the SR98 (also known as AW) was also extremely accurate and in the right hands could produce a tight group at 1,000 metres. This weapon is fitted with a Schmidt & Bender variable power scope. But for this course we used the L96.

Every course starts with theory lessons in ballistics, optics and the weapons you'll use. Each student needs to have a good understanding of the equipment, and ballistics is taught in depth. He must understand what will happen to the projectile in flight and in different conditions so he can make the necessary adjustments to his scope before firing. Once the theory lessons finished we spent a week or so on the range, sometimes conducting judging distance (JDs) or observation (OBs) practices in between. After the range week we then concentrated on tactics, navigation and stalking. During the 'static nav' (fixing your position by reference to the surrounding topography) the DS often pointed out small buildings and track or creek junctions far into the distance that we had to plot on a map, give an eight-figure grid reference, a back bearing and also a magnetic and grid bearing, all timed. This proved to be quite difficult at times but I enjoyed mastering the art.

There was a lot of emphasis on field craft and they ran a couple of exercises running for 36 hours. One scenario was a possible enemy meeting taking place at a prominent point on a series of cross-country tracks. We were given a six-figure grid reference and had to 'yomp' into the area at night, identify (ID) the possible meeting point and dig in a belly hide with some OHP, which had to be finished by first light. It was quite a demanding task as we were working only in pairs.

I was paired with 'Keith' who turned out to be a top bloke. We finished the hide before first light but were absolutely knackered and there was no time to sleep. The rain started as usual and for the rest of that day lying up in the belly hide we worked on our range cards and continually observed our arc and reported on any activity. In darkness we still had to maintain our security, so only one of us slept at a time – hour on, hour off. We also had to keep an ear out for the radio. The night seemed to drag on forever, but shortly after first light our targets appeared. We were given the 'stand by' over the radio and then came the command to fire. All four shooters of the two-man teams fired at the same time, which is quite a good option to guarantee a hit. The DS then came around to critique our hides and give further advice. We got a kick in the arse for our radio antenna being visible.

We conducted a couple more stalks on Woodbury Common towards the end of that week. The common can be a nightmare at times to conduct a stalk, as in places the ground doesn't offer much cover or freedom of movement from the observers. This meant your movements had to be slow and deliberate. Most of the common is covered in heather and gorse; the gorse can be helpful at times to mask movement, but when it grows higher than usual you need to avoid it because it becomes a prominent reference point that attracts the eye of the observer. The height of the foliage meant that more often than not we had to find a firing location that suited the prone position. Sometimes we could find a 'keyhole' that allowed us to shoot through gaps in the foliage from behind a rudimentary tripod made from sticks lashed together. In fact that's the firing position I used to pass my badge stalk.

The following week we travelled to Torpoint to use the Tregantle rifle range, which at that time went as far back as 800 metres. The facility is in quite a nice location, situated on the western side of the River Tamar and not too far from the coast. It made for a nice break in the routine and I scored well on the range.

Back at Woodbury Common we continued with observation practices, JDs, nav, panoramic sketching and stalks. Because Woodbury is open for civilian use it's not uncommon to see day walkers passing through the area and that can lead to some amusing situations. During one stalk two middle-aged couples were slowly making their way along one of the dirt tracks that criss-crossed the common. The track ran between us and the observers, who were sitting in folding chairs up a small hill trying to observe us with binoculars. They were approximately 300 metres from the track; all I had was around 30 metres of knee-high heather between me and the well-worn dirt track.

The two women paused and let their two male companions walk on. I had been slowly making my way towards a firing position that wasn't too far from the edge of the track. The two women then proceeded to look around the immediate area. I was crouched down but motionless and heavily camouflaged with cam cream on my face and wearing a ghillie suit (a heavily camouflaged suit) with some local foliage placed behind the elastic straps around the shoulders and in my hat. My weapon had been camouflaged using a combination of scrim and hessian. They looked straight at me but appeared not to see me. Suddenly one of the women dropped her trousers, squatted on the track and started to relieve herself. I cracked up laughing but had to do it quietly due to the close proximity.

She finished and moved off, then I heard movement to my left; it was one of the walkers, an observing DS who acts on command of the observer. He had seen me moving towards my final position and was coming across to confirm what he had just seen. The walkers are in clean skin (standard olive drab shirt and trousers) armed with only a radio and pointer. Not giving my position away we had a childish giggle about it and so too did the observers via hand-held radio.

Woodbury Common was also the home to a small population of roe deer, and during another stalk I got within 10 metres of a small buck. I lay motionless and enjoyed the moment.

The best phase of the course was conducted at Sennybridge, South Wales. This was a field firing week with some night nav thrown in. We put into practice most of what we had learnt to date. We had to sketch a 'panoramic' adding prominent features and key ranges. Once finished, we shot from 100 metres out to 1,000 metres, making adjustments for range and wind, recording every adjustment. We would record weather conditions, light, temperature, wind strength and direction, range, type and weight of rounds used. All this detailed work would provide a reference in similar conditions to guarantee a first-round hit.

We would also record the characteristics of the first round fired. This is known as a 'cold barrel' or 'cold bore' shot. Rounds fired through a warm barrel have slightly different characteristics. A selection course for 22 SAS had started while we were there and they stayed at the same camps as us. We didn't see too much of the selection course but we did have a few beers with some of the DS at a local pub. Their stories fuelled my desire to join them.

Soon came badge week, the final testing period. If we failed one test during this week we failed the whole course; it didn't matter how well we had done previously. The final test is a 2,000-metre approach to a designated area between 200 and 400 metres from the observers. Sniper instructors are equipped with standard issue binoculars to observe between the arcs of the stalking zone.

At the start of the course we all make the same mistake as young apprentice snipers and will try to get as close as possible to the target because we are not yet confident of our skill. As the course progresses confidence picks up in marksmanship and field craft, allowing us to work out the optimum position within the zone.

The further back you are, the less likely it is that you're going to be seen. In fact, when I reach a position where I have clear line of sight to the target, I turn 180 degrees so I can take in the scene from the observer's viewpoint. I look for positions that provide me with better cover, more depth, avoid silhouettes, a good background, and a position that will allow clear trajectory of the round without striking any objects during its flight. Once in position I make a practice of removing the bolt from the rifle, and then with the correct range set, I place the scope's cross-hairs on the target. Without moving the rifle, I look through the barrel checking to see if there is any foliage in the way of the initial path the round is going to take. If there is you're going to have to go out and cut it, or if possible and time permitting change your position. Looking through the scope will give you line of sight from your eye to the target – an imaginary straight line. The flight path of the bullet (projectile) is different. It will be an arc. This is due to various reasons, muzzle velocity and gravity being the two main ones.

The successful stalk is getting into an area undetected, finding the target or observers, finding a suitable hide or concealed position and calculating the correct firing solution to the hit the target. You may even have to construct your hide from foliage or material brought in from some distance away, always making sure you remain concealed and that the foliage is the same as your surroundings. You build your fire position checking you have a clear path for the projectile's course. You adjust for wind if you have to, add the range then, using all the marksmanship principles correctly, fire the shot – obviously you're using blanks. The sniper is being assessed on his application of field craft and his understanding of weather conditions and distance with only his binoculars and rifle scope as aids.

If you have been detected by an observer at any stage during the stalk a walker is coached on to the suspected sniper position via radio. The walker will not assist the observer in any way, and will only act on instructions he is given until he places his hand on the suspected sniper.

Army and Royal Marine snipers are awarded the same qualification badge: crossed rifles with the letter 'S' to be worn on the left sleeve of the dress uniform. A Royal Marine sniper is also accredited with the Platoon Weapons 3 (PW3) qualification.

From our course of 16, eight of us passed – a 50 per cent pass rate is quite common. There had been previous courses where only one bloke had passed, which was pretty tough on the lads who had performed well all course but then had one bad day when the pressure was on. As a sniper on an operational task, you can't afford to have one bad day. This may sound tough, but you are the most hunted and feared opponent of your enemy, and there is nothing they'd like more than to kill a trained sniper. And a lack in concentration or laziness will give them this chance.

During the course of my time in BPT I had submitted my notice for discharge, which back then was 18 months notice. So in March 1996 I went back to 40 Commando and then joined them in April for the final six weeks of their Northern Ireland deployment. This time we were based in County Tyrone, but a ceasefire had been called and the tour wasn't as active as the 1993 trip. The patrolling and security programs continued as normal but my heart really wasn't in it.

For the six weeks I was away I really missed George. When we returned to Taunton it was terrific to be back with her again but the truth was I'd had enough of living in the UK. I'd been there seven years and it was time to go home.

George and I began planning our future together. I had an idea for an outdoor lifestyle operation in New Zealand where I'd be able to put all my training to good use. I thought about buying a few acres to set it up as a training ground getting the young and adventurous fit, and older people back into shape. There was an area on the Coromandel Peninsula, a short boat ride from Auckland Harbour that I reckoned was just right. So in late 1996 I headed back to New Zealand for five weeks leave. George would follow a few weeks later when her holidays came through. It would give her the chance to look the place over before we made any final decision about where we'd make our life together. What I didn't see before I got there was that New Zealand had recently been the subject of a property and housing boom and land was now well out of my reach.

While I was waiting for George to arrive I took the opportunity to do some hunting with my mates and had an absolute ball. When George arrived she took to New Zealand immediately and after two weeks of showing her around we flew to Fiji where we'd decided to get married. The honeymoon came first, at Musket Cove resort on an outlying island, Malolo Lailai. We snorkelled, scuba dived and enjoyed the friendly island life. The wedding day started with a flight back to the Fiji mainland, and we made it official on 16 December 1996 at the Nadi registry office. I didn't make it the best experience for George as I was suffering a huge hangover at the time given to me care of the two-dollar bar. The subject does surface from time to time.

By this stage we had definitely made our minds up to move to New Zealand and to make a go of it. Once back in the UK we celebrated our marriage with a big party at the rugby club's function room with friends and family. Over the next few weeks we talked for hours into the night about what we were going to do when we reached New Zealand and came up with a loose plan. I didn't have any real savings behind me and I knew I'd have to work hard for a while to save up a deposit for that block of land.

8

COLD COMFORT

Arriving back in New Zealand was like falling out of bed and hitting the floor with a thump. In the seven years I'd been away land prices had gone through the roof. They had even increased since we were there last on holiday six months earlier. Now not only was the Coromandel totally out of the question, I didn't even have a deposit for a house. All of a sudden I found myself thinking, 'Have I made the right decision? Now what am I going to do?'

We quickly went to work on a Plan B. The New Zealand defence force wasn't really an option. They didn't pay anywhere near enough, and had next to nothing on the operational front. Opportunities were very restricted. The best alternative seemed to be the police force, since they had a counter-terrorism unit, the Special Tactics Group (STG). I had all the necessary qualifications to become a Kiwi copper. The only problem was we didn't have the savings to see us through to the start of police training, so to build up a bank I had to look for a job as a mechanic to cover the gap and pay the rent. Fortunately, that wasn't too difficult and at the same time George got a nursing job in Intensive Care at Middlemore Hospital, South Auckland.

Recruit training at the police college couldn't come quick enough, and as soon as I got a date the mechanical workshop where I was working couldn't see me for dust! Unfortunately I can't say that I enjoyed my time at the police college in Porirua and was glad to see the back of it. I was posted to the Wiri police station in Manukau City, South Auckland, the busiest station in the country, but also spent some time working out of the Papakura station, all familiar ground to me. Shortly after starting at Wiri we moved into a rented police house, George became pregnant and her parents came to New Zealand to spend six months with us.

One of the first guys I got partnered with in the police, Russ, was part-time STG and he organised an interview for me with the inspector in charge of Auckland STG; Russ would also be present at the interview. He was the sniper supervisor and was interested in my sniper background from the marines. For a while prospects looked pretty good. However, I had a gradual falling-out with the inspector. He told me a few porky pies and then took somebody else on when a position became available within STG. He once said to me, 'There's a sniper course coming up; what gear have you got?' I told him I had the lot. 'Put it all in a pack and bring it. You're on the course.'

When I turned up the bloke running the course, Russ, said, 'What's in the pack, mate?' When I told him he said, 'Well, you're playing enemy. Sorry, mate, you're not on the course.' I took a deep breath and thought, 'That bloody arsehole inspector has really led me down the garden path,' not to mention also embarrassing me. Furthermore, it wasn't even a course; it turned out to be a sniper concentration involving STG snipers from Auckland, Wellington and Christchurch.

The idea was to amalgamate all their skills and keep everybody up to speed. There were scenarios where the 'enemy' – me – could be involved in a hostage situation or be a guy with a gun who was very threatening. I played the game and took it seriously and it played out well. Some of the other 'enemy' guys were prospects for STG also and they saw it as a chance to make a good impression. So at the end of the day's training we were all asked for our comments. They all said, 'Yeah, great, good training.'

I stuck my hand up and told them a few home truths about some of the very basic tactical errors they were making during the exercise, like not to silhouette themselves and using depth for cover. Just because they were police snipers, it didn't mean that they wouldn't become a target. I also shared other tactics that I had learned in the Royal Marines. Maybe I shouldn't have done it because it didn't sit well with them, but they asked me for my thoughts and I passed on my experience.

As it happened I was called away from the concentration because George had gone into labour. Our daughter Lauren came along on Tuesday, 27 October 1998, and although I hated to see George in pain, it was pretty special to be there for the event. Lauren was born in the same South Auckland hospital as my son, Lee, who had remained in the UK with Carla, now remarried. I stayed in touch but tried not to interfere and cause any problems for him or his mother.

The police gave me two weeks compassionate leave to look after George. I tried to help as much as I could but her mum was doing a great job fussing over her, so I sat back and took it all in.

Back at work I realised that as well as my falling out with the inspector, the Auckland STG team were very tight and resentful of outsiders; whereas the Wellington crowd and the Christchurch boys were a great bunch of blokes. However, I was stuck in Auckland and it looked as though I'd have very little chance of moving into the area where I had most to contribute.

I quickly became disgruntled with day-to-day

policing. You could virtually set your clock every weekend for domestic violence, the fights in the pubs and the burglaries. The majority would start at the same time every weekend and you'd tick them off one after the other. I found the domestics tough – obviously, you've got to protect the woman from harm but half the time it was the woman causing the dramas; and once you step in you can cop it from both sides. There was one time I really felt sorry for this guy – a Maori fella – he was a truck driver doing extended amounts of time on the road trying to raise some capital to buy a house. They had two lovely kids, and twice his wife took the savings from the coffee jar and went to the casino and blew the lot. The second time she was gone for four days.

When she finally came home he went ballistic and knocked her around bit. It a was hard one but I had to arrest the guy because he'd committed an assault. And since it was 'male assaults female' the offence was a lot more serious than a normal assault. He got remanded for 24 hours and then had to front court, pleaded guilty, copped a fine of $2,000 which he couldn't pay, so went further into debt.

There are some fantastic blokes in the New Zealand police, but it just wasn't the road for me. At heart I was a soldier. It wasn't my place to reason with people and show compassion. I had become accustomed to a life lived by the sword shown to me by the Royal Marines. And I also needed more.

I couldn't just settle for staying as an ordinary infantry soldier. So that meant Special Forces, and for me the Australian Special Air Service Regiment (SASR) was perfect. I knew of their reputation through the Royal Marines, and knew they were originally modelled on the British SAS and that they had the same motto: 'Who Dares Wins'.

They had a history of their own from the 'Z' Special Force that did some terrific work behind the Japanese lines in World War II. Their biggest win at that time was Operation Jaywick in the converted Japanese fishing boat *Krait* in 1943 when they quietly slipped into Singapore Harbour in kayaks and attached limpet mines to seven enemy ships, blew them up and escaped back to Australia. It was reminiscent of Operation Frankton in 1942 by the Royal Marines who severely damaged five German ships in the port of Bordeaux. These men were called the 'cockleshell heroes'.

'Z' force returned the following year on Operation Rimau but this time their luck ran out and all were either killed in action or captured and later beheaded just as the war was about to end. There were other 'independent' Special Forces companies operating in the South Pacific and they too had a great record. But the Australian SAS wasn't officially established until 1957, and even then it was only a company. They later expanded into three Sabre squadrons and were given regimental status in 1964. The regiment saw action during the Indonesian 'confrontation' the following year in north Borneo where according to the official history they 'inflicted at least 20 kills on Indonesian forces' through ambushes and contacts on both sides of the Malaysian border. Three SASR operators were killed during their time in Borneo: two drowned in a river crossing and one 'gored by an elephant'. What a way to go.

However, it seemed that they really came into their own during the Vietnam War when 3 Squadron SAS deployed as part of the 1st Australian Task Force. They operated mainly as a reconnaissance force acting as 'the eyes and ears' of the task force. And I was pleased to see that the Kiwi SAS had sent a troop to work alongside the Australians, keeping up the Anzac tradition.

The squadron rotated through Vietnam with deployments lasting a year and they became known as 'the phantoms of the jungle' because of their field craft. The Kiwi SAS were known by the enemy as 'the Grey Ghosts'. The Australians and Kiwis were responsible for taking out somewhere between 492 and 598 of the enemy and lost only two men in action, and unfortunately three from friendly fire. Despite this, it was a fantastic record.

The main problem for me was that you couldn't apply directly to join the regiment because all recruits had to come from the Australian Defence Force. So there was nothing for it but to apply to join the Australian infantry. George and I talked about it and she was all for it so I sent in my papers in late 1998.

The process seemed to take forever. I had to travel to Sydney in March 1999 for a week of testing and interviews. I took the chance to shoot up to Brisbane to catch up with Craig and head over to Stradbroke Island for some fishing and copious amounts of beer. Craig was now a plumber with his own business.

When the good news finally came through I signed all the official papers on 6 June 1999 at army headquarters in Oxford Street, Sydney – my own D Day exactly 55 years after the Allies landed at Normandy. After a rollcall and some last minute admin, I was one of 22 brand-new recruits on an army coach bound for Kapooka, outside Wagga Wagga, in southern New South Wales.

Kapooka is the army's all-corps training centre, so everyone who joins does their initial training there. Sitting on the coach watching the countryside go by, I remember feeling a distinct lack of anticipation or nerves, unlike when I joined the Royal Marines. The other young new recruits on the coach reminded me of that day back in '92 as I headed off to Lympstone.

Wagga is about 370 kilometres in a straight line from Sydney, and the coach journey took about six hours. We arrived late in the afternoon and were met by most of the training staff. The first thing that caught my eye was a big feather that was stuck in the hat of a SNCO's parade uniform. It turned out to be an emu plume, first worn by the Queensland light horsemen in the late 19th century. It was later adopted by all light horse units in Australia, and is still worn today by the armoured units of the Australian army.

As we stepped off the coach the shouting and assertiveness from the DS started, which didn't have the same effect on me this time round. But I was back in the forces now and had to comply with their demands all the same. They got us into three ranks as quickly as they could and called the roll, separating us into two groups.

They showed us our accommodation then marched us down to the mess for dinner with the instruction that we could only choose just one of the meat courses on offer. This provided a good opportunity for the young cooks behind the bain marie to exercise some authority that they didn't usually have. And the spread was quite a shock to the new recruits. All they could see was free food and stacks of it, so naturally they wanted to gorge.

The first bloke through loaded his plate with every type of meat. 'What the fuck are you doing?' came the cry from behind the bain marie. 'One choice only. Listen to the brief next time!' I had my eye on the lasagna, which looked very tasty but as I got closer the guy in front of me got the last piece. 'Is there any more lasagne, mate?' I said politely to one of the cooks.

'Is there any more lasagne . . . private!' he replied snidely.

'What!' I said.

'You will address me as private!'

Fuck you, I thought. There was no way on this earth I was ever going to address anyone as 'Private'. I looked him in the eye and leaned forward slightly and said, 'Is there any more lasagne . . . mate!'

I could see the anger building up in this bloke, but the poor fella was at a loss to know where to take it next. A corporal nearby heard and saw what was going on. He approached me and said, 'There's more coming out.' Then he asked, 'Have you been in before?'

Since I was now 32 and was the oldest of all the new recruits, I said, 'Yeah, mate, I was in the Royal Marines.' I didn't bother acknowledging the young private as he was now probably feeling a bit sheepish. It dawned on me there and then that my time in these training establishments was going to be very painful.

Luckily the army was trialling a six-week training course instead of the usual 12. This suited me down to the ground but six weeks is nowhere near long enough to convert a raw civilian into a soldier. In fact, the training was slack by comparison with the marines and I guess I didn't handle it very diplomatically.

However, the initial process was quite similar to

that of Lympstone in regard to kit preparation and maintenance, drill lessons, weapons training, fitness programs and history lessons. One thing that did stand out was the PT regime and just how much focus the instructors placed on showing us the correct techniques to tackle an obstacle. This was to minimise the risk of injury, not just during training but hopefully on operations as well. I totally agreed with this, as injury would only prolong my agony at Kapooka.

It was quite an eye opener for me seeing these young civilians ever so slowly getting turned into something that resembled a soldier. It triggered memories of my Lympstone days but without the fear of pain. I put myself in their shoes from time to time and knew exactly what they were thinking.

After a while I was pretty much left alone at Kapooka. I just had to toe the party line and put in when required, although I often helped out the others with their map reading, field craft and other trade secrets if they were struggling.

I was amazed by the amount of bird life around the training area and just how noisy galahs can be. The cockatoos and the crows can be pretty vocal at times as well. There were a few emus knocking about too, and during one of the first overnight exercises I had one pecking at my boot. He started to push the friendship when he began to peck at the bottom of my trousers to get at the elastic band that helped blouse them.

Shortly after the march-out parade at the end of training we were herded onto separate coaches bound for different destinations. Mine was going to Singleton in the Hunter Valley where the infantrymen learn their trade. The school of infantry also run promotion courses, the sniper team leader's course and an assortment of other infantry-related courses.

As soon as we stepped off the bus at Singleton I instantly noticed the temperature difference; this place during the day was definitely warmer than Kapooka in the south. The next thing I noticed was that the camp was almost being overrun by kangaroos. They were everywhere, and reasonably tame. We met the training staff and were put into sections, then shown to our accommodation. The school of infantry was also trialling a six-week training package. But again, this is nowhere near enough time to learn all the skills to become well rehearsed in your trade.

Once again we went through a series of lectures and kit issues before we got stuck into training. There are eight men in a British infantry section – a third of a platoon. That is then broken down into two four-man teams so when you pepper-pot forward, you will always have security. As you move, the other half of the section will stay firm and cover you. The Australian system of nine-man sections broken into three manoeuvre groups is, I think, a lot better. The section is split into the two forward scouts, three in the gun group where the 2IC is situated and four in the assault group.

This meant more moving parts for the section commander to control, but it also brought more flexibility. I also liked the idea of having two scouts working together because as a single scout your personal arcs are restricted, making your job quite hard work at times and mentally draining. Having a second scout relieved a bit of that pressure, but also provided that all-important additional security and visibility. But being the lead scout is by far the best job in the section, or even patrol: it carries a lot of responsibility, but you are the eyes and ears of the section, or patrol commander.

The weapon we used was a 5.56 mm semi-automatic Steyr, with the capability of switching to fully automatic by applying extra pressure to the trigger. The two trigger pressures were four and eight pounds. There is a single shot-lockout button that stops heavy-handed firers from passing the first trigger pressure and letting off an unexpected burst. But when I was lead scout I always had the lockout button pushed in so if compromised I could initially return a heavy weight of fire in two- to three-round bursts. Then on the completion of the contact immediate action (IA) and a change of mag (magazine), I would go back to single well-aimed shots by just manipulating the first trigger pressure.

Initially a heavy or an aggressive weight of fire will get the enemy's head down in fear for his life, but sending just one or two shots his way will alert him to where you are, and then you'll be on the receiving end of his anger. Aggression is a vital ingredient in any attack or contact. It helps overcome the fear, but also lets the enemy know that you mean business.

It did actually take me a little while to get back into the swing of things at Singleton, and to start remembering how to be an infantryman again. It doesn't take long before your skills start to perish. Sniping is a prime example of that; your expertise diminishes very quickly if you haven't done anything practical for a while, and takes some good training to get back up to an acceptable standard.

One thing I'll never forget about 'Singo' is the inch ants. They are everywhere, and they deliver a very painful sting. You don't necessarily notice they are on you until halfway through a section attack after you've crawled over one of their nests. However, you do notice the prickly pear that you've just crawled through, sat on, put your hand on and walked through, embedding its thorns everywhere. The thorns are not easy to remove either. As you try to pull out these sharp, needle-like weapons they break off and stick into your fingertips. It's a bit like trying to get a piece of very sticky tape off your fingers; all you do is transfer it from one hand to the other. Then there are the small brown scorpions under rocks and of course plenty of snakes in case you're tempted to relax. The range and training area also has a big population of feral pigs, but hunting is banned.

Aside from each man's all-important rifle, the infantry section was armed with the 66 mm rocket launcher and the M79 single-shot 40 mm grenade launcher, which looks like a big single-barrel shotgun: the breach opens the same way and a cartridge is loaded in the same manner. The M203 40 mm grenade launcher was only just coming in at that stage; the battalions had them but not the school of infantry.

The gunners carried a light machine gun, a fully automatic, belt-fed 5.56 mm Minimi light machine gun also known as an LSW and supported by a bipod. This is the hardest job in the section. As a gunner you have the responsibility to provide an enormous amount of fire power to suppress the enemy so the rest of the section can close with them. Your drills also need to be very slick to rectify any stoppages or problems you have with that gun and get it operating again. Your kit is generally heavier than everyone else's. The Minimi weighs twice as much as the Steyr, and you'll carry 800 to 1,200 rounds of link in your webbing and pack.

Other lads in the section will also carry a few hundred rounds of link to be given to the gunners if needed. Each man will carry an M18A1 Claymore, which is 680 grams of C-4 plastic explosive with 700 small steel ball bearings embedded into the explosive, and packed in a hard plastic case. It comes in a green carry bag with a firing device and electrical cable with detonator attached. They are primarily used in ambushes and as an anti-infiltration device, and can be used singly or as several banked together.

They put us through quite a punishing regime of patrolling, section attacks with different scenarios, and defensive exercises. This culminated in a section competition they called 'Hard Core' that ran for 12 hours. It was designed to test how much individuals and complete sections had learnt over the previous weeks. We would pack-march between stands where we would have to complete certain activities that were either timed or scored. The activities included radio communications, observation stands, weapon drills and first aid. In truth there was nothing hard about it at all, except having to listen to the DS 'gobbing off' at you!

My mate Jon who was in the regiment at the time had organised for me to meet Sully, a WO2 from SASR who was based at Singleton in a training position. I was keen to have a chat about the unit and the best way to approach getting on selection – and hopefully 'back-dooring' it once I had marched out of training. But when my training team found out what I was attempting to do, the troop sergeant threatened to charge me if I set foot anywhere near the Special Forces Training Centre (SFTC). I don't know where that outburst came from, but when this bloke had me 'heels together' at attention in front of him it made me even more determined to get into the SAS. I was told to pull my head in and had my chest poked a couple of times over the course of the six weeks.

I was a happy man to get away from that training establishment and to pick up my position in the 3rd Battalion Royal Australian Regiment – 3RAR.

George was back in New Zealand for those first three months and they were pretty tough for her. Once I left the police we had to give up the police house we had been renting. And like the police, the army recruit training pay is the absolute minimum so keeping a pregnant George and one-year-old Lauren housed, fed and clothed was almost impossible. She stayed with my parents for three months, which almost drove her mad.

She arrived in Australia in September 1999 with Lauren and our two dogs, and we stayed in a hotel on the Hume Highway while waiting for a house in Holsworthy. The dogs had to be kennelled and George had to take an hour's train ride to walk them each day.

Finally we moved into a house on Yengo Court, one of the Defence Department houses available for rent in the area, and 200 metres from Holsworthy camp. We were lucky enough to get a brand-new one. But word had already come through that 3RAR was to be deployed to East Timor. Fortunately, George's mum and dad were back again from the UK. Even though money was very tight I was glad to be back in the forces. I'd taken the first step towards my goal of joining the SAS. I knew there was a bumpy road ahead but at least I was on the way.

9

COOLING IT

Just across the Arafura Sea from Darwin, East Timor was descending into chaos. You had to feel sorry for the East Timorese. They had been under the colonial heel of Portugal for about 400 years before they cleared out in 1974. The colonial power had exploited the place without giving them either education or the means to run the show economically or politically. So no-one was particularly surprised when the Indonesians took over in 1975.

The Indonesians did a lot to develop the place economically for the next 20 years but it was really run by the Indonesian Army (TNI), who also ripped them off. The Timorese set up an armed resistance under Xanana Gusmão that gradually won a lot of international support, especially after the Dili massacre in 1991.

When Suharto was forced out in 1998 and Habibi took over, he offered the Timorese autonomy inside the Indonesian state. That only encouraged the resistance, who wanted full independence, and in 1999 Habibi agreed to give them a referendum. That happened in August and nearly 80 per cent voted for independence, which really pissed the TNI off. When they left they torched and trashed just about everything they'd built – the water supply system, the electricity grid, schools, the university and just about every major public building in Dili.

They had backed a local militia who tried to disrupt the referendum; when that failed the militias retreated over the border to West Timor but returned from time to time to settle scores and stir things up.

Before we deployed there we were briefed on the background to the conflict and since we were basically peacekeepers, our job was to act as a deterrent to the militias and to any locals who might want to use the situation as a cover to settle family feuds. It's a role that requires special skills. You need to assert your authority in any given situation and to use your weapon only as a last resort. This is where my experience in Northern Ireland was useful. I was used to the constraints and similar rules of engagement. Even though the tropical battleground was much more like Brunei than Belfast, it was a similar scenario.

Because I had just been posted to the unit I didn't

deploy with the initial push. I still had a bit of admin to sort out and was deployed to Timor two weeks later. A handful of us from 3RAR flew to Darwin to join other members of the task force then loaded onto a big motorised catamaran, the *Jervis Bay*, built in Fremantle for the Americans. On 8 October it took us about 14 hours to reach Dili, where we would become part of the Interfet force.

The WO2 in charge gave us a heads up before we arrived on what had occurred in the area over the previous couple of weeks. The militia were the bad guys and were very lightly armed, more often than not carrying machetes, but casualties were still high. In the ranks there were plenty of stories of blokes finding dead bodies at the bottom of wells and caches of hundreds of Indonesian weapons that had been burned. We all thought it could get rough, especially since all the news reports suggested that the situation was hostile.

So it was a bit of an anticlimax getting off the boat to find the place quiet and relatively peaceful. Dili looked like a battle site due to all the rubbish everywhere and all the burnt-out buildings, but I felt quite safe and secure as we were transported to battalion HQ on the back of an open Unimog. The HQ was set up in a burnt-out school. From there we were sent to form up with our respective platoons.

I was in 1 Platoon of Alpha Company and at that time 3RAR was responsible for securing the Dili heliport. Alpha Company occupied the main entrance and a couple of other areas around the base. In between normal security details we rotated through shifts as guards for detainees. The shifts were long and tedious and I couldn't wait to get out and see some action – if there was ever going to be any.

Our first operation outside Dili was to secure Bobanaro, a Falintil stronghold in the hills, and we flew in by Blackhawk helicopter. Amongst the pilots was a bloke I'd get to know and like a lot in the years ahead – Mark 'Bingers' Bingley. As soon as we were settled into Bobanaro we started a day and night patrolling program and even conducted a few two- and three-day patrols.

The Timorese did everything they could to help out and make life a bit more comfortable. When we moved to their villages in the hills they built shelters for us using palm fronds thatched together for the roof, and cleared areas overgrown with lantana. It might take two or three days to build a decent-sized shelter but nothing was too much trouble. There were times when we would patrol to some outlying villages which had been abandoned following militia attacks, so we would use the vacant houses for temporary shelter to get out of the elements due to the wet season.

The patrols were fairly uneventful, although you could never relax. We were in Bobanaro about a month before we moved again, this time to Gildapil near Tapo, which was closer to the West Timorese border. The SAS had the village under surveillance and had cleared it well before we got there. But, as usual in the battalions, the left hand doesn't talk to the right hand and we also ended up clearing the entire village. We never did catch up with any militia in the villages, because as soon as we arrived in the area most of them took off back across the border.

Every now and again some locals would come up and point out a guy they said was militia, so we'd apprehend the guy and send him back to Dili where the MPs would interview him. The locals had quickly cottoned onto the idea that if you called some guy 'militia' the Australians troops would come along, grab him and he'd disappear for three or four days. It usually turned out to be the result of a feud, and he wasn't necessarily militia at all.

When we became used to the scene we found that if a militia member did come into the area from West Timor it was like stirring up a beehive. You could see how agitated the locals would become and the intruder would realise that his mission in East Timor was compromised and he'd soon be gone.

My section conducted a three-day observation post just outside of Gildapil overlooking the border. One night while I was on sentry duty I heard gunshots and screaming about 3 kilometres on the other side of the border. The rest of the section woke but unfortunately we couldn't react because West Timor wasn't our jurisdiction. All we could do was listen to what was going on and report it. This frustrated the whole section. There was something quite significant going on within our reach and we wanted to get there. Gildapil was rat infested and thankfully we didn't stay too long.

We did have a few laughs while there, usually at someone else's expense. Our troop boss was burning rubbish one lunch time which set the village meeting house on fire and burned it to the ground. He was in a state of panic. All we could do in between fits of laughter was to just put out the spot fires in case everything else went up. This meeting house was quite large and had been there for many years.

From Gildapil we flew to Occussi, an East Timorese enclave in West Timor, where we provided OPs and border checks on individually displaced persons (IDPs) who were coming back in from West Timor. This started to wear thin after a while and when Christmas and New Year came along it was a welcome relief to get some beer inside us. As usual we ignored the normal two beers per man and ran with 'Drink as much as you can get your hands on'.

Alcohol was very hard to get hold of, but one day our section patrolled up to the edge of the border, which was defined by a large river. Once at the main crossing bridge two Indonesian soldiers approached us. One had a blue plastic bag in his hand with something heavy in it. As we struggled through the language barrier a can of Bintang, Indonesian beer, was pulled from the bag. 'For you,' they said and handed us half-a-dozen cans of beer, which we protected with our lives. Eventually succumbing to the pressure, we drank the beers at room temperature. Bear in mind room temperature in Timor is approximately 34 degrees; the tepid amber liquid never touched the sides.

There were militia troubles inland from the border that we reacted to. Our new CO, who was a bit of a clown, got quite excited about this and addressed the unit as we were awaiting the Blackhawk helicopters, saying in rather an authoritative voice, 'I am taking you to battle, men!' We were all stunned and looked at each other mystified.

Even my OC rolled his eyes back. Surely this guy wasn't for real! Once on the helicopter and still confused about what the CO had said, we headed straight for the hills to Nefelete.

When we got there my patrol was tasked to put in an observation post (OP) and monitor the troubles. On the 8-kilometre walk in we met a couple of very agitated and frightened local men. They said a militia gang was terrorising the returning refugees and had killed some East Timorese. So we went in to check the situation.

Using the dead ground we got into position about 80 metres from the border. We observed five men with .303 type bolt-action rifles about 70 metres on the other side of the border. They were indeed antagonising a group of terrified refugees and the situation was suddenly critical. One of the militia saw us and deliberately pointed his rifle at us. Once that happened, our rules of engagement required a response. Unfortunately I missed that window and he realigned his weapon across the border to the local East Timorese.

I still had a bead on him in case he needed to be neutralised. You could see the cogs clicking away in his mind as he very deliberately turned and aimed his rifle at us again. I steadied my aim and fired one round at him. I was confident that I'd hit the target as he was only 150 metres away. However, the 55.6 round is so small it will sometimes pass through a human who will be left wondering what hit him. If it doesn't hit bone it will cause minimum damage. In this case he went down into the long thin grass.

I switched my focus and took a bead on the other guys who had weapons, but by that stage they were running back into the high cornfield and looking for cover. They were no longer an imminent threat so I held my fire.

A man's body was brought into a border checkpoint with a single gunshot wound the following day. It was my first killed in action (KIA) and I have to say that mentally I took it in my stride. I simply felt I had done my job with a proper level of expertise. For the next two nights the militia continued to harass the locals at the border. They fired weapons and even burnt down huts on their side. Another section arrived and took up a separate location and we monitored the area for five more days until the situation quietened down.

We continued to patrol the area and occupy OPs until word came through that we were going home and were to be replaced by a Jordanian unit. We had become good friends with the locals in the hills and they became noticeably upset as we started our prep for leaving and the handover with the Jordanians. The Timor trip had its moments, and I knew there was better out there and started to reignite my desire for doing the SAS selection course.

We ended our tour on 28 March 2000. And in Dili Harbour we boarded the *Jervis Bay* again for the trip back to Darwin where we stayed at Larrakeyah barracks for two nights. There wasn't enough accommodation to go round so some us slept outside between the accommodation blocks. We flew home to Sydney on a Qantas 747, a special flight that was put on by the Australian Government. The plane was painted in Aboriginal designs. After we landed it taxied into a huge hangar where our families were waiting. It was terrific to see George, Lauren and baby Ashley. We got straight into the car and drove home. I briefly exchanged pleasantries with George's parents then jumped in the shower. George and I spent the next couple of days and nights in the city and got to know each other again. We ate at restaurants in the Darling Harbour area and even took in a musical at the theatre.

It was hard to get my head around the fact that I

was back in civilisation. We'd been living in the field for five months and now suddenly I was back in the concrete jungle. One night I must've been dreaming I was still over there and nearly hit George. When we were up in the hills – in fact through the whole Timor trip – we were living really close to each other; at Nefelete the hut they built for us was long but there wasn't a lot of room for the blokes inside. So the stretchers were probably only 6 inches apart. George rolled over and put her arm on me and I damn near hit her with a right cross.

As I sat crouched over her with my fist raised I suddenly knew something was wrong, I thought, 'There's walls here. Where am I?'

George said in a rather frightened voice, 'I thought you were going to hit me.' No way.

This did worry me though, and I wondered if it was ever going to happen again.

On Anzac Day the whole battalion marched in full dress uniform. The streets were lined with banners saying, 'Welcome back 3RAR' and 'Good on ya boys'. The reception we got from the public was really fantastic. After the parade we hit the beer and were slowly making our way to the pubs in The Rocks area of Sydney. As we passed a wine bar there were 20 to 30 of the lads inside and they beckoned us in. About five of us went inside and ordered a beer. When we tried to pay for it the barman said it was already paid for. I asked who had bought the beers for us, but he said that the gentleman had wanted to remain anonymous. The drinks were free for approximately one hour, which would've cost this bloke an absolute fortune. We really appreciated this, and in appreciation we drank as much beer as possible in that time. We then went down to The Rocks to the Observer Hotel and got on it there. It was a good night.

My night was cut short though, because one of the blokes was making a bit of a scene. He'd obviously drunk too much, and had spewed up all over the footpath and then passed out on one of the benches across from the pub, and was asking to get rolled by an opportunist. People were walking past looking quite unappreciatively at him and muttering, 'Look at this drunken bum.' So I picked him up and tried to get him in a taxi. Not one taxi would take us back to camp so I carried him to Central Station and got him on the train to Holsworthy.

I was still very keen to get out of 3RAR. The Timor experience only reinforced my desire to try and crack selection. When we were on the helipad in Dili we saw British SBS, the NZ SAS and SASR getting into helicopters and flying out to a job. They returned later after a successful patrol. I remember thinking that I really wanted to be a part of that organisation.

We had about four weeks leave when we arrived home from Timor and it was during this time that I found out I had malaria. I did come down with a fever over there but by the time I got to a medical facility the virus had withdrawn back into my liver and a blood test didn't diagnose it. So I just carried on as normal. The eradication drugs didn't work on return to Australia, nor did they on many other soldiers from 3RAR. So after a couple weeks back in the country I started to feel the effects of the malaria getting stronger every other day until I began shivering uncontrollably. The temperature outside that day was 40 degrees but I felt so cold that I had to wear a thick jacket to control the shivering. George took me to the army hospital on Holsworthy camp where I spent the weekend. A nurse took a blood sample and the pathology lab confirmed I had vivax malaria.

Malaria can be quite debilitating and is very hard to shake. The symptoms come on gradually. At first you feel lethargic; the next day you can feel fine; but the following day your joints ache, you've a backache and you develop photophobia as your eyes become very sensitive to light. It comes on in stages increasing in severity. Some people have slightly different symptoms and different strains of the virus have a variety of effects.

When we returned to work the battalion had started its internal posting cycle, which is designed to broaden your experience in other areas. The choices ranged from the HQ Admin Company, the fighting companies or Support Company, which included the pioneers (battalion engineers), the reconnaissance platoon, heavy weapons (including machine guns and 84 mm rocket launchers), the mortar platoon and the sniper section. I had focused my attention on the sniper section.

First I was panelled to do the parachute course. I had already completed the British course at RAF Brize Norton and had to produce evidence of this. It was now the end of April and they sent me down to the Parachute Training School in Nowra. I was starting to feel the effects of malaria coming on again and knew I would be in the hurt locker in a few days' time. While waiting to start the course I saw one of the instructors, Easto, who was from 3RAR. When he saw me he said, 'What the fuck are you doing here?' in his rough sounding voice. I said, 'They told me I've got to do the course again.' He said, 'Mate, get back in the car and fuck off.' Barry Rhodes drove me home that afternoon. Barry is an Australian lad who also served in the UK. In the early 80s he had joined the Royal Green Jackets, a light infantry regiment. He had also spent some time in Northern Ireland with them and on return to Australia he joined 3RAR. He was the parachute expert in the batallion.

I have no idea why they didn't initially recognise that qualification, but I'm glad they did in the end, as parachuting isn't one of my favourite pastimes. That was the only qualification from the marines that was recognised. They wouldn't have a bar of my sniper or reconnaissance qualifications. Whatever the cause, they made it known that I had to complete the 3RAR four-week basic sniper course and reconnaissance course to get back on track.

In June 2000 I had my first opportunity to do the barrier/pre-selection test for the SAS. A team from the regiment visited Holsworthy on their regular annual recruiting drive and they held the testing at 4RAR, a regular infantry battalion that had recently changed its role to a commando unit.

I had prepared myself reasonably well for the three-day course and I felt good the first day and achieved some good results. But the following day I was struck with another malaria attack during the long early morning pack march. We had to complete a minimum of 24 kilometres and a maximum of 28 kilometres in four hours carrying 32 kilos of kit. I started towards the front but gradually got slower and watched everyone pass me. At the 14-kilometre mark I could hardly talk and it was a struggle to stay upright. The medics there thought I was out of my tree – everything I wanted to say was jumbled and they couldn't understand me. I withdrew from the course and the next day George had to take me back to hospital again. Two days later I returned to 3RAR with my tail between my legs. I was gutted.

10

HOT SHOTS (2)

I resumed my 3RAR routine and a few weeks after the reconnaissance course I started the four-week basic battalion sniper course. I had already completed a far superior course in the Royal Marines but in a way I was glad that I had to do it. At least it would prevent people from whinging about me being a member of the sniper section without doing their course, plus it got me on the same net as everyone else. I did struggle at first during the stalks as the foliage in Australia, unlike the UK, is generally above knee height, so finding the effective prone position I was accustomed to was difficult. I now had to rely more on aids like the tripod and also tying my weapon to a tree to use as a support for the standing firing position.

During the course we used a civilian range facility at Mittagong in the New South Wales Southern Highlands. It was an 800-metre range with very different wind conditions from those I was used to. The wind would zigzag its way down the range and oddly enough this meant the rifles hardly required any windage adjustments, maybe one or two clicks left to compensate for spin drift, or Magnus drift as it is also known. For the Schmidt & Bender variable 3–12 power scope, one click at 100 metres equates to a 1-centimetre adjustment, so applying the rule of subtension, one click at 800 metres equates to 8 centimetres; two clicks at 800 metres is 16 centimetres and so on. This adjustment applies to elevation and windage corrections.

During the course I became good mates with Lee W, an ex-Grenadier guardsman from England who joined 3RAR not long before I got there and was also a veteran of the first Gulf War. Lee is professional soldier, but not very diplomatic when it comes to letting someone know that they've either screwed up, or are just not up to Lee's standard. We got on well and developed our own little competitions throughout the course.

It wasn't long before I suffered another hit from malaria. We were judging a few distances around the camp when it came on rather quickly. I could feel my back aching and had a horrible taste in my mouth. It wasn't long before I started to shiver, so Flynny, one of the instructors, took me to hospital. It was a good thing it was Friday afternoon and we were not too far away from knock-off. On Monday morning I left the hospital and rejoined the course. This time the doctor gave me a trial drug that the defence force was looking at implementing. It worked for about six months until I suffered from malaria again on the Sniper Team Leader course at Singleton.

I have read quite a lot about the art of sniping since my first sniper course in the marines and there is widespread misconception about the role of the sniper. The media have managed to rubbish the true professionals' name by calling everyone who's managed to shoot someone with anything other than a handgun 'a sniper'. So now the whole identity of snipers has been tarnished and the sniper trade looks somewhat cheapened. The actual word 'sniper' came from British soldiers in India during the colonial days. If someone was lucky enough to shoot a bird called a snipe as it flew they were regarded as a sniper. But the role of a sniper didn't really catch on until World War I. This is when Australian Billy Sing made his name. Billy Sing shot between 150 and 200 Turkish soldiers during the Gallipoli campaign.

Billy's mother was English and his father was Chinese immigrant who'd hung on after the gold rush days. Billy was born in Claremont, Central Queensland, and was already a highly ranked target shooter when he enlisted. On Gallipoli they teamed him with a spotter named Ion Idriess, who would later become one of Australia's better known authors, and they caused havoc in the Turkish ranks. In fact, the Turks sent their best man, 'Abdul the Terrible', to hunt him down. Billy was too good for him. He spotted Abdul under cover and fired first. He was decorated with a Distinguished Conduct Medal in 1916 and returned a hero in 1918. Unfortunately, his life ended sadly. His marriage broke down and he died broke and alone in a Brisbane boarding house in 1943.

Lance Corporal Simo Häyhä, a Finnish sniper known as 'The White Death', is credited with killing an amazing 542 Soviet soldiers (an average of five a day) during the Winter War using a SAKO m/128–30 (Pystykorva) and iron sights. He's regarded as the most effective sniper in the history of warfare.

Zhang Taofang, a Chinese soldier during the Korean War, made 214 confirmed kills in 32 days without using a scope. And a New Zealander, Alfred Hulme, won the Victoria Cross after he stalked and killed 33 German snipers in the Battle of Crete during World War II.

But the bloke who really impressed me was Gunnery Sergeant Carlos Hathcock in the Vietnam War. He had 93 confirmed kills but the real figure was very much higher of unconfirmed KIAs. For 35 years he held the record of the longest confirmed kill – a distance of 2,250 yards made with a scoped M2 Browning machine gun. It was finally beaten in 2002 by a Canadian, Corporal Rob Furlong, in Operation Anaconda, Afghanistan, with a confirmed kill at 2,430 metres using a .50-calibre McMillan TAC-50 rifle.

Carlos Hathcock was a marine corps scout sniper who became one of several American sniper heroes from Vietnam, not so much because of the number of confirmed kills or because he was an incredible marksman but because of his extraordinary all-round skills. Being a good or great sniper isn't measured by your number of kills; it's by being able to use your skills to the highest of standards. The real test is to be able to carry out successful missions time and time again, varying your modus operandi and living to tell the tale.

Carlos Hathcock's tactical application and sheer guts set a new standard and paved the way for the next generation. He became a role model for modern day snipers around the world. I tried to mirror his practical application and knowledge in my own sniper career. His greatest asset was his patience; he was also a brilliant marksman. A book was written about his experiences and documented an occasion where he pinned down an entire enemy company, which took cover for three days in a rice field before attempting a breakout. When they did he was waiting. He hadn't moved. This is a great example of what highly trained snipers are capable of. I have read this book a few times now and realised that everything about the 'dark art' suited my character and outlook.

I am a bit of an individual, but it's the tactical sense of sniping and the stealth that I find most engaging: getting yourself into the right firing position without being seen, taking the shot, the result and your extraction. You take everything you've been taught, put it into the one package and make it tactically sound. About 70 per cent of the sniper trade is no more than basic infantry skills but applied at a very high standard. It is the other 30 per cent that makes a good sniper and I believe this is where the 'dark art' lies. This is the area that the enemy find most sinister and where you have to put all emotion aside because you are planning in great detail to stealthily kill a specific person on the battlefield, leaving only a dead body as an indicator that you were around. Temperament is important in all forms of soldiering, but especially in sniping. It is a trade where you really have to stay calm. Your field skills have really got to be exceptional, and you've got to apply yourself to that skill. You can get yourself into position unseen or unheard easily enough, but if you can't judge distance or read mirage or wind then you're not going to be able to hit your target. It's all those little factors that all add up to complete the package.

Having a steady hand is also important, but other skills like tracking are also valuable; or at least have an understanding of tracking so when you're moving through an area you're not leaving any sign for anybody else to see. If you do leave signs you've got to cover them up somehow. If you break a twig or leave muddy boot prints on freshly fallen foliage which indicates your route, the enemy may see that, so you've always got to be mindful of the disturbance you are creating to the environment. If you're stalking with a ghillie suit on it's got fabric attached to break up your outline, so you've got to be aware of it becoming snagged on obstacles and getting pieces ripped off. Any soldier seeing that will know immediately there's a sniper in the area or one has moved through, which will bring more attention into your AO.

You've got to have the fitness and the techniques to get to unusual positions. You've got to be able to read maps proficiently, have a good sense of direction, be able to read shadows and how long they'll be at a certain time of day and use them to your advantage.

If you present yourself in an area where there's a lot of sunlight, movement is likely to catch someone's eye. It's about moving slowly and stealthily and using the terrain to your advantage to cover your movement.

You've always got to be able to see what's coming up and be aware of what's around you. So every now and again you might have to get yourself into a position on a bit of high ground where you can ob-

Me with an average Bathurst goat.

Waiting for a night extraction by Black Hawk in East Timor.

Airborne rappelling from a Black Hawk during a
training day, Moleana, East Timor.

The end of a patrol in East Timor – this was a patrol
where we used a tracker dog.

Tying off to a tree during a live fire field exercise.

In the Afghan mountains – looking north from an elevated
Observation Post from behind a .338 sniper rifle.

On a 6×6 Polaris ATV in Afghanistan.

Destroying ordnance from a severely damaged long-range patrol vehicle after being hit by an IED.

An American AME Black Hawk coming in
to pick up Sean McCarthy.

Providing security while the specialist engineers
cleared a suspect area of the track.

Looking down over IED alley. It was at the top of this feature
that we found three decapitated locals from Saraw.

Riding through the villages just outside of TK.
Dave O'Neil is on my left.

Typical Oruzgan terrain. The vegetation and high mud brick walled compounds provide excellent cover for the Taliban, and high and inaccessible mountain ranges give them perfect observation conditions.

An Australian Forward Operating Base named after Lockie.

A 5AVN Chinook landed for extraction after a night patrol.

Leaving from a tight valley after successful patrol and – one
Taliban KIA.

serve or listen to see if there is any enemy movement, or even to get an indication that someone has noticed you're around.

In March 2001 I started the Sniper Team Leader course in Singleton with my good mate Lee. We were joined by several other snipers from infantry battalions that were based in Darwin and Townsville. This course was very similar to the Royal Marines course I had completed six years before and was thoroughly enjoyable. However, my malaria raised its ugly head several times over the six-week period. By now I was really starting to get pissed off with it. It just seemed like every time I got to a certain level of fitness, or was physically run down it would hit me again.

About two weeks into the course I woke up in a pool of sweat and shivering. I put up with it through the night and by morning the virus had left my bloodstream and melted away back into my liver. This was one course that I couldn't afford to leave, as I was looking at having my own sniper team for the next trip to East Timor.

Two days later I had a full-blown fever during a navigational exercise where we were just using aerial photography, and narrowly escaped failing it. I started to feel the effects as I was gridding and scaling my aerial photograph. To grid and scale an aerial photo requires measuring the same two known points, one on a map and the other on the photograph. By using a mathematical formula with these two measurements you will get the size of the grid squares required for the aerial photo. Once you have your scale, you can lightly draw on the grid. As we individually set off I could feel myself starting to burn up. The previous times I had been admitted to hospital with malaria my body had a reached a temperature of just over 41 degrees, which could be quite dangerous and trigger convulsions. Anything over 42.5 degrees could permanently damage the brain.

I had to lie down in the shade and open my ghillie suit top until I could bring myself to start walking again. I was really struggling to make sense of what I was doing but I managed to plod on in the right direction. We had to hit six checkpoints and I had only got four, which had taken me all day to get. The others had finished long before.

That evening I managed to get hold of some doxycycline, hoping that the drug would subdue the virus long enough to complete the course. Four days later came the day/night navigation exercise and I had a bad fever the night before. The navex was conducted during some bad weather, which helped keep me cool. I started off okay but it got to the stage where I could only walk about a kilometre then had to stop for a break. I just lay on the side of the road in the rain. I couldn't hold down any food so I just sipped away at my water. Part of my route saw me walking underneath high tension powerlines, which should have been very easy going, as

the track was a firebreak, wide and cleared. However, the clay was quite sticky due to the rain.

I'd gone about 200 metres under the powerlines
when I fainted. I fell backwards onto my pack,
which weighed 32 kilos. I can't remember how
many times that happened during that nav leg, but it
seemed to take forever. The final checkpoint for the
day nav wasn't too far from the end of this clay track
but I was absolutely exhausted. Somehow I mus-
tered up the energy to slog away to the end. Once
there I was able to get some food on board and after
a rest I started to perk up a little. Pete, one of the
DS, walked with me on the night navex as he was
concerned about my wellbeing, but I finished the
nav exercise and went on to finish the team leader
course.

Towards the end of the year 3RAR did a series
of build-up exercises in and around Townsville in
preparation for our second Timor deployment. Lee
and I were now promoted to lance corporals. Lee
went to Bravo Company as a section 2IC and I
stayed on in snipers as a team leader. Sniper section
conducted a reasonable amount of our own training
as did most of the battalion, only coming together
for the final exercise. One day during the course of
this exercise I was riding in the back of a Land
Rover with Paul as we were being driven out to the
range. Our colleague 'Monty', who was driving,
was obviously fatigued and the reconnaissance platoon boss was asleep in the front passenger seat.

Monty's driving deteriorated by the minute, so I suggested to him to stop and take a rest. He said he was okay but then drove straight past the turn-off to the range. Paul knew something wasn't right but couldn't quite put his finger on it and asked Monty if he knew where he was going, to which he replied, 'Yes!' So for a while we sat there and said nothing.

Monty was nodding off momentarily and Paul angrily told him to pull over but he wouldn't, and next minute he drove into a severe dip in the road way too fast, panicked and hit the brakes, which sent us into a 50-metre sideways slide before we hit the bank on the right side of the gravel road and rolled the vehicle onto its side. I got catapulted onto Paul, who hurt his back badly. My first thoughts were to get hold of Monty and punch the hell out of him, but I had to help Paul first. As I got Paul out I noticed this Monty idiot standing beside the Land Rover having a smoke. 'You fuckin' bastard!' I shouted. 'Give me a hand!' He was in a state of shock, so I got him to get the accident forms out and start filling in the paperwork. He had to go back inside the vehicle to get the accident forms out, but didn't even bother to help the reconnaissance platoon commander who was still trapped inside by the seatbelt. I had to get in from the driver's door that was facing skywards to help him out.

We had no form of mobile communications and

luckily a civilian turned up who had a winch on his 4×4. We hooked up the winch cable to the Land Rover and turned it back on its wheels and then pushed it to the side of the road. The young lieutenant got a ride out with the civilian and told range control what had happened. I remained with Paul, who was in severe pain and four hours later a recovery team turned up to survey the damage and tow the Land Rover back to base. Monty got off this reckless accident scot-free; meanwhile Paul is still having trouble with his back.

One good thing about our return to Timor in 2002 was that I'd achieved my aim to be sniper team leader on operations, even though the operational environment was very quiet. I was among the advance party from 3RAR that flew to Dili on an RAAF C130 Hercules, and then was driven to Moleana. The humidity hit us as we walked off the back ramp of the aircraft and to a small fleet of trucks. We were to work from Moleana for the next six months. On arrival at our location we quickly orientated ourselves to the camp and received a good handover from the 2RAR guys. During the first couple of days we met up with the Blackhawk crew briefly before they rotated out. I was pretty sure Bingers was there again also.

As snipers we operated as two four-man teams with the ability to break down into pairs if needed. My team consisted of Paul, Chris and MP, who I worked with again when he joined me at SASR. We lived in porta-cabins that had been joined together and had the centre wall removed. Conditions weren't bad. We had hot and cold running water, good cooked meals every day we were on base, and real toilets! Most of our work involved observing border crossing points where the TNI were controlling movement back and forth. West Timorese locals would trade fuel and other items in the tactical coordination line (TCL), which was the designated border. The TNI would let the locals cross to the other side in the mornings to trade their goods, but when they returned in the afternoons they'd charge them a fee for the privilege.

The Indonesians swore this wasn't happening so we set out to gather the evidence. And on this particular job there were only three of us: MP, Paul and myself. We inserted at night by foot from one of the checkpoints that was manned by a section from Bravo Company. The locals don't particularly like the dark so we got into our final location undetected.

But as we pushed through to our OP location we got covered with this very fine hair from a bush which worked its way through our clothing and stuck into our bare flesh. This made us itch furiously for the next 24 hours and we all broke out in rashes. The observation post was too good to leave so we set up our optics and cameras with long-range lenses in among this extremely aggressive foliage. It wasn't long before we started to see some activity across the border.

We got perfect shots of the TNI taking their cut – often in American dollars – and hiding it in the roof of the shelter they'd made. On our return we sent our evidence up the chain of command and they produced this to the Indonesians. They did make an attempt to control the black market checkpoints after that but it was a hopeless task. There was virtually no fuel in East Timor for local use, but it was readily available over the border. So they did bring it across, and they charged a fortune for it.

We did do some good work throughout the trip but nothing that would place your life in any serious danger. Tensions between us, the militia and the Indonesians had virtually come to an end in 2000. There were a few minor bun fights between locals at a couple of checkpoints, but nothing too serious.

As a result of the lack of conflict, sniper section got on the wrong side of the company hierarchy, as we would always question the reasoning behind painfully pointless tasks. We all had high personal standards, and begrudged being sent out into the field because someone was too lazy to do their job properly. Soon we found ourselves constantly tasked and this kept us in the field and away from the command structure. In the end it suited us to be away from Moleana and all the bickering and ridiculous rules that were being thrown around by the bored battalion and company hierarchy.

The pattern that developed was a two to three day OP operation, back in camp for a few days and then out again. During our time back in base I used the Kiowa helicopters of 161 recce squadron to conduct a visual reconnaissance of the ground where we were to operate, which worked a treat. Because the foliage can be quite sparse throughout Timor we spotted the best possible locations to place OPs just about every time. The helicopter pilots were very good to us and always keen to help us out. I think they enjoyed doing something different from their normal TCL runs and joy rides for officers.

I also worked closely with the Blackhawk crews organising the insertion and extraction of our next task. They had started a database on all the LPs (landing points) and LZs (landing zones) within the Australian AO. And when I was given one of these 'pointless' tasks I was talking about earlier, I just popped in to see these guys and they gave me all the information I needed with 15 minutes. When I produced this information to the company hierarchy it sent them into a rage. They thought I was going behind their backs and being obstinate. I thought I was being practical and showing some initiative.

The task was for my sniper team to walk a 26-kilometre circuit of several helicopter landing points and landing zones, to check on their condition and report back. The Blackhawk crews were even prepared to fly to each LP and LZ, which would have been completed in approximately one hour from start-up to shut-down. The result was that we were inserted by vehicle for a long and tedious walk. Both 'superiors' very quickly lost what little respect I had for them.

On another occasion we were ordered to occupy an OP on a very large bare rock in the middle of a wide river on the border. It had no cover from view or fire, and no escape routes. If for some reason we had come under fire in that location we would have had to run straight into the open to a feature which faced the enemy. Paul even pointed out a track on the aerial photograph that ran right through the centre of it, but the officer in charge was hell-bent on putting my team on that rock. It was thoughtless planning like this that inspired me even more to move on to better pastures. We did the job, but didn't go anywhere near that suggested location.

This trip wasn't all bad news. It was frustrating, yes, but we did have a few laughs in between. At one OP location we killed a snake and decided to take it back to Moleana for the 'prevent med' guys to identify for poison antidote, as they had limited information on the flora and fauna of East Timor. It turned out to be a python. I felt like a real mug and the boys didn't let me forget it.

On what little time we had off we managed to get into the township of Maleana to check out the markets, which were about a slow 15-minute drive away. Some of the blokes bought trinkets for family members, but more importantly we had sourced a little local bloke who would sell us beer for double what we pay in Australia. We tried to haggle but he knew he had the monopoly and wouldn't budge on the price. So we parted with the cash. This was one of our personal little wins over the army, and as soldiers do, we love to down a few amber nectars from time to time.

Towards the end of our tour I bumped into the RSM, Peter Tyrell – or 'Squirrel' as he was known. He was a good bloke and we got chatting. He asked me what I wanted to do that next year so I said I wanted a posting to Perth, as near as possible to Campbell Barracks, the SASR headquarters. By now I had only one object in mind – to join the regiment. My plan was to get out of Sydney and position myself for the selection course. He supported me, and pulled all the right strings to help me secure a position as a lance corporal in 16RWAR, a reserve unit based about 6 kilometres from Campbell Barracks.

My team managed to produce some good results from our observations of Indonesian army activities over the six months and I was proud of them for that, even though the situation was benign. However, we did go on high alert just before the Bali bombings and for a short time afterwards. Elections had been held the previous year for a constituent assembly to draft a constitution. That was completed by February 2002 and East Timor became formally independent on 20 May, with Xanana Gusmão sworn in as the country's president.

I would get to know XG, as we called him, a few years later as a member of SASR. Dramas did arise in December 2002 when rioting students set fire to the house of Prime Minister Marí Alkatiri and advanced on the police station. The police opened fire and one student was killed. The students carried his body to the national parliament building where they fought the police, set a supermarket on fire and plundered shops. The police opened fire again and four more students were killed. But 3RAR had been home two months by that stage. Alkatiri called an inquiry and blamed foreign influence for the violence, a typical response from him.

11

MAKING THE GRADE

As soon as I got the posting order I applied to do SAS selection. I had a friend in the regiment who was trying everything he could to give me a heads up on what I needed to concentrate on for the best chance of success. But in reality there wasn't a lot he could do. I began completing the paperwork, stringent medical examinations, written tests and psychological evaluations.

First came 'barrier testing' back at Holsworthy, the physical endurance work that gives the training staff a good idea if you have the makings to attempt selection. What worried me was that I'd hurt my knee running around Moleana and it wouldn't heal. By now I was pretty sure I'd beaten the malaria off and I trained hard for the barrier testing with a mate – RS – who also wanted to join SASR. The barrier was a combined test with 4RAR and, as it turned out, RS did his barrier testing a couple of days before me and he passed with flying colours. In my group of six candidates for SASR only two of us got through. Step one down and dusted!

3RAR was winding down for Christmas leave, and I had my sights firmly set on Perth and selection. I continued a tough training regime I designed for myself interspersed with organising our relocation to Perth, although I did slip over to New Zealand with Lee for one week for a hunting trip.

With George and the girls, I arrived in Perth on a Saturday and our first impressions were good – it seemed clean and quiet. We stayed in a hotel until we could move into a defence house close to Campbell Barracks. Early the next day we went for a walk around the CBD until lunch time then caught a train to Swanbourne and walked to the married patch to check it out. It was very hot and the girls – by now three and four – were getting tired and grumpy, but we gained a good idea of the area, which was close to the beach. When our gear arrived we moved in.

I had a couple of friends from 3RAR who were also posted to 16RWAR including their training warrant officer. When I told them I was doing selection they let me do my own training, which I was very thankful for. In fact, I was only at 16RWAR for five weeks before I started selection.

Selection began on 18 February 2003. I met up

with RS and a couple of others from the old battalion and we were transported to a hangar in the training area at Bindoon where we and our kit were thoroughly searched. We didn't get much sleep that night due to nerves and the bloody snorers, and were woken at 0400 hours to start the 15-kilometre timed pack march to another camp.

During this walk a huge blister developed on my right heel. I was surprised this happened as I had walked a lot of miles wearing the same boots and never had a problem. I wasn't happy about this, particularly at such an early stage. We were to stay at this camp for the next five days conducting several lessons and a three-day continuous navigation exercise. I was ever mindful that the malaria might resurface at any stage, and also did everything I could to make that blister as comfortable as possible. After this phase we spent a fair bit of time at Lancelin, a very scrubby area north of Perth, and although that phase was very hard I began to enjoy it. The tests were a series of solo pack marches from point to point over quite long distances carrying about 32 kilos in a pack plus webbing. It was quite tough because it was midsummer and temperatures were mainly in the high 30s; we even had days at 41 degrees.

During this phase I tackled it more systematically than most other candidates as I knew I wasn't a bad walker with a pack on my back, and my nav was pretty good. So just before dark I'd find a spot and settle down for the night. I'd get my wet sweaty gear off and get inside my sleeping bag, as the nights were quite cold. I would cook up a feed and knock up a brew from the ration pack while it was still light, then get a good night's sleep to start fresh and early in the morning. There were times when I was woken up by blokes stomping past me in the dead of night, tripping over and cursing because they were walking into things or falling flat on their faces – an easy way to acquire an injury and be withdrawn from selection.

Endurance is all in the mind. If your mind becomes corrupt when you're on selection you're finished. For example, when I started to think, 'I'm starving right now and I could really tuck into a pizza,' I had to blanket it with other thoughts and press on. You can be big, strong and extremely physically fit but if you're not mentally tough enough you won't pass. As long as your mind keeps telling your body to keep on going and to put one foot in front of the other you'll be there at the end.

Of course, sometimes the body will just simply give up. One of the lads in my syndicate passed out with exhaustion but then got back on his feet and finished selection.

By the end of the ordeal in early March I was absolutely exhausted and very happy to finish. We had to wait until the following day before they told us who had passed and who hadn't. Then suddenly I was in. Strangely, it felt like a bit of an anticlimax, probably because I was so knackered. I'd expected to feel much more excited about passing. George was really happy for me. In fact she was more excited than me. She did know of the potential dangers of the job as I didn't keep any secrets from her about what would – or could – happen if I got selected. I wanted her to know exactly what we were getting into and she supported me. Being in the regiment probably gave her a sense of security as well, because this would mean we could live in Perth for as long as I stayed in the army.

George brought some beers, pizza and chocolate biscuits to the main gate of Campbell Barracks and I shared this with RS. I put the biscuits in the fridge for the next day but RS decided to have a midnight snack and ate the whole packet. I was annoyed; he is a bloody eating machine.

Selection just gets you through the door. Waiting on the other side was the 'reinforcement cycle' where the real training occurs. Some blokes from the previous selection, which ran in September 2002, had joined us for the start of the 'reo cycle'. We started by learning to operate the majority of the weapons the unit owned, from the 5.56 mm M4 to the Javelin rocket launcher. Directly after that we went on to the patrol course to learn special reconnaissance and close country warfare. Other specialist courses followed and the entire reinforcement cycle was to take us 14 months to complete, but that time flew by as we were always busy.

My knee was giving more trouble and I had to have an operation on it three months into the cycle. This meant I had to miss roping course, which I had to pick up later on. There were complications with the operation that gave me no end of trouble during the most feared course on the reo cycle, close quarter battle (CQB). The standards were exceptionally high and extremely hard work, the instructors took no prisoners. I'd be driving home at the end of the day mentally and physically exhausted. Christmas leave was rapidly approaching and I was looking forward to the break. A few didn't make it to the end of the cycle, and one was sent on his way shortly after it completed.

When you join the regiment you lose whatever rank you previously held from your parent unit, and have to earn your stripes at a new level. But there's mutual respect between officers and operators and the organisational pyramid is quite flat, which means there are a lot of chiefs and not many Indians. If someone comes up with a job, everyone has an idea of how they want to conduct it. There might be a few arguments but inevitably the result will be a better plan. There are highly motivated soldiers at all levels and opinions are valued and listened to. Some of the lads have degrees behind them in a variety of subjects, and some more practical than others, but it's the way they apply themselves to soldiering that makes them better than everybody else.

A sense of humour is important. Sometimes it can be pretty black, but that's inevitable in the work we do. When you're out on a live job you concentrate on the task at hand. If you're not concentrating you won't last the distance and you might take some of your mates with you. If there's a sudden attack it's got to be dealt with there and then, but you have to have the ability to relax again afterward and have a laugh.

The other hallmark of the SAS is controlled aggression. You've got to develop the ability to remain calm and relaxed but to turn on the aggression in a flash, and then to turn it off just as quick. If you don't already possess this attribute it is built into you during the reinforcement cycle when live firing or conducting close quarter battle.

After the reo cycle I was posted to 3 Squadron and familiarised myself with the normal regiment routine. The squadron was running a mobility course and I was panelled on it as a student. This was to become my insertion skill. Generally you will only pick up one insertion skill; some may get lucky and become multi-skilled. There are three insertion skills in SASR: mobility, which deals with all types of motorised transport and special reconnaissance from all terrain vehicles (ATV); water ops, the divers with the ability to insert by boat or submarine and can provide coastal reconnaissance; and freefall, covering specialised parachutists who are inserted by aircraft at varying altitudes.

Every operator in the unit is basic parachute qualified, which means we have the ability to insert from an aircraft using the round static line parachutes only. These are deployed at an altitude of 800–1,000 feet. We generally parachute into the ocean as the unit cannot afford to lose blokes due to injuries sustained when landing on hard ground.

My first exercise with the regiment was a mobility exercise, part of a wider ADF exercise that ran during June and July 2004. At the start, we had a fair amount of planning and preparation time, which meant we could mix business with pleasure. As usual we started crawling before we could run and conducted a couple of overnight patrol-sized activities, and then built up to squadron size. The primary objective was to square away our mobility and special reconnaissance capability, but we also managed to conduct several live fire exercises.

I hadn't seen so much ordnance in my life. But we needed this to be able to train to the high calibre of the regiment, and also to remain very proficient in our vast array of weapon systems. We conducted plenty of live fire vehicle-mounted and foot patrol break contacts withdrawing from an enemy engagement under fire and then culminated in a live fire deliberate attack (DA) combining the two. Because I was the driver of our long-range patrol vehicle (LRPV) one of my weapon systems was the Carl Gustaf, an 84 mm Swedish recoilless anti-tank weapon. I placed this on the outside of the vehicle just by the steering wheel for easy access, so if need be I could rapidly remove the 84, grab two high explosive (HE) rockets and move off to a flank, then in quick succession send each rocket into the target.

In between activities we were stood down for the weekends and were able to catch a taxi into the centre of Darwin for a few well-earned beers.

The main exercise was starting and it was time for us to insert into the field. Nev, my patrol commander, had decided we should use the 6×6 Polaris ATV instead of our traditional LRPVs to keep a low signature and to increase our mobility. There was a downside to this: we were up against an armoured unit with Leopard tanks. We packed the ATVs to carry six days rations, water, fuel, spare parts, field kit and an assortment of weaponry and ammunition. This wasn't enough to keep us going for the whole 10-day exercise, so we had to organise a resupply for the night of day five.

It was late in the afternoon as the patrol loaded the four ATVs onto the waiting C130 Hercules at RAAF Base Darwin, and would be dark before we inserted onto a private airfield in the Katherine region. We prepared our night vision kit for the dropoff before departure, making sure it was focused and had fresh batteries. Once in the air, the pilots turned off the white light and started tactical flying – keeping the aircraft low, almost contouring the ground. It's not a smooth way to fly and it wasn't long before I started to feel a little nauseous and wishing it would come to an end.

Soon the back ramp of the aircraft was cracked, letting a rush of warm air into the fuselage and we got the two-minute signal from the aircrew. We started the vehicles to ensure a smooth and rapid deployment and I sucked in as much fresh air as possible to try to stop myself from being sick. The engine revs dropped right off and suddenly we felt the thud of the C130 touching down on the dirt airstrip. As it braked hard the back ramp fully opened, filling the back end with dust and we came to a brief stop. On the load master's signal we drove the vehicles down the ramp and entered the orange dust. Initially it was very difficult to see into the night through our night vision goggles (NVGs) as our eyes weren't adjusted to the dark and the aircraft had disturbed a lot of dust from the airstrip. The air temperature was about 26 degrees and relatively humid as we watched the C130 turn around then take off in the direction that we had arrived. We had found some dead ground just off the runway that was big enough to conceal the ATVs until we felt secured enough to start patrolling.

The hum of the aircraft engines was fading away under the sound of frogs and crickets when Nev put up one hand splaying his fingers, indicating to each patrol member that we were moving in five minutes.

We travelled cross-country all night through the

varying Northern Territory bush, tackling natural obstacles and dodging termite mounds to insert deep inside the exercise AO, and just before first light we found a suitable LUP where we could harbour up for most of the daylight hours. Once we deemed the LUP was secure, JB and I refuelled and checked the maintenance of the vehicles while the other patrol members were either on sentry duty (piquet), conducting communications checks or making a brew.

After a good rest we decided to make a move mid-afternoon to find another LUP that would be suitable for us to conduct a night foot patrol to seek enemy activity. Unfortunately, once in that LUP the enemy found us. The 2IC didn't do his job of covering our tracks properly where we crossed a small single-vehicle track that had looked like it was regularly used. An enemy Land Rover used as a light reconnaissance vehicle saw the tracks and decided to follow them up. We were compromised, but got over it by using some stealth and aggression and ambushed them as they headed on foot towards our LUP.

We had to move from that location, which meant travelling all night to a different area where we would get some rest and then conduct some reconnaissance patrols by day.

During another move we found a tank troop harbour. I was the lead scout and on foot for our six-man patrol, ATVs trailing quietly behind. Suddenly to the left at about 40 metres from the corner of my eye I saw a main gun barrel from a Leopard 2 slightly protruding from a heavily vegetated area. We back-tracked slowly taking each step deliberately, making sure we didn't step or drive on anything that would make a noise and alert the enemy to us. It was a very slow process to move the hundred or so metres away from where we initially saw the enemy. We went into all-round defence and conducted a listening stop for approximately one hour to try to pick up some of their routine.

These tanks have to start up every now and then to recharge their batteries, so you can count how many tanks or at least get a rough idea of how many there are when they start up one after the other. Once we had a fair idea we quietly slipped away even further and Dave called a notional air strike onto them.

By now we needed a resupply so we headed off to a pre-designated area that Nev had organised for the C130 to drop our requested supplies to us by parachute. It was very dark that night but everything ran smoothly.

Soon we were coming towards the end of the exercise and had to make our way to our extraction point. Pick-up was by C130 at night, and as I drove my ATV up the back ramp and into the belly of the aircraft I felt quite proud that I was part of the regiment and finally doing something where I felt a sense of achievement.

After the exercise, 3SQN was going to drive back to Perth cross-country via the Canning Stock Route. I had to miss this, as I needed to get back for the start of the SF sniper course. This was by far the best sniper course I had been on. We covered all the basic principles at the beginning and then rapidly moved on to more advanced tactical applications and a variety of sniper weapon systems, including the 7.62 mm semi-automatic, the .338 and the .50-calibre suite. As well as collating ballistic data in log books we also used a personal digital assistant (PDA) to calculate firing solutions. This uses specifically designed software to give you elevation and windage settings by analysing the data you input. Some of the data you need to apply is range, wind strength and direction, muzzle velocity and projectile weight. Of course it's only as accurate as the data you program into it but if done correctly you can safely guarantee a first-round hit at 1,000 metres. The percentage of hits will start to drop after that range; for example at 1,200 metres it generally drops to about 85 per cent. But even then if your round misses it would still be close enough to make a very small adjustment and hit with your second shot.

We spent a lot of time on the ranges shooting out to 1,000 metres with the 7.62 mm weapons, and out to 1,800 metres and 2.5 kilometres with the larger calibre rifles. I gained valuable knowledge on different wind conditions at the Perth ranges as the sea breeze gets quite strong and is never constant. It even does a complete 180-degree turn at about 1100 to 1200 hours at certain times of the year. This is all very valuable experience for the sniper. Learning about wind can quite easily turn into what seems like a science: for example, if the rifle bore has a right-hand twist, the projectile will spin clockwise on its trajectory and if the wind is coming from 9 o'clock it will push your round slightly low and to the right, while a wind at 3 o'clock will throw the round a little higher to the left as it climbs the fingers of the wind. How far the round is pushed depends on the wind strength.

We also incorporated shooting with a spotter as much as possible, rotating between tasks after each shoot. This gave the spotters confidence in adjusting the sniper onto a target, calling wind strengths, directions and 'mirage' with increasing accuracy. A lot of time was dedicated to shooting moving targets; this was a big part of the counterterrorism (CT) phase.

The course ran for eight weeks and encompassed the 'green' (field) side of sniping, and domestic CT. We shot a lot at night using thermal imagers (TI), and image intensifiers (a night observation device that amplifies ambient light). We also experimented shooting through different types of glass with a variety of rounds and studying the effects.

Apart from the first stalk, every one was a 'live fire' stalk, by day and night. This is where we really needed to calculate the trajectory over the range of the shot, because if the round didn't have a clear path through foliage or buildings it would be deflected and you wouldn't hit the target. As the course progressed we did more in an urban environment, learning different applications for camouflage and concealment, tactical movement and approach shooting. We also practised helo (helicopter) sniping from a Blackhawk.

Much of the course was centred on Lancelin and Bindoon. Lancelin is full of saltbush intertwined with a really fine vine, like a creeper that runs through the scrub at ankle level. It is public land but there's a naval gunfire impact area and the live fire range extends out to several kilometres. It's really ideal for the task except for the ticks – little red ones – which are absolutely everywhere and in plague proportions. They get in mostly around your belt area, we've tried many methods of prevention and extraction but nothing seems to work. You are supposed to twist them off so they don't leave their head buried inside your skin, but this never works either. Some blokes do get a bad reaction from them, but generally you'll end up with a small and very itchy sore that can last up to four weeks. They feed on the kangaroos and often you'll come across a mob that will be in very poor condition; some may not even hop off like the others because they've got so many ticks sucking the life out of them.

At the end of the course we were presented our

crossed rifles – my third – and proceeded to get pissed at the bar. On return to 3SQN we concentrated on overseas recovery operations, similar to what the American Delta Force does. The OC did an exceptional job raising our capability on overseas recovery to a comparable standard to that of the US and British Special Forces. Obviously, we would never get right to the top without the kind of assets and weaponry they had but we were improving our capability all the time. We trained aggressively and tried to cover every scenario.

Then suddenly in Iraq the Australian businessman Douglas Wood was taken hostage. We reckoned the timing couldn't have been more perfect.

12

MISSION ABORTED

We heard about Douglas Wood's capture on the news the day before we left Campbell Barracks for a hostage rescue exercise in Adelaide. Initially, I thought, 'He'll be released very shortly,' but when we got to the airport at Adelaide and came together as a group the CO was there. He told us the good news – good for us because it was looking highly likely that we would get the chance to execute the regiment's first overseas recovery job; not so good for Douglas Wood at the time.

This was a big deal for the Australian Government also. The set-up we had been developing was untested in combat conditions at the time so Adelaide was a good exercise for us to prove our capabilities. It was more along the lines of a domestic CT response, which involved the police, emergency services and others. But we could still include what we had been working on.

The police were the first responders. They evaluated the situation: hostages were taken in a violent fashion and automatic weapons were involved; that meant the threat to the hostages was quite high. If the captors threatened to shoot them or had shot one and thrown him out the door as a statement, then we would respond.

In the event, the exercise was successful; our tactics worked well under pressure and we learned some valuable lessons. We returned to Perth and prepared to embark four patrols to Baghdad. We were all raring to go. Then suddenly four patrols were cut to just two and we wondered how we were going to handle the job with so few of us.

When they announced the names of the two patrols, I was glad to see mine there. We conducted further training together to get back 'on net' because as a patrol we had not worked together directly. We went through the specialist skills designating each operator to particular tasks and I was designated the patrol sniper. I was armed with my M4 and a USP 9 mm hand gun, I also took my SR25, a 7.62 mm sniper rifle. This gave me the ability to either shoot at long range or conduct close quarter combat.

Defence engaged a civilian charter plane and we flew direct to Kuwait, where we put some gear together at an Allied base that had been maintained there since the first Gulf War. We then boarded an

Australian Hercules and flew straight to Iraq. We landed at Baghdad international airport around midday and transferred to armoured vehicles for the drive to where the Australian Security Detachment (SECDET) were staying.

They were based in an American facility – formerly the old Ba'ath Party HQ – just on the verge of the Green Zone. SECDET were a detachment of battalion soldiers who were responsible for the Australian Embassy's security. My patrol was attached to the Delta boys from the US. The other patrol stayed in our hasty accommodation where SECDET were and were attached to taskforce (TF) Black, the British Special Boat Service – the SF unit of the Royal Marines – and commuted to and from the SBS quarters – all in the Green Zone but a stone's throw from each other.

We had ideas of integrating us into the Allied teams and working with their guys, but we wanted to get the operation out of the way first. The CO told us we'd be there for three months regardless. 'As soon as the operation finishes you'll start working with the other SF groups,' he said. This would have been awesome, as they were doing some fantastic work. But as it turned out we found ourselves caught up in what we called the 'intelligence game'.

The Australians, British and Americans were spreading a lot of cash around trying to buy intelligence about Douglas Wood's whereabouts. Not surprisingly, the Iraqis were coming forward with information that was no good, taking the cash and doing a runner. Then there were two Iraqi doctors, a married couple, who were selling a lot of information to anyone who was prepared to pay for it, and they were pulling in a lot of cash. But they were walking a very fine line; it's almost like being a double agent – which they probably were – if you were found out supplying information, you would lose your head. They gave information about Douglas Wood but it was very vague because they knew they could come back and get more money. In this case it didn't do anyone much good and these two finished up dead.

But every now and again you would get what the Americans call a 'walk-in'. These are locals who would approach American soldiers with information. Nine times out of 10 the response they get would be 'Forget it, buddy, piss off'. It is very rare that someone is genuine but occasionally it really pays off. That's what happened with the Italian journalists recovered in 2005. They had a walk-in by a guy who said he had information. The Americans initially said, 'Bugger off, mate, you're taking the piss.' This bloke came back shortly after and offered information regarding some Europeans. He was interviewed and the captives turned out to be Italians.

Our teams rehearsed nearly every day in building clearances, insertion and extraction and shooting just in case we got confirmation of the whereabouts of Douglas Wood and we'd able to react accordingly. There was a lot of information coming forward but nothing of substance. We were working on the basis that if we were 80 per cent confident in its provenance we'd act on it, whereas the Americans were working on a much lower level of proof. In fact, they would respond on very small amounts of information, which is probably not a bad idea when a hostage is in great danger, but they did end up hitting a lot of dry holes. They would hit target after target and gain very little. It did put their guys at risk but at least they could then take that information out of the equation. They were as keen as mustard to help us out.

To secure our 80 per cent confirmation with some of the sources coming forward we would buy them a camera and tell them to go away to get a snapshot of Douglas Wood. These are guys living on the edge, so you have to expect some pretty weird results. There was one guy, an absolute nut case, who had heard that the Americans were looking for an Australian so he made himself known. He was given money to buy a camera and take a picture of Douglas Wood. He took the money but bought a phone – not a phone with a camera, just a phone.

The Delta guys were not happy. These fellas are firm but fair, and said to him, 'Do that again and you'll end up in prison!' He was given more money

– this time to buy a camera, and was told, 'Get a photo of Douglas Wood, and tell us where he is.'

So he went away and bought a camera, but then came back and asked for more money. He was now pushing his luck. 'Go and get some proof of identity,' he was ordered. He returned with some bogus information about some Turkish hostages in the same place who were being anally raped.

'Go and get the address.'

'Back soon.'

You've got to admire the Americans' patience. I don't know where he went but when he came back he displayed a photo he'd taken: 'This is your guys,' he said. It showed a TV screen of some male porn, but you could see the outside of a TV set on the edges of the photo!

The Americans said, 'Thanks very much, mate. You're going straight to prison.' It turned out this guy's family had been killed during a significant battle and he was after a bit of payback. They figured he was setting us up to assault a compound or a house which may have been wired full of explosives, and on detonation would collapse the house on the team.

Our Australian intelligence guys in Baghdad worked hard to get information also. It was the first overseas recovery job the Australians were involved in, so the agencies really wanted to do a top job. They were really working hard to get some good intelligence as to where Mr Wood was. They got close – they worked on an informer who said he wasn't too far away, which was actually the case, but we just couldn't pinpoint the right spot. The Americans also had intelligence that he was in the general area but they couldn't discover the exact building either.

However, just as some really good information came forward a combined American–Iraqi operation swept through an area and found him. We were happy for Douglas Wood but disappointed we were not able to help with the recovery.

It was a big anticlimax for all involved, because everyone on the project had worked hard. We were trained to do the job and we'd have done it well given the chance. We did a little bit of security for Douglas Wood at the hospital and the other team did security for him when he was transferred to Dubai, but that was it. Game over.

Before leaving we conducted a security survey on the Australian Embassy in Baghdad and put together a contingency plan if unwanted guests were to break through the physical security.

We wrapped up the survey in about five days and left shortly afterwards. Debriefing was important on our return. Everything you do first up always provides lessons. This operation was entirely new to all Australian Government agencies and we figured there was probably a good chance that we would change the way we went about it next time. Maybe the government saw it as a bit of a tester, as they too were probably concerned about how it was all going to run. Douglas Wood himself was a bit of a rarity in that he had an American wife and was living in the US, and his captors saw him as a source of income, not a political statement.

We returned to Australia in July and resumed our normal training pattern for about three months. At the time some of the squadrons were well under their nominal strength. So it really came as no surprise when word passed around in October that reinforcements were needed for 2 Squadron in Afghanistan. I was on the east coast on a special recovery operations (SRO) exercise when the OC called in six of us and told us we'd been chosen. 'Any dramas with that?' he asked.

'Nope, no dramas.'

'Okay, you're leaving tonight. Pack your bags; don't say anything to the other blokes. You have to go to Randwick barracks where they're conducting pre-deployment lectures.'

We sat in these ridiculous lectures for three days before we rebelled. The lectures aimed at the wider army and were totally irrelevant to what we do. They might have helped people in an admin role who didn't train for conflict, but not frontline soldiers. Towards the end of day three there was a lesson on Afghan culture, and were amazed that a

Sydney taxi driver was brought in to talk to us. I thought that was quite appropriate for Sydney, but not ideal considering the circumstances.

However, the guy who was running the pre-deployment package was really good. When we told him we'd had enough he said, 'No worries, you've done enough for me to sign you off anyway.'

Back at Campbell Barracks we did some more build-up training before departure. There was probably half the patrol who hadn't worked with each other before. So we developed some patrol integrity and worked up some drills to get accustomed to each other's idiosyncrasies. This would also be beneficial when working in the dark – you could identify someone by the way they moved or conducted their drills. Of course, we knew when we got there we'd all get farmed out to different patrols but it's good to work closely with as many members of the regiment as possible. You never know when you'll be thrown together on an operation, and knowing each other's strengths and weaknesses can mean life or death.

We took the same chartered plane that had flown us to the Middle East earlier that year. And from Kuwait we travelled to Qatar where there was quite a large contingent of admin staff and RAAF personnel. This was the base for the C130s in the Gulf. They were attached to a huge American camp big enough to support several messes. We weren't there long before a C130 flew us directly to Tarin Kowt,

Oruzgan, Afghanistan. It was like walking into a reunion as we were led around our compound and shown the accommodation. We were briefed by the troop sergeant, PG, who reckoned it was going to be on between us and the Taliban up north. Our first patrol was to take us through the area where 2 Squadron had previously been viciously contacted by the enemy in the Khod valley. So with that in the back of our minds we spent as much time as possible on the range.

Three days later we were heading out.

I was in RH's patrol; a bunch of magic blokes. Four were straight off the reinforcement cycle that had been sent to 2 Squadron and immediately overseas. But they were good soldiers. One was an ex-clearance diver and the other three had infantry backgrounds.

Once we left the gates we headed north to a place called Saraw. I rode on the back of the LRPV as an extra shooter as we drove through villages every 10 to 15 kilometres apart. At the side of the road I saw an old T55 Russian tank half buried on a river's edge, a reminder of the history of Afghanistan, which has been at some kind of war for longer than we've been writing history books.

The countryside was a mix of stark, bare, rocky mountains and valleys – 'the green' – is the lush vegetation either side of a large river usually stretching out to 1–2 kilometres at right angles to the river. The wind rose and fell unpredictably and changed direction as it whipped around the mountain passes. There were no trees on the hillsides to act as indicators of wind strength or direction, so when calculating adjustments for your scope a sniper had to rely on small puffs of the fine dust from the shoes of moving targets or from the tyres of vehicles. You could also get an idea of the wind strength as the target's clothes flapped in the gusts. Sometimes if you were lucky you could get an indication from a small flag or piece of cloth that was hanging from a compound wall.

Generally the women stayed inside the compounds, but we would often have kids staring at us as we passed. The men – bearded and surly – would be in the fields with their crops or gathered in small groups lazily seeing the day out. You'd never get a friendly grin out of any of them. If you wanted information, you paid, and you could never be sure if they were telling you the truth. At best, only 25 per cent of the population seemed to be on side with us. Many of them said they hated the Taliban and they probably did, but at least they provided some kind of law and order. Some spoke very broken English, so we would communicate through an interpreter hired from an American company. They treated the government in Kabul with the contempt it probably deserved. And there was never a minute outside your own base when you could relax.

It took two days to get to Saraw in the blazing sun and dust because the patrolling program was quite slow and focused in the surrounding area. To get into the valley where Saraw is located you first have to move through a mountain pass we called IED Alley. It is quite steep and very narrow towards the top. All the way up the pass there are burnt-out shipping containers and truck bodies.

This was very nerve-racking and everyone anticipated an ambush as it was a perfect area for it, so we cleared it by foot. This took a long time and NC, the troop boss, decided that we would harbour up for the night at the top of the pass. He also wanted an OP on the high ground to act as overwatch using the TI. I was part of this patrol and streamlined my pack by just taking my sleeping bag, warm kit and a thermos of coffee. I also carried my SR25. The going was steep and treacherous underfoot due to the loose rocks. The ridgeline at the top was narrow and comfortable sleeping spots were nowhere to be found. The wind was also bitterly cold. No-one got much sleep that night.

On return to the troop harbour position we had a quick feed and a brew then continued on task.

We had 'eyes on' Saraw for a few days and were now awaiting the arrival of the Afghan National Army (ANA) for the second phase of the operation. The night they came we could see their headlights as they were driving down the mountain passes, 'Oh shit, here we go,' we thought. The lights were a clear indication to the Taliban that someone was coming; the locals rarely travel at night or in convoy.

So we had to race out and get them to turn them off. We taped their headlights and all the other lights on the outside of their cars with black masking tape. But since they couldn't see where they were going, we drove their cars for them wearing our night vision goggles. They loved it. They thought it was magic.

They were a pretty ragtag bunch. Their vehicles were bursting at the seams with all the guys inside; their utes on average had eight blokes on lookout duty with RPGs, and there was an AK47 protruding from every window.

That morning the 4RAR guys were dropped off by Chinook, and a Canadian Special Forces (CANSOF) unit also joined the convoy. When the combined units started to conduct their sweep, we went through Saraw and moved north up the valley. We could hear a bit of small arms fire but figured that it was the ANA shooting at shadows. Pretty soon we had the area consolidated and waited on the ANA to interview the locals and detain suspected Taliban.

We all ended up spending the night to the north of the village and just before it got dark we saw a Taliban 'retrans' (remote signals) location on the top of a very high ridgeline to the east, and called in a Spectre gunship to destroy it. The following morning we departed that location leaving the attachments behind and driving through some very dodgy areas where everyone was on edge. We could see the enemy's spotter network operating on the high ground. They had their radio systems going and we knew we were being watched. We were tuned into a captured enemy radio and could hear their chatter. The spotter network would hide themselves on a high feature that provided great fields of view and could see up to 20 kilometres with the aid of binoculars. They might not be able to see anything in great detail, but would easily spot the huge clouds of dust our vehicle would create, allowing the Taliban plenty of warning of our arrival.

As we came into the Khod Valley it was late in the afternoon and we were entering the area where 2 Squadron had been involved in quite a big contact. There was a lot of intelligence coming in. Our Afghan interpreter was updating us via a captured radio, saying, 'Right, they're forming up, they're going to attack.' There was clearly a certain Taliban leader trying to organise his fighters, but the chatter was all over the place; they couldn't seem to get themselves together properly and we actually drove through their proposed ambush site before they could form up.

It wasn't until a few days later that we actually had rockets fired at us. We had gone north to what we thought was a secure area. One of our tasks was to suss out the allegiance of certain villages in that location. In one village we had extremely good OBs, and after checking it out thoroughly we drove in and spoke with their leaders. When we got there we could see a big Dushka – a 14.7 mm heavy machine gun – lightly concealed and pointing towards the troop harbour. That would have caused us an absolute headache if it had opened up. We got talking to them and they seemed to be on side. Apparently the reason why most men were armed was because of tribal tensions – and not our presence in the area.

There were four villages in the immediate vicinity, anywhere from 2.5 to 10 kilometres apart, and we visited each one. Each had a different feel about it, some more unsettling than others. When speaking to the locals the standard response was 'Taliban, there hasn't been Taliban here for 12 months.' And the other was 'Yes, that village down the road is full of Taliban.' So we treated every village with care.

Mid-afternoon we positioned ourselves about 4 kilometres way from the second village we looked at. The area between was quite open so that if they wanted to take us on by foot we'd have prior warning and see villagers coming. At this stage we were about 8 kilometres away from Khod in a very large and open area we called the oyster shell because of its shape on the map.

We were back far enough to be out of the way of small arms fire and maybe even heavy machine-gun fire. But we were wary of Taliban 107mm rockets that have a range of about 7.5 kilometres. We hadn't seen any in the villages but they are easily hidden and when they want to fire them they throw together a wooden firing platform in the shape of a V.

They have a very crude aiming device – they get down behind it, add or remove rocks for elevation and aim it in your direction.

They have explosive charges or detonating cord that runs from the base of each 107 mm rocket that will set the charge off to fire it. A timer initiates an electrical charge that sets off the detonating cord. They can set it up so that each individual rocket is on a different timer. Half the time these rockets are okay for line on target, which means it will land in a straight line anywhere between them and the target. But range is generally off. It's rough and ready but they pack a hell of a punch.

The Taliban know from years of experience that if they hit you late in the afternoon they stand a good chance of getting away with it because it will soon be dark. So by 4 p.m. everyone was on edge and waiting for something to happen. Suddenly they opened up. The 107s make a huge noise as the rockets are coming in that is chilling. This particular time they fired four that landed close enough to cause concern. One rocket went directly overhead and dropped off into dead ground and exploded right next to a kuchie (Bedouin nomads) camp. This didn't worry the occupants in the slightest; they live with it all the time and just shrug their shoulders and say 'Inshallah' ('if Allah wills') and go back to their business.

By the time we reacted and reached the village it was getting close to dark and of course no-one knew a thing. Next day we headed for the village of Manare to see what we could find, as at least one rocket had been fired from a knoll on the side of a hill close by. As we entered the outskirts of the village the enemy chatter started; our awareness was heightened – there was a good possibility of contact with the enemy. I was still a passenger in the back of RH's car but I had also become the troop mechanic, not by choice. Babbs, the driver of our car, was also mechanically sound and at times both of us worked long hours replacing CV joints and diffs and repairing other mechanical failures. We had just got word that one of the other patrols had noticed a few 'squirters' – Taliban shooters who head for the hills to evade capture. So we decided to hunt them down.

Bang! Our car had just broken a left front CV joint. I started ratting around in the back of the car to locate the replacement while Babbs began to jack the vehicle up and remove the wheel. We felt quite vulnerable as we were well within range of small arms fire and caught between two high features. It took about 45 minutes to replace the broken CV joint, then we got moving again.

A patrol was despatched on foot to follow up the squirters but it didn't get far due to the severity of the terrain. One of the lads shot at these guys with the .50-calibre sniper rifle and the .50-calibre machine guns but because they know their backyard they got away.

We spoke to the locals to try to develop some intelligence, but got the same answer every time: 'No, there's no Taliban here, we haven't had Taliban in the village for years. The rockets must have been from Taliban passing through the area.' The fact was that the Taliban had a very firm hold over them, and most were very sympathetic. The Taliban pay their fighters – not very much but they do pay them – which is a rare source of income for these locals. It saves them having to scrimp and scrape from the land trying to sell dry roots for firewood.

But that's only part of the story. Their way of life is very different. Afghans live by vendettas but they are the most patient people you'll ever come across. If one of them commits a bad act against a family, the victim will seek revenge. It may not happen overnight but the culprit will eventually get his comeuppance. That's something you learn on the ground. The Sydney taxi driver left that bit out of his cultural awareness lecture.

After fruitlessly chasing the squirters up in the hills we decided a patrol should stick around and monitor the village. So we gave the impression we were moving away, which we did, but we dropped off Stodds and his patrol at the base of one of the hills that provided good OBs into the village. But as far as the villagers were concerned the Australians had cleared out.

In the morning we heard from Stodds, his voice crackling over the radio: 'There's a Taliban fighter coming towards us with a .303. We're going to have a crack as he's going to compromise us anyway.' As it happened, this bloke stopped just over 300 metres out and squatted for a dump. Two of the patrol's snipers were tracking this guy through their scopes. As the target became static they took aim and fired, but they missed. This bloke instantly leapt off the small cliff face with his trousers around his ankles leaving his rifle behind. I don't know what happened, but at that range it should have been a gimmie. They reckoned the wind was very strong and pushed their rounds off target. Stodds was not impressed and recovered the .303.

After that we moved back into the bowl and talked about the combat indicators – such as movement in the hills and in the green, radio traffic and the actions of villagers. You piece them together to give you a picture of what is going to happen or can happen. You learn with experience to read the signs but some soldiers seem to have a better developed instinct than others. Sometimes you just *know* when the shit's about to hit the proverbial.

The next day we took a break for a game of cricket and to do some repairs on our ageing LRPVs in the middle of the dasht (the bare, strong Afghan landscape desert). We were halfway through the game when we got engaged by several 107s, which we aggressively followed up. NC, the troop commander, had had enough and we advanced to contact, pepperpotting forward. Half the troop's vehicles would move, while the other half provided cover for them in case we were engaged again. Upon reaching the edge of the Khod Valley where this set of rockets came from we positioned the cars to give us all-round security and the other half of the troop drove down towards the green belt. There they were contacted by small arms and RPGs; we provided fire support. A couple of enemy RPGs exploded quite close to our vehicles and we engaged their main firing position, which was in a dry creek line behind a cemetery. We could see the enemy moving around inside this creek line, which gave them some good cover from fire. The boys on the flanks adjusted their .50-calibre machine guns onto the creek line catching some Taliban in the crossfire.

The Canadians were quite close to our location and joined in, providing 60mm mortar fire onto these positions. Our MK19 – 40mm grenade launchers, .50-calibre sniper rifles and machine guns also joined in. I arced up the Javelin rocket launcher in order to take out any other 107mm rocket firing positions. The Javelin rocket locks onto heat, but due to the temperature trapped in the rocky landscape I couldn't make out any distinct targets. So I ended up holding the bloody thing on my shoulder for four to five hours hoping that the landscape would cool down enough for me to get a lock on a target.

As I sat there scanning for a target I could hear the chatter from the Taliban coming through a captured radio in the background. I realised that the voice was getting rather excited. Suddenly from the radio, 'Allahu akbar! Allahu akbar!' Then two more rockets were fired at us. Both went over our heads. One screamed just metres above our car. I had seen the dust cloud created from the back blast of the rocket and knew instantly what it was. I dropped the Javelin and lay flat on the stony ground. As I hit the deck the rockets passed overhead. I couldn't get the Javelin back on my shoulder quick enough to look for the firing pad. Two of the cars engaged with their .50-calibre machine guns to try to provoke another reaction or some movement. Once again I couldn't make anything out due to the warm lunar-type landscape.

The light was fading by this stage and the other half of the troop had moved a little further north of our location. We called in US air cover to help destroy the enemy positions. They sent an A10, a fighter bomber known as a Warthog, which has two engines at the very back of the aircraft. It is a very agile piece of machinery. At that time their call-sign was 'tombstone'. Our joint terminal attack controller (JTAC), HM, got on the radio to get in touch with tombstone and gave them the grids of the main locations where the rockets were coming from. He also organised for them to conduct a couple of gun runs using their 30 mm canons to suppress the enemy fire.

However, that night intelligence suggested that the bad guys were still in the hills, so HM got the

aircraft to drop a 500-pound bomb on the main location. As the US aircraft came in, our boys put a
laser spot on the target. Then the aircraft lit up the
whole area with infra-red. HM gave him 'Clear
hot!' – the signal to drop his ordinance. He came in
and dropped the 500-pounder right on target. There
was a huge flash that lit up the whole valley and we
could see through our NVGs extremely hot shrapnel being thrown all over the hillside, then a second
later, *Bang!*

We stayed in location that night to see if anything further would eventuate. Everything had
gone quiet, so NC made a decision to move. We
continued to snoop about this area gathering more
information. We were contacted several more times,
and on one occasion the car I was travelling in was
targeted by 107s. Luckily they dropped about 150
metres short, but when I had a look around I could
see piles of rocks about 1–1.5 metres high that
seemed to be placed at 100–200-metre intervals.
Smart bastards: they were using them as range finders, and we were parked right in the centre of them.
Using these markers they could very easily bracket
us with their rockets until they were on target. So
I shouted to RH, 'Let's get out of here quick!'
Through the captured radio we had determined
that there was a spotter guiding the enemy onto us.
We did have a scout around for him, but it was uneventful.

Task complete, we drove the two-day journey

back to Tarin Kowt. We had been living in the field now for a full month and in contact with the Taliban a quarter of that time. So it was good to get back not only to relax, but to get stuck into a decent hot feed, have a warm shower, but more importantly get a few beers inside us to release built-up tension.

One week later we were back in the field. We had decided that we had some unfinished business in the areas surrounding Saraw. This time I was in a different patrol and riding one of our Polaris ATVs. Dave O'Neil and MR were on ATVs also and Dave was the 2IC. (Unfortunately Dave died in a Melbourne car accident a couple of years ago. He was a great bloke, always happy and keen for a laugh.) Once again we found ourselves at the base of IED alley and began to clear it by foot. Shep was using a handheld metal detector to sweep the road for possible IEDs and their components. We gingerly followed behind him. On reaching the top Shep had made a gruesome discovery. Three locals with hands bound had been beheaded and just left on the side of the road.

We gathered as much intelligence as possible and moved on to set up OPs in strategic locations around Saraw. We remained in that area for a few days, becoming very aware of the spotter network in the hills. At night we could see where they were camped because they had lit fires and you could see the faint glow several kilometers away. It was rapidly approaching winter and the nights were becoming extremely cold especially for those spotters at altitude. They were well out of range for the weapon systems we had, and access to these locations could only be achieved by local knowledge. Even behind a stone wall we could still see the glow from the fires through our NVGs or thermal imagers. The nights were generally very quiet, the peace only broken by a distant barking dog or burst of machine-gun fire.

Just before dusk we would prep ourselves for the night routine of sentry duty and rest. We had already had a hot feed and a brew, and there were no fires or white light once darkness fell. The level of threat at the time determined just how many blokes we would have providing security. If we were very secure we could reduce the number of sentries and get more rest. The 2ICs made a roster that included every man at various stages throughout the night. I didn't mind doing piquet at night as it was so peaceful; the night sky became alive with light shows in the way of shooting stars as they entered the Earth's atmosphere. Reveille for the locals was at 0500 hours when they were woken by the wails of their call to prayer through a cheap PA system.

On the third night I was woken by radio traffic from RH whose patrol was on an opposite feature 2.5 kilometres away. Through their thermal imager they were watching three Taliban fighters planting an IED into the gravel road. Two Taliban were doing all the work while the third was keeping watch. We knew that an American convoy was going to be travelling on that road in the coming hours so RH decided to contact the fighters. To make sure that the Taliban were killed and all the IED components destroyed and explosive burned, the Javelin was chosen because of its accuracy. Suddenly I heard the thump and whoosh of the rocket being launched and nine seconds later it impacted on its target. After the initial explosion I could make out the home-made explosive (HME) burning as it sparked and flickered in the night. A couple of bursts of .50-calibre and 40 mm followed the javelin rocket to make sure that the enemy was neutralised.

Just west of Saraw we had good intelligence that there was a medium-value target (MVT) who was operating from a small village and was watching us. As well as keeping in regular contact with commanders and his own fighters he had revealed a few other patterns. One particular pattern we had picked up was that every morning around the same time he would move to a similar position to radio his commanders or his spotter network.

We decided to set a sniper ambush on the high ground about 800 metres away, and the weapon of choice was the Barrett semi-automatic .50-calibre sniper rifle. Due to our being the prominent sniper patrol we were given the task and split into two three-man teams. My observer was Dave O'Neil. The PC came up with a plan and ran it past us.

Once we'd given it the nod he went away and wrote his orders.

The plan was to get another patrol to drive us towards the high ground, stopping about 3 kilometres short, where we would dismount and walk the rest of the way. That vehicle-mounted patrol would then remain in that location and become our QRF. At the base of the high ground we would split and move to two key locations we had previously identified that were around 500 metres apart. Once in location we would set up a firing position that had good fields of fire and OBs onto the approximate area the MVT would go to that morning. On the call from the PC the two snipers would simultaneously engage the Taliban leader, continue to observe for a short time, then extract.

So once the PC had delivered his orders to us, we went to work getting our gear ready for the short task. EH and I were the shooters so we made sure our .50 calibres were clean and serviceable. I pulled the barrel through as a matter of course. Because of the short duration of the task we only took day sacks with minimal food and some water. It was early December and the start of winter so we resigned ourselves to the fact that we would freeze up there. We took a windproof smock, a beanie and a pair of gloves each. I also took a flask of hot water to add to the dehyde I took as food for the following morning. I took 20 rounds for the Barrett and carried a browning 9 mm pistol. Dave had his M4 and carried the optics in his day sack; MR carried a 5.56 mm Minimi light machine gun as he was to be our rear protection. We all carried personal radios.

Once we had completed our battle prep and actioned our weapons, we got stuck into a good feed and a hot brew. Darkness fell, and shortly after we were on the back of the two LRPVs moving slowly towards the back end of the village. On reaching our drop-off point (DOP) we all went silent for 10 minutes to establish if there was any movement in our immediate area. After that we conducted a quick comms check and set off on our foot insertion.

The going under foot was quite treacherous when crossing the dry wadi (river bed), but once on the other side we made good time. At the base of the large hill we confirmed a few 'actions on' and then we split to our respective positions. The night was very dark and when we approached the top of the hill we began to look for a suitable firing position without silhouetting ourselves. The other team was lucky enough to get into position almost straight away upon reaching their final location. We had a bit more of a climb.

MR got into a good position and started to provide security, which gave us a little more freedom of movement to pinpoint a good firing position. Dave and I still weren't happy with the final position we'd selected, but we were running out of time and it was quickly approaching daylight. This position offered a good platform for me to shoot from, but cover from fire and view was minimal, which was going to make it extremely difficult for us to move around once daylight broke. The escape route we had identified wasn't the best either. If we were compromised and started to take rounds we would have had to momentarily expose ourselves to the engaging Taliban in order to get away – far from ideal!

Just before daybreak we saw some human movement which we observed like hawks as we felt quite exposed. When the light was sufficient I ranged my scope into the likely area our target was using – 850 metres, an easy task for the Barrett. I assessed the wind, which was blowing gently on an oblique angle from right to left up the valley, and added a couple of clicks right to compensate for that.

After an hour of daylight a lone male approached the area where our target was supposed to be. He stayed for about 10 minutes and didn't seem to be doing anything out of the ordinary. This gave me time to recheck the range and wind. He turned out to be slightly closer and the wind had picked up a little. I made the necessary adjustments and then continued to observe him through my scope.

The other half of our patrol confirmed via radio that he did not appear to be a threat; but we continued to observe on chance that he was our guy and became the target. As it happened, he never did pose a threat and the task was called off. Even though it was dud, all the excitement and adrenaline was present. It is these very emotions that need to be suppressed before you pull the trigger on a live target, because if you don't, you will miss.

The order was given to move back towards Saraw, as a combined clearance was to take place. Once in location 4RAR were dropped to the east of the village behind a huge feature and walked to a blocking position on high ground. Their mortars were dropped off in front of our location. The ANA conducted a sweep from the south with some of our blokes in support. It wasn't long before the ANA had found some enemy and started shooting. I and some other snipers took up a position on the high ground to provide overwatch and commentary, and to engage any threats. We located some likely enemy positions and gatherings but did not see any weapons at that stage.

As the clearance progressed we moved locations to another feature, which allowed us to see right into the village. We could also see the 4RAR blocking position but nothing else came of that clearance at that stage. We RVd back with the rest of our patrol, who had been watching a possible MVT on an adjoining feature some distance away to the one 4RAR had just walked around. This bloke was quite fidgety and talking into something regularly. He would run from position to position as though we were shooting at him, which wasn't the case, as he was well out of range.

We scanned the feature in detail from left to

right to ascertain whether or not there were more individuals up there. This guy was on the far left, and 4RAR had somehow 'seen' someone on this feature also. Orders for a mortar fire mission were being given by the mortar fire controller (MFC) to the mortar section, which had three 'tubes' (mortars). *Bang!* One mortar was released and splashed onto the right-hand side of hill. The MFC gave a correction to his section.

Dave and I rode down to them on our 6×6 Polaris ATVs to see what they were firing at, and to my amazement they described the bloke we had been observing for the last hour and a half. *Bang!* Another spotter round was sent flying to start the MFCs bracketing procedure. Dave politely let the MFC know that the bloke they were trying to target was on the opposite end of the ridgeline. The MFC didn't want a bar of our advice, so we sat back with our binoculars and watched the show.

'Fire for effect!' the MFC ordered his section and round after round was sent flying. All the time we were watching the area to see what our man was doing. The MFC then corrected his mortars onto a new location which saw his rounds disappear over the back of the ridgeline. Dave and I gave each other a very confused look. The MFC then declared, 'Target destroyed, end of fire mission!' Dave turned to me and said, 'How do you call "target destroyed" when you can't see if it has been destroyed – that is if there ever was a target up there!' I had my doubts also. We rode back up to the rest of our patrol and they couldn't see what the MFC was firing at either, but our man had disappeared over the back of the feature. Someone had given these guys the wrong target indication.

That was pretty much the last contact of that trip. It opened my eyes to the command structure of the enemy, which was quite loose. Some of the commanders were old-school from the Mujahideen days against the Russians, and good at wheeling and dealing their fighters; some of the younger guys coming through weren't as confident or as aggressive. Either way, when rounds are winging past your ears it doesn't matter who they are coming from; they are just as dangerous.

By the time we left Afghanistan it was January 2006 and when we reached Kuwait on the way home those of us who had come over as reinforcements picked up another job: personal security detail (PSD) for the Chief of the Defence Force (CDF), Angus Houston. He was on a tour of Iraq and Afghanistan and we were ready and waiting for him when he arrived in Kuwait. We had a small enclave inside an American base and he met us there. It was no more than a meet and greet but even at that early stage we all took to him immediately.

Myself and one other bloke were the recce party for this job and with the help of a liaison officer from the regiment we visited all the venues on his schedule a week before to ensure the smooth running of the PSD. Once the task had started we were the daily reconnaissance team that moved ahead to every venue and approved the route. If there was an incident or blockage on the route, the PSD would be diverted and we'd have to approve another. At the venue we would clear it and give the team leader the 'all clear' for the motorcade to move in.

The CDF invited us to have dinner with him one evening, to share ideas on kit and equipment. This was also an opportunity for him to guage how things were going with us, and a chance for us to express our ideas.

To protect someone's life by sacrificing your own plays on your mind a fair bit. It certainly ran through mine occasionally as we travelled through Baghdad and I rehearsed a multitude of scenarios in my head. We were constantly alert, always seeking dodgy looking areas, vehicles or characters and thinking, 'What if?'

The PSD was incident free and now I was looking forward to getting home to George and the girls.

13

CRASH!

I had completed both my corporal's courses by 2005 and promotion came through early in 2006, just before my return to East Timor. It was a big jump from the deserts of Afghanistan to the sweltering tropics of Timor but at least I was with the SAS this time.

In February, 404 Timorese government soldiers, out of the regular strength of about 1,500, deserted their barracks and towards the end of the month they were joined by 177 more. The troops were ordered to return to their posts in March, but refused, and were relieved of duty. They were later joined by some members of the police force.

Foreign Minister José Ramos-Horta said early in April that a panel would be established to hear their complaints but said, 'They are not going to be brought back into the army, except on a case-by-case basis when we establish the responsibilities of each individual in this whole incident.'

On 25 April, the former soldiers and their civilian supporters, mostly unemployed youths, marched through Dili in protest. The march turned violent when they attacked a market run by people from the east of the country. The protests continued over the next few weeks and on 28 April the former soldiers clashed with government forces. Five people were killed, more than 100 buildings were destroyed and about 20,000 Dili residents fled the city.

On 4 May, Major Alfredo Reinado, along with 20 military police from a platoon under his command and four other riot police, defected and joined the rebel soldiers, taking with them two trucks full of weapons and ammunition. After joining the soldiers, Reinado made his base in the town of Aileu in the hills south-west of Dili. There he and some military police guarded the road leading into the mountains.

Violent gangs roamed the streets of Dili, burning down houses and torching cars. The civilians who fled Dili camped in tented cities nearby or in churches on the outskirts of the capital. On 12 May, the then Prime Minister John Howard announced that although there had not been any formal requests for assistance from the Government of East

Timor, Australian forces were standing by, with HMAS *Kanimbla* and HMAS *Manoora* moving to northern waters in preparation.

The violence escalated late in May, as one government soldier was killed and five wounded in a skirmish. Ramos-Horta sent out an official request for military assistance to Australia, New Zealand, Malaysia and Portugal.

We had already strategically moved up to Darwin and had begun planning and training for the job ahead. A company of 4RAR (now called 2 Commando Regiment) joined us as our cordon force. The majority weren't airborne-rappel or fast-rope trained, so we spent a couple of days getting the boys up to speed. It also meant myself and a few other guys gained valuable instructor qualifications during this time. Shortly after that, things in Timor calmed down slightly and I was sent back to Perth for a week to complete the SAS roping course that I had missed in 2003 due to my knee operation.

About three days into the course the boys deployed to Timor; I was disappointed that I had missed it and was keen to get over with them. As the boys arrived, there was trouble in Dili and they reacted soon after.

I flew there direct at the end of the week and was assigned as 2IC of a patrol commanded by SE. We were responsible for Xanana Gusmão's close personal protection and security for the next two months.

XG, as we called him, lived up in the hills with his Australian wife Kirsty and their children. We would travel there from our accommodation at the airport each morning to escort him to his office. He's very much a people's man and that made it tough to protect him. We'd ask him to change his routine, vary his route (which is not easy in a place with so few roads) and vary timings. We also asked if he could close his car window because it was all too easy for someone to walk or ride up beside his car and drop a grenade into his lap. But he wouldn't do it. He said, 'I love the people and the people love me. They wave to me, I wave back.' And he did that every day, to and from the house.

There were a couple of crowd situations that had the potential to be dangerous, but the locals just wanted to get up close to him. However, we had a job to do and couldn't afford to lower our standards. We formed an outer cordon around him close enough to respond to any threat. He also had his own trained security team alongside him, so he was pretty secure. After a while we figured we'd be hard pressed to find someone who'd attack XG at that stage, although it did happen a year or so after we had left the country. On 11 February 2008, national television reported that the motorcade of Gusmão had come under gunfire one hour after President José Ramos-Horta was shot in the stomach; according to the Associated Press, the two incidents raised the possibility of a coup attempt. I suspect whoever fired the shots was paid an awful lot of money to carry out the task.

XG's office was well protected and his own East Timorese guards provided 24-hour security for him. On arrival at his office in the mornings the recce team would talk to the guys on the gate asking them if anything had happened or if they'd noticed anything out of the ordinary overnight. Most of the time they said no, so the boys would go ahead and clear the office to make sure there was nothing planted there waiting for him.

We also had to look after Ramos-Horta and Prime Minister Alkatiri as well because we couldn't be seen to be showing political favouritism, but they had separate teams. However, the fact is that Alkatiri was organising people from outside Dili and paying them to travel to the capital to stir up trouble. Half of them didn't even know who Alkatiri was, they'd just take the $20 and do as they were told.

SE was the personal security officer (PSO) and placed himself in a position so he could react to any threat or danger to XG's safety but also maintained his freedom of movement as much as possible. I organised the boys into shifts for the jobs we had to fulfil and maintained a link with SE.

A couple of weeks into the job, John Howard and Angus Houston came to visit XG at his office. The Australian Federal Police (AFP) arrived a few days earlier to do their security evaluation and received a brief from SE. The AFP also had a unit from their overseas recovery team.

These blokes were dressed almost identically to the GNR (Portuguese special police), who were also involved. Every man wore black boots and black military-style cargo pants and a black T-shirt two sizes too small, black sunglasses, a belt kit and a chest rig. Everything was black and tight enough to stop you from producing kids. It might look cool but not the most appropriate gear for that heat in Timor, I'm afraid.

I was providing security at the door by that stage and John Howard was as pleasant as always. Angus Houston recognised me from the PSD I did for him, so he stopped for a quick chat.

Part and parcel of working in the tropics is the constant war against harmful bacteria, especially when sanitation is overlooked, so 24-hour stomach upsets are very common. And when I went down with one I just wanted to curl up and die. The heat and humidity didn't help things and neither did spewing and shitting myself at the same time at XG's office. I would've normally been embarrassed but I was too sick to care.

From what I could gather on the ground, the political trouble really arose from a power struggle between Mari Alkatiri on the one hand and XG and José Ramos-Horta on the other. XG forced Alkatiri to resign in June and Ramos-Horta replaced him as prime minister but even then the new prime minister also had his eye on the presidency. But he and XG got along really well and they weren't going to start fighting each other. They knew that would have torn Timor apart.

The place had calmed down by the time we left, but it's always going to be a problem until they sort out the economy and stop the corruption. The East Timorese are nice people but we were all anxious to get home once the job was done. We flew direct to Perth and George was waiting with Lauren and Ash. We had bought a nice home in the northern suburbs of Perth within easy travelling distance of Campbell Barracks. And by now we were getting financially sound and house prices were on the rise which meant we had a bit of equity behind us. George continued her studies and started a degree in psychology at Edith Cowan University, which wasn't too far away.

I had always answered any questions she had about my work but being from a military family she knew what not to ask. And of course she knew the risks that came with being in the regiment. But neither of us were prepared for what happened next when, out in the Pacific Ocean, death tapped me on the shoulder.

The crash of the Blackhawk helicopter off Fiji that killed two guys when it smashed onto the flight deck of the *Kanimbla*, spun out of control, landed in the ocean and sank has always been presented by the authorities as simply a training exercise gone

wrong. But in fact we were on core business, preparing to rescue Australian citizens. When the call
came, 1 Squadron was picked to carry out the task.
I was instructing on the SASR sniper course at the
time, but 1 Squadron were short on snipers so the
whole course was deployed. We flew east and
boarded the *Kanimbla*, which reached the standby
area off the coast of Fiji four days later. There we
began rehearsing several scenarios that might present themselves should the need to conduct the recovery arise.

The Blackhawk guys were working up their own
training of dry roping serials while we were conducting aerial fire support activities. The dry roping serial involved positioning the helicopter over
the *Kanimbla* while the crew practised the calls
they would make to each other when our guys fast
roped down from the helicopter to the surface. On
the approach to the *Kanimbla* the pilot would turn
and flare, taking the nose up to bring the speed
down, then level off above the deck. The two 'loadies' on board would go over their hand-signals and
calls over the radio, the pilots would acknowledge
this and go through their calls as well.

At the same time I was supervising a sniper scenario where we would provide fire support from
the helicopter. I followed the standard format – the
sniper supervisor tells the pilot where he wants to
position the aircraft, and once there the snipers can
engage designated targets. Arcs are limited from

the door of the aircraft and you also have to be mindful of the step fitted to the underside and the rotor blades above. You can get the pilot to roll the aircraft 10 or 15 degrees and he'll do that quite happily to get a door shot. Otherwise you can tell the pilot to move the tail left or right, or whatever you need to open up the arcs.

On the day of the crash I took the place of one of the other PCs who was crook. We were going to do a few dry roping serials and then we would practise a dry helicopter sniping serial. Before we boarded we went through the mandatory briefings and safety precautions. There was a little bit of waiting around before we headed out to the aircraft, which was being wheeled out of the superstructure onto the flight deck. I noticed Bingers chilling out and relaxing towards the back end of the hanger. When the time came we put our life vests on and moved out to tail number 221. I sat on a coiled 90-foot (27-metre) fast rope that was secured to the floor by a ratchet strop just inside the right side door and clipped my strop to one of the rings on the floor; Bingers (now Captain Mark Bingley) was in charge and he and Grizz started their pre-flight checks.

I had borrowed a set of Peltor earmuffs from one of the blokes that I could plug into the Blackhawk communication system to talk to the crew and pilots. Comms worked fine until the engine was started and then I couldn't hear a thing.

We went into an orbit to wait for the other two

aircraft to get airborne, and flew about 10 kilometres in front of the ship. We then turned and came back approaching the bow. This approach was going to be the first of a series of dry roping serials for the crew to square away their calls and drills. No-one was actually going to fast rope. There were two ropes coiled on the floor, one on either side, and just in from the doors. There were two blokes sitting on the floor in each doorway and Shep, who was on the rear seat recording the action on a video camera. The sliding doors were open and locked into place.

It all went according to plan until we approached the ship. We came in from the bow and turned hard left in the direction of the flight deck. Bingers tried to put the aircraft into a flare over the deck, and then I suddenly noticed that the engine started to make a really high-pitched noise, and then realised that we were rapidly descending.

I remember hearing someone shouting 'Shit!' over the headphones. We were going to crash. The flight deck was rushing towards us and I thought, 'This is going to hurt; if I'm sitting up I'll smash my back,' and I tried to make myself horizontal to the floor but I didn't quite make it. As it hit the flight deck I smashed into the floor of the aircraft face first, probably making the impact even worse for me. I can still remember hearing the impact of the crash, and a high-pitched screeching noise, then a feeling of centrifugal force as the aircraft began to spin. My quick-release strop tightened, stopping me from being flung out of the door. I could hardly breathe. I bashed my face quite badly on impact and then lost consciousness as the helicopter plunged into the water.

I came to underwater with a lung full of ocean. I remember initially seeing lots of silver bubbles, realising how quiet it was, then realised what was happening. The Blackhawk was sinking fast and I was being dragged down with it by my strop. Both side doors had been locked in the open position so we could conduct our practice, and luckily they were still open. I carried out a drill which is used for emergency braking while abseiling. If you run into difficulty and your hands have come free from the rope or figure 8 descender, the drill is to clap your hands onto the rope in front of you and drag them to the body to make contact with the descender and regain control. I used this to find the quick release device that was clipped onto a steel ring on my belt.

It released instantly as I pulled on the lanyard, but the aircraft was sinking so fast that I hit the roof on the inside. I could see the opening of the door, as the light was still coming through. As I reached towards the door I grabbed hold of the roping anchor point and pulled myself out. I was now about 20 metres deep and could see the bottom of the ship. I was in serious trouble. I instinctively reached down and pulled the toggle on my life vest to inflate it from a CO_2 canister, but it just hissed for what seemed like ages. It didn't inflate because the gas had been overly compressed due to the water pressure at that depth. Initially I thought that I'd be lucky to make it to the surface, but I wasn't going to die like that. I had too much to live for.

I believe at this point your life is supposed to flash past your eyes. I did get a flash image of George and the girls. Maybe this was my subconscious telling me to get a move on. I kicked and clawed my way towards the surface. My body was making involuntary muscle movements trying to breathe and I was semiconsciously trying to stop myself. I knew if I was to take on any more water it'd be all over. My vest started to inflate around the 5-metre mark and I came up touching the starboard side of the ship.

On the surface I initially had extreme difficulty in breathing and blood was starting to reach my eyes from a cut on my eyebrow. The wind and the current didn't help either and was pushing me into the side of the ship causing seawater to splash back into my face. The 'wateries' (divers) from 1 Squadron, had actually just exited the water after conducting a diving exercise. So we were probably lucky in that regard as most managed to get back into the water to help the survivors who were struggling with the current. It was also lucky the squadron sergeant-major (SSM) was skippering a safety boat for the divers and was also still in the water. One of our lads who was an ex-clearance diver,

CW, came swimming over to help me. Still struggling for breath I said, 'Mate, get me on that fuckin' boat!' He said, 'It's okay, mate, you're in shock.' I replied, 'Fuck off, mate, I'm not in shock. I can't breathe. Now get me on board that fuckin' boat!' He replied, 'Okay let's have a look at you first.' He was genuinely concerned; I'd gashed my eye and the skin had been taken off much of my face. I thought I might have damaged my chest due the difficulty I had in breathing, but I'd also taken on a large amount of water. The life vest, which had finally inflated, was on top of my chest and was constricting my airways.

I was hurting all over but I was relieved to be alive so pain took a backseat. CW asked, 'Let's have a look at your chest.' I told him, 'Mate, don't worry about it; just get me into that boat.' So he dragged me over to the boat and Cal and the SSM pulled me aboard.

Bingers and Josh (Trooper Joshua Porter) didn't make it, but eight of us did, with various injuries. I didn't blame Bingers for the accident – not then and not later. The board of inquiry said Bingers got his helmet snagged on a plastic antenna outside the door. He drowned. When Bingers came to the surface. I heard, 'Oh shit, there's one.' One of the lads who was in the water swam over and started CPR until we got him on board our boat; then the corps medic took over. I remember noticing Bingers' stomach was quite distended, full of water; basically he'd passed away long before that. All the survivors had been picked up and there were people looking around for Josh.

We strive to be the best and Bingers was no outsider to this; he was always looking to enhance his ability to provide us with a capability that was second to none, and sometimes to enhance capability you need to push the boundaries of risk otherwise you don't progress. But unfortunately that day something went wrong, and two good soldiers died. It could have been a lot worse.

Once I had climbed the rope ladder on the side of the ship they led me to the galley. On the way I passed several matelots (naval personnel) who were sitting cradling their knees with their heads bowed and crying. I couldn't understand why they were so upset. A navy nurse tried to dress the cuts on my face. She was shaking so badly I told her not to worry about it; I would try to control the bleeding myself. I had a few cups of coffee and a yarn to the boys from the other chopper about what had happened and also general chit chat; then they took me to the sick bay. The boys on the Blackhawk behind 221 had originally thought that their aircraft was in trouble, because when ours spudded in it set off all the warning alarms in the others. They went into a mad panic for a few seconds until they saw our aircraft disappear into the Pacific Ocean.

At our debriefing, one of the first things the CO said was, 'Were the life jackets sufficient?' We said,

'No!' Had we been wearing our body armour we would've lost more blokes. One of the water operators back at Campbell Barracks tested it later – he put body armour on then jumped into the pool, which is only 4 metres deep. At the bottom he pulled the toggle. It slowly inflated but it didn't bring him to the surface.

That was a lesson learned. But the cost was too high.

14

LONG SHOTS

I had been working in Afghanistan on a still secret mission for the previous five months when 3 Squadron requested I join them in Tarin Kowt for three weeks for their last patrol as they were short on numbers. Shortly after my arrival there we deployed into the field in the old LRPVs to drive to the American forward operating base (FOB), Anaconda. At the time there was quite a high concentration of enemy fighters up there and the Americans were getting hammered. We deployed as part of a big operation in conjunction with 4RAR to give them a helping hand.

We left well before the commando contingent, heading into some pretty open country that started to close in the further north we drove.

The trip from Tarin Kowt to Anaconda is a big

drive so we took everything carefully as the LRPVs were gradually becoming more fragile. Early the following day we headed for a village that we needed to pass through ahead of a tight pass in the mountains. As we gradually closed on the village we started to pick up a lot of radio chatter. The interpreters said there was a lot of movement in the village; they'd picked up that we were coming and they were getting ready for a fight.

We said, 'No worries; bring it on!' We split the troop on either side of the village and the guys on the northern side covered a large feature. This was unfortunate for some of the Taliban who from that feature tried to engage the cars. Our guys pinged them and used the heavy weapons – .50 cal machine guns and Mark 19 grenade launchers – to stop them in their tracks.

You could see them running through the hills with their PKM 7.62 mm machine guns, their old RPK Russian assault rifles and RPGs. In fact, most of their weapons were Russian made apart from the ageing bolt-action rifles. They had quite a variety of them. We've even come across jungle carbine .303s. Where they came from is a total mystery.

Most of the more modern weapons were definitely taken from the Russians – either from their dead or what they left behind. The Soviets just walked away from large warehouses full of kit, including tanks. We assessed the situation and decided that the majority of the bad guys were in the hills, as the ones that were left weren't going to fight inside the village; we decided to cautiously move through it.

The route we had selected was very tight, but it was the most direct. We did our best to avoid the outer compound walls but we finished up driving into a few of them and knocking a couple over because the vehicles aren't very manoeuvrable.

The atmosphere was becoming quite tense. Some of the vehicles were having a lot of difficulty navigating the narrow pass, and the chatter was suggesting that they were looking at coming out of the hills to hit us. But, as happens a lot, nothing eventuated.

Once again we didn't see any women in the village. If they see soldiers coming they tend to hide their women or send them out of the village with the very young kids. The male children from about 10 or 11 will hang around with the men. Whenever they can, the Taliban take them under their wing and try to groom them as prospects. Then when they come of age – very young by our standards – they give them the tools of a fighter: the AK.

Once on the other side we drove about 12 kilometres beyond the village, harboured up and spent the night there. The following morning we drove to the pass. On the way we received more chatter from the captured radio from spotters up in the hills who were keeping tabs on our progress. As soon as we got into the pass one of our guys saw a spotter, so one of the vehicles in front stopped and their snipers engaged him. I don't know whether they got him or not but once that was resolved we drove to the top of the pass. It took longer than we had expected as it was really narrow, and we broke a few CV joints. So the decision was made to spend the night up there to fix the cars and start early the following morning. The CV joints were still the weakest points of the vehicle. And the following day we blew four more getting down this particularly steep gradient. When a CV blows it's very hard to operate the steering so you've got to somehow get the vehicle to a piece of flat ground to replace it. In an emergency you can take the CV joint out and remove the axle; you have to take out all the broken pieces from the inside of the joint before you can put the CV back in place. You won't have drive to the front wheels because the axle has been removed. But if you engage six-wheel drive, both the rear axles will have traction and you will become mobile again until you have a chance to replace the CV.

Because the LRPV produced a lot of torque at low range something had to give. You weren't able to change gear going up hills because they're so heavy and the sudden loss of drive between gears would slow the vehicle down too much, then when reapplying power the weakest point of the vehicle would give in. So we had to nurse the vehicles, particularly when there was a chance of contact, because if you lose your vehicle in an emergency situation like that you're in deep shit. From 2005 the vehicle didn't improve but the drivers did, becoming more educated and more sympathetic to the vehicles.

We started the steep descent to the bottom of the pass, which took until lunch time, but we made it without a shot being fired. However, a couple of kilometres further on, the road narrowed by a wide river. From the road across to the other side of the river must have been about 180 metres to the green and a strand of tall trees. We got a bit of chatter as we came through that little area so we stopped by the river and made a decision to send a patrol into the village.

On the left, a big bank came right down to the roadside and on the right there was a little drop-off of about 10 metres to the river. The cars were moved away from this spot and some lads occupied the high ground. Our six-man patrol plus interpreter made our way on foot down over a ford then into the village. We had a bit of a scout around and talked to a couple of the locals. As we got to the end of the village we turned around to come back. That's when one of our boys on the high ground got on the radio and said, 'There are three or four blokes across the river with AKs and chest rigs heading your way.'

From where the boys were on the hill the river came past them and went into an 'S' bend. We patrolled with stealth to the bend. Kabes (the lead scout) and I were up front. We both stepped into the knee-deep river covering each other as we cautiously moved forward. We were almost halfway across when two armed fighters who were lying in the grass on the other side of the river bank jumped up and ran off. We instantly engaged with our M4s but the targets didn't drop.

With a sense of urgency we cautiously approached where they had been hiding and found only a long scarf that they had left behind. They had retained their weapons and their chest rigs, so we took cover the best we could while waiting for the rest of the patrol to catch up before we split to follow them. I went left with one other into the open fields where small patches of chest-high corn were growing. We kept eye contact with the other half of the patrol as we followed up in extended line. This was pretty tense since we knew there were others around – they'd sent those couple of guys to see what was going on and to report on our position.

We pepper-potted forward in case these guys were flushed out in front of us. About 40 metres into the green, Kabes caught up with one guy and engaged him at close range – about 5 metres away. He stood up in a bush, AK in hand right in front of Kabes who instantly engaged and killed. We recovered his AK and his chest rig. It was a Chinese-style chest rig with little wooden toggles used to secure the flaps of the magazine pouches – the Russians wore them as well.

The other guy must have heard the shots: he ran

up the strip of green parallel to the river and came out into the open. The boys on the other side of the river engaged him with .50 calibre and 40mm grenades, which landed around him. He was a bit of a mess and dead when we reached him.

We searched the bodies then left them for their people to bury respectfully. But while we were with the second body we discovered just how lucky we'd been. They'd had word that we were coming up through the village towards the American base so they had started digging a trench system in the strip of green to give themselves some protection. It was quite a long trench, about 50 metres. They had tied ribbons in the trees about 10 to 15 metres apart – probably positions for machine guns or RPGs. It was about a metre deep and was all fresh, so they had probably started digging it that night. They're hard workers when they want to be.

They had cut foliage between the trench and the road we'd just driven along to give them good fire lanes. It was a perfect ambush spot because there was nowhere for us to go. From a soldier's point of view it was a very well thought out ambush position.

We have had a tremendous amount of luck over the past few years, but from time to time we do get caught out, and it's usually due to a bit of complacency. The enemy does set patterns and things do go in our favour for such a long time that you forget how unforgiving the Taliban can be at times.

Once we ascertained that the other Taliban had

slipped away we headed back up to the cars. But one guy, who must have been down there in the green as well, came up to our location looking for medical treatment. He reckoned he was down there farming and we shot him through the calf. Lying bastard – he was one of the guys down there all right, but he wasn't farming. It was a small 5.56 mm hole that went through his lower leg, so it must have been either Kabes or myself who clipped him as they were running away. But all that meant was that there were more guys down there; this bloke had dropped his weapon and chest rig then sneaked across the river. There was no way we could prove that he was a fighter so one of the medics treated him, gave him some antibiotics and sent him on his way.

When we moved off there was quite a long strip of urban area to pass and we did so without further incident. We spent the night about 4 kilometres beyond the green, and the next morning, while still under the cover of darkness, we drove through a narrow pass between two mountains. On the other side the Americans met us to guide us into their FOB where preparation began for the next phase of the operation.

We stayed at Anaconda for about five days before we went out and into the second phase. By this stage 4RAR's convoy of close to 40 cars had taken up what little space there was at the FOB. They had close to 120 blokes, not all shooters though: they took along a lot of support members like Q staff and mechanics; in fact it was a bit like a small mobile version of Tarin Kowt.

At Anaconda my PC had hurt his back; this meant that Gumps, who was the 2IC, would step up to take the patrol, and I moved up to take the 2IC's position. This part of the operation was purely an Australian show, and soon we were being inserted to a drop-off point in the dead of night by vehicle approximately 5 kilometres outside Anaconda. From there our SAS element would move by foot carrying packs and weapons to various OP locations throughout the mountain range to get eyes on a village for a clearance conducted by 4RAR. The operation was to last 36 hours.

We started walking. It was quite slow going as the ground was very steep. Our packs were heavy, with items like surveillance equipment, radio components, two days rations, 8 litres of water, warm gear and spare ammunition. After hours of walking we reached a dispersion point and split up. It wasn't long before we came to our final destination: troop HQ was in a good location about 200 metres behind us and could provide rear protection.

Our patrol had pretty good OBs of the eastern side of the village and to the north; the other boys went to the west of us in a horseshoe configuration. In the morning 4RAR inserted into the AO and started their sweep to clear the village, which ran up a valley and then turned left and opened up.

This was the only area we could see. It took a long time before we saw the first soldiers appear from 4RAR, but we knew that they had a very large area to clear.

It turned out that they started to do it very tactically and methodically but it was just taking too long as the task they had was massive. So they decided to speed things up, otherwise it would have taken about two days to complete – with some extremely exhausted soldiers. Even by this stage I'm sure they were absolutely knackered because they were suited up with body armour that was loaded with magazines and grenades – twice as heavy as our kit.

Shortly before we noticed the first 4RAR soldiers rounding the feature to our right-hand side, one of the lads, with the naked eye, saw three blokes walking down a track towards them about 1,500 metres away. He said, 'Have a look at those blokes down there; one looks like he has something across his shoulder, I reckon it could be an RPG.'

I could hardly see them, so I put the binoculars up and after a slight focus adjustment I could see this bloke was carrying a tube across his shoulder. There were also a couple of other guys with him who looked to be carrying rifles under their long clothing. What gave them away was the barrels protruding over their shoulders, and the fact that they were not swinging their arms. Seeing this you immediately think, 'What's he carrying under his shirt?' It's a dead giveaway.

We adjusted the sniper spotting scope onto target, 'Yeah, it's an RPG tube he's got.' Then you could see two rockets poking out from underneath his shirt. They got to within about 1,300 metres when Gumps engaged them with his .338 sniper rifle. He got close but missed because there was a hell of a wind through the valley and it was hard to judge its effect on the projectile. But the round landed close enough so that they knew they were pinged.

They split into two packets – two guys ran into a large creek line that stretched for about 200 metres. The older guy with the RPG went up onto a small knoll and hid in some rocks. He presented himself again and Gumps re-engaged and thought he might have winged him. We got on the radio to 4RAR and gave them an indication of where they were. But unfortunately they were pre-occupied with their clearance task. There were a couple of easy kills to be had so we asked their mortars to agree to a fire mission. SG, the patrol JTAC, had eyes on and could bring the mortar fire directly onto the target. 'No,' was the response, 'We'll conduct the fire mission because our JTAC has recorded a few targets in the area.' We said okay, if the mortars are off target, our JTAC can help your guys adjust. 'That's not necessary,' they said.

But when it came to the crunch their mortars

landed 400 metres away from the target. We suggested, 'Hand it over to our JTAC, he knows exactly where they are, he can adjust the mortars on target.'

Wary of wasting more rounds, they decided to cease the fire mission. But then about 15 minutes later without warning they decided to fire more mortar bombs – and once more they landed nowhere near the target. It was a bitter pill to swallow.

Suddenly we noticed the bad guys walking very cautiously out of the creek line. It was about an hour after the initial contact when they decided to make a run for it. They seemed to be coming towards us so we thought, 'We'll wait until they get to about the 700–800-metre mark before we engage.' SG and I both had our SR25 sniper rifles. SG was lucky enough to have one of the new Schmidt & Bender two-turn 3–12 power scopes on his rifle. This scope allows greater elevation adjustment, which is needed when using the .338 or .50-calibre rifles. I still had the single turn scope, which took my 7.62 mm out to 1,000 metres; beyond that I had to start making adjustments using the mil dot reticle pattern.

We both made the necessary adjustment for the range where we would engage these guys, and calculated the wind. We were going to wait until they walked in front of a large hill that was on an oblique angle to our right-hand side. This would shield a lot of the wind and give us a better chance of hitting them first shot.

But as they came out of the creek line two snipers from 4RAR engaged them. They fired two shots that landed about 20 metres in front of them and about 15 metres to their left flank. SG and I were dumbfounded and also pretty annoyed. We wouldn't have minded if they had both been killed, but now there were two armed men in the creek line, and one beyond them with an RPG with several rounds, and 4RAR were still working their way towards them.

We watched these positions, waiting for them to make the next move. After about another hour and a half we saw another guy who was hunched over with what looked like a sack on his back. He quickly scurried from where the mountainside ran into a track, crossed the track and ran into the creek line. 'What's this dodgy bastard up to?'

Anyway, these guys presented themselves. They must have been hiding just out of sight from us and when they stood up they were in plain view. They were 1,150 metres away. By any standard that is a very long range and a real tester in those conditions for a 7.62 mm rifle. We said, 'They're not going to be in range again so we're going to have to engage them.' We made the necessary adjustments, 1,150 metres for range, and 30 clicks right to compensate for the strong wind. We watched as the new guy opened his sack and began to take out some items of clothing. The two armed Taliban took their tops off and replaced them with the ones from the sack. Gumps said, 'That's it, fellas.'

I raised the crosshairs directly above my target's head and used the mil dot reticle pattern for a point of reference. I had previously shot this rifle out to 1,200 metres before we left Tarin Kowt and recorded my adjustment, so I knew exactly how much hold-off I needed.

Gumps, who was assessing the wind for us, gave the 'ready, ready'; we both started our breathing cycle. 'Ready, ready, now relaxed, ready!' We took up the final trigger pressure. 'Stand by . . . fire!'

Bang! We both fired at the same time but each round hit a metre to the right-hand side of them. We had slightly over-compensated for wind. Instantly we made a quick but slight adjustment by shifting the point of aim a fraction still using the reticle pattern as a reference point. The next two rounds found their mark and they fell to the ground. We could see they were still alive so we fired a few more rounds.

You could see the effects of the wind on the rounds because as a gust came through it pushed them off target slightly to the left and when the wind dropped they landed just to the right. The atmospheric conditions were also good enough for us to observe the swirl from the rounds. This meant we could see exactly how the wind was affecting our rounds on their trajectory. So getting a round back on target took several attempts.

The third guy with the RPG was still hidden in

the rocks and they sent some kids to see if the two guys in the creek line were still alive. They knew we wouldn't engage the kids, and shortly afterwards we observed several males walking into the creek line. They were carrying a large blanket to recover the deceased, and as they came out the bodies had been wrapped in the blanket and were being carried off.

They also sent two kids up to the older guy with the RPG to shield him from us as they walked him away from his hiding spot. He was walking quite gingerly so it seemed like Gumps' second round had winged him. The other guy who took the clothes in came out of the creek line with about six kids shielding him. The kids were also carrying the rifles of the deceased to be put back into circulation.

4RAR had now entered our field of view and were continuing with their clearance. Soon after, it began to get dark and we decided to cut away from our OP locs under the cover of darkness, and walk back the 6 kilometres through the hills to where the vehicles dropped us off.

Back at FOB Anaconda we were given a warning order for the drive back to Tarin Kowt. Our patrol was to conduct a night patrol through the village to the south to provide awareness of any enemy movement and early warning should the Taliban decide to hit our cars as they drove for the mountain pass early next morning. The territory was hostile but working at night was to our advantage. Wearing NVGs we could stealthily move in and around the green without anyone knowing we were there.

4RAR were leaving that night so we got them to tactically insert us from one of their Bushmaster vehicles. As soon as we stepped out of the vehicle I instantly noticed how cold it was. Most of the boys had only packed a thin jacket into a day sack, as we didn't anticipate it being that cold. Anaconda wasn't all that far away and the nights there were quite comfortable. SG, who loves his comfort, was the only one who took out his big green puffy jacket that we had been issued. He also carried the TAC/SAT – quite a heavy radio used by the JTACs to call in an aircraft. I had to borrow a thin fleece jumper, which hardly provided any protection from the cold at all.

As we patrolled we noticed that all the villagers were inside, it was now late September and the night temperature was freezing. A couple of times we held our breath as a local farmer exited his compound to have a shit in his field. We stayed motionless, but at the ready. When you're on edge, as we were, every noise is amplified. These situations can be quite unpredictable as some of the locals carry firearms for their own protection and if startled could start blazing away blindly into the darkness, which would compromise our patrol.

It was now 0200 hours and the air temperature was starting to drop rapidly. Gumps had decided to go 'static' for a couple of hours parallel to a well-used track to see if there was going to be any foot traffic. Within minutes I was absolutely freezing and had started to shiver. This was going to be a very painful two hours but Gumps cut it at the hour and a half mark as we needed to get the circulation going again. By that stage my ears were stinging and I could hardly move my hands.

I was glad to be moving again but wasn't warming up at all. We patrolled uneventfully the rest of the way and RVd with the troop at the mouth of the pass that we had been observing for the last hour. One of the boys who was very warmly wrapped up told us the temp was minus 2 degrees then smiled at us. No wonder I was so bloody cold! Back with our vehicles we could source some more cold weather clothing. One of the lads had thoughtfully made us a brew in a thermos flask before they left and handed it to Kabes.

Late that morning we had reached the same steep and winding pass where we had all the trouble with the CV joints. We did survey the area for other avenues, but this was our best option. In Afghanistan even the best options can be bloody dangerous and this one was no exception. By now we had started to attract a fair amount of attention from the bad guys, and the radio chatter was running on full auto. There wasn't a lot we could do about it; we just had to be super vigilant.

We had started to climb the mountainous pass

and it wasn't long before a car had broken the first CV, which had to be fixed in place. The LRPVs generally weighed about 6 tonnes fully fuelled and loaded, so this was an enormous amount of strain on these cars, which weren't designed to carry such a heavy load. We broke several on our journey to the top of the pass, but luckily we had been resupplied at FOB Anaconda. At the top of the pass our patrol saw some enemy movement close to 1,700 metres away. They looked like they were getting into a position where they could either observe us, or hit us with mortars.

DM and Kabes put forward a plan of action to stalk them and give them the good news from across the valley. DM took his .338 sniper rifle and Kabes had his M4. The lie of the ground was extremely steep and the temperature that afternoon was around 34 degrees. They travelled very light and carried just one water bottle each in their chest webbing. As they got halfway towards their target I saw two blokes at the base of a tree on the ridgeline they were travelling. We warned them by radio and gave them a target indication. This meant that DM and Kabes would now have to disappear over the other side of the ridgeline and out of our sight. After a short time DM got back on the radio and informed us that they were approaching the enemy position.

During a stalk we set our scopes to 300 metres in case we got unexpectedly compromised and we could then battle shoot quite effectively using the mil dots on the reticle pattern. DM and Kabes got within 80 metres of these blokes. DM got into position, placed the crosshairs on the target, and fired but the round missed. We saw the splash of dust, which seemed to land near; this spooked them and they vanished from our view. At that range and with the elevation set at 300 the barrel was pointing too high. So when they engaged, the round went straight over the top of the bad guy's head. But it was enough to get these two blokes running, and they ran straight towards Kabes, who dropped both of them with head shots.

They recovered an AK and a .303 with about 200 rounds per gun. We had been awake for 36 hours straight by now and DM and Kabes were members of the night patrol.

With the boys back in location looking very drawn in the face and vehicles all fixed, we decided to hit the road again. That was when we got word via a captured radio that the enemy wanted someone to lay some IEDs in the road for us, and they needed it done in a hurry. As we crawled towards the bottom of the pass, the front car, which was Gumps', stopped right in front of where a small creek line ran across the road – a favourite spot to plant IEDs. I was in the car about 20 metres behind them. All the combat indicators were there, but sometimes it's not until something happens that you say, 'Fuck, I saw it coming but didn't actually realise it was going to happen so soon.'

Gumps' crew saw a guy about 50 metres in front of them sitting on a rock with a black bag in his hand. I couldn't see him because we had just come around the corner but I heard Gumps say on the radio, 'We're going to move forward and talk to this guy.'

As soon as they moved forward the guy legged it, and as they drove into the ditch, *Boom!* The bastard had laid an IED in the road, which exploded right underneath the gearbox. I think the right front wheel drove over the pressure plate.

The pressure plates are made using a wooden box containing two saw blades with batteries connecting wires from the blades to a detonator. Once the saw blades are crushed together it completes the circuit and sends the electrical pulse to explode the detonator.

The gearbox took the full force of the explosion and this protected our guys. The bad guys try to position the IED to go off under one of the front seats or to get the gunner in the back, which is what happened to Sean McCarthy in 2008. We also reckon that this time they used double Russian anti-tank mines, one stacked on top of the other. It caused a terrific amount of damage, but fortunately only threw the guys out of the car with minor injuries.

I went to run forward but one of our guys shouted, 'Stop!' He was concerned about the threat of a secondary device being planted there as well. Initially I thought, 'Yeah, good call, mate.' But then

I thought, 'No, bugger it, my mates are injured and they need help.' So I ran forward with one other guy from my car and checked on the blokes.

They were bruised and battered and one had cracked his elbow. They were all grey and black from the blast, which we thought was quite funny and had a bit of a chuckle at their expense – they looked a bit like the black and white minstrels. I shouted to SG, who had been in the back of the car and was a bit disorientated, 'Where's the bloke with the black bag?' He tried to give me a target indication but he was slightly confused.

He said, 'I'll shoot at the area. Watch the splash.' Where he hit was like the entrance to a cave. 'Good, he's gone in there. Let's go round the top and come in behind him.' So three of us crossed the creek line and made our way onto the high ground tactically pepper-potting forward. As we got close I threw a grenade off the high ground and it landed at the entrance to the cave and exploded. We then quickly pepper-potted down to the entrance.

We covered each other into the overhang. There was nothing there. One of the lads who was a tracker said, 'Let's go down and see if we can pick up this guy's tracks.' We did but only managed to track him about 20 metres where we could clearly see that he had climbed onto a motorbike and ridden off. The re-entrant that he rode up was so deep it had absorbed the sound of his bike. He got away to fight another day.

As we moved back, the troop sergeant had already started to organise an air medical evacuation (AME) for the injured blokes. A couple of patrols had also organised themselves into providing security for us on the high ground. We jockeyed a few cars around and tried to make the damaged car towable. Some of the lads were picking up all the broken bits while scouting around for pieces of kit that were strewn over a large area. There was still the smell of HE in the air mixed in with diesel and engine oil from the damaged vehicle.

It didn't take too long to make the car towable. We then hooked it up to a solid 'A' frame and secured it to the rear of my car. The AME came in, which was a couple of American Blackhawks, and landed right beside us. The Americans run the AME and do an absolutely fantastic job over a huge area. They are always flanked by Apache gun-ships for their protection. The injured were carried to the aircraft and once on board they took off.

We had intelligence suggesting that there had been a second device laid further down the road. Generally the Taliban will place an IED in an area that is constricted and no other way around, forcing us to drive through it. We had a couple of specialist engineers attached to us who had a bomb disposal dog able to sniff out small traces of explosive or firearms. The engineers set about clearing the rest of the road to ensure a safe exit from the mountain pass.

This process was very slow and we inched forward to within 1,600 metres from the dasht. A few of the boys had remained on the high ground looking for the spotter who was reporting on us. We heard him report that we were coming up close to the next IED. Everybody instantly became extra vigilant, anticipating another device.

The dog handler and his dog Razz were out front together with another engineer who was sweeping the ground with a mine detector. The mad thing was that Razz wouldn't go any more than 20 metres away from his handler. We were about 500 metres down the track when suddenly the dog got all excited.

He was interested in a spot similar to the location of the earlier IED: the road dipped down into a shallow creek line where the ground was quite loose, which would have made it easy to plant an IED. Razz became increasingly excited. I must have been about 150 metres back at this stage, and there were a few cars ahead of me. Razz then ran back to the engineer wagging his tail, letting him know that he had done a good job, but then ran back to the device and started to dig for it. *Boom!* – Razz was vapourised and we were briefly pelted by small stones that had been thrown into the air; a couple of the front cars were covered in Razz's fur. The explosion blew the engineer over and knocked him out. This was a double whammy for him as he'd been sitting on the back of Gumps' car when they drove over the first one. He was pretty upset about his dog but it was a good thing that he was still alive. Not a good day for him.

He was able to continue without an AME and was extracted from the field by Chinook when it came in that night to lift out the damaged car.

The next morning we headed for the same village where we thought we were going to get contacted the previous week. This was undoubtedly the home of the IED facilitator, and they were already talking it up to attack us. They realised they didn't do a very good job of it a week ago and all indications suggested that they were up for it this time. Sure enough, the bad guys came up on the radio again saying, 'They're coming towards us. We're going to attack them this time.' This was translated through our interpreter. I thought, 'Christ, here we go.'

We sat off the village observing it for some time trying to make an assessment of what the Taliban were actually going to do. We didn't have any other option; we couldn't drive around the village, as the topography wouldn't allow it. We pushed closer, arranging the vehicles into fire support position, and two patrols went in on foot to clear the route. As there were only three of us left, with the other half of the patrol now in hospital, we joined these two patrols to boost up the fire power slightly.

It was an eerie feeling entering the village, as everyone was hidden indoors. We tactically approached the bazaar, which seemed to be the hub of the village and where small groups of fighting-age males congregated. We expected to be hit at any moment; I could hear my heart pounding as I looked for any sign of trouble.

Step by step we moved closer to these young blokes, who seemed to be taking our advance rather casually. This put me a little more at ease but I wasn't going to drop my guard. We cleared all the buildings in the bazaar and searched the young males; all the more mature men had disappeared. It was possible that they had used an unseen 'rat line' (escape route) that ran into the hills. Maybe they planned to attack us from there.

Once we cleared a small proportion of the village we got the cars through and harboured up about 3 kilometres on the other side. It was now getting dark. One patrol went back into the village at night to scout around to see if there was any activity. However, there was nothing doing, so the following morning we packed up and headed back towards Tarin Kowt. The Taliban tend to talk themselves up a lot and hardly ever seem to follow up on their tough talk. This can eventually lead you into a false sense of security.

Back on the road and four hours later the chatter started again. We were about to enter the next village when we heard, 'Get ready, we're going to ambush the infidels.' As it happened we got through the village again without incident as they couldn't organise themselves fast enough.

4RAR were about an hour behind us at this stage

and the plan was to marry up with them before we entered the dasht, our last leg of the journey. We placed ourselves in a position of overwatch just in case the Taliban came good with their word of an ambush, which to my surprise they did! They waited until half the massive 4RAR convoy came through and then opened up on them with small arms fire and a possible RPG from the opposite high ground.

The first half of the convoy took off and headed towards us. The others were static for a bit until they got their head around what was going on. By the amount of fire they received there can't have been any more than seven shooters up in the hills, but all of a sudden half the countryside was being shot at from the 4RAR boys who were itching to get among it.

We were in quite a good position to observe into the green and provide fire support, but we were taking a few rounds also. These rounds seemed to be coming from the village. I was half expecting the 4RAR OC to come up with a quick battle plan to enter the green to see what was there, because he was in the perfect position to do so, but nothing ever came. They decided that they were going to shoot on the move and re-join the rest of the convoy.

I was pretty disappointed at this stage: we had a massive force on hand of highly trained soldiers who could have rolled up these bad guys easily. One of our patrols was securing the entry point to the dasht down on the low ground. We were stuck up on the high ground, and copping a few rounds from the green. We were almost on the crest of the hill so I got on the radio and said, 'We're sitting ducks here, we'll drive down to the other patrol and help them out in case they need it.'

Upon reaching the other patrol we saw two bad guys running from the cover of some thin bushes to seek refuge behind a small square mud brick building. 'Get the 84s out and we'll send two HE over the top of that building,' I told MR and SP.

You can dial a range onto the nose cone of an HE rocket and it will explode in the air once it has reached that range; otherwise it will explode on impact. The boys grabbed an 84 mm each; I ranged the target and they dialled in the elevation for the scope. I gave them the command: 'Ready, ready'; 'Ready, ready, ready! Stand by, fire!' They both fired at the same time and the rockets exploded directly above the Taliban hiding behind the building. If the blast didn't kill them the shrapnel would have. There was no movement after that.

Then we saw another guy walking through the green. He had kids around him for protection and was carrying an AK and wearing that very recognisable Chinese-style chest webbing. He was only about 450 metres away so I thought, 'I can get this guy and not hit any of the kids.' I put my M4 back in the car and grabbed the SR25 setting the range and adjustment for wind. He was walking at an oblique angle so I had to keep adjusting the elevation to keep up with his range. I kept on losing sight of him as he passed through soft cover – green foliage – but when he did produce himself he would be with the kids. When I decided I was ready to take a shot, he slipped into some bushes and vanished.

Conditions needed to be perfect for the shot before I would take it. I didn't want to risk hitting one of the kids, and they were very close to him. Scenarios like this do happen from time to time and you can walk away from it feeling quite disappointed, but I'd rather that than have an innocent death on my conscience.

There was a Canadian infantry mortar section with 4RAR. They were now beside us and had started to send 60 mm mortars onto the hillside. The situation should have been controlled a lot better, but unfortunately it was the last patrol of that rotation and everyone had their sights set on going home. The seriousness of the contact had now died off, and we all thought that this was rather pointless, it was time to get out of there and head for Tarin Kowt.

15

ANOTHER
BLACKHAWK DOWN

In 2008 I did a number of supervisory courses before we began the build-up for our rotation to Afghanistan in June. It was tough saying goodbye to George and the girls again, especially because young Ash was finding it difficult to deal with my absences. But when you head out for a combat zone you have to try to put these concerns to one side. We were able to contact our families from our base in Tarin Kowt but that can be a double-edged sword if they're doing it tough at home. I'm very lucky that George is such a champion. She tries not to worry me, even when the situation becomes stressed. She knows I have to be totally focused on the job.

I was in 3 Squadron at the time and we left on the same charter plane that had taken us across the previous years. When we reached Kuwait we stayed for a couple of days organising kit and preparing for what lay ahead. We had all seen action, but we had no idea just how close we would come to being KIA ourselves. In fact, some of us would eventually become involved in one of the biggest Australian battle against an enemy force since Vietnam.

I went on the advance party to Tarin Kowt with about 10 other lads – a command element of the troop and 2ICs. In our patrol, three of us went early. When we got to Tarin Kowt we met up with the 1 Squadron fellas and they gave us a very good handover. It consisted of a couple of days of briefs and PowerPoint presentations, culminating in a combined patrol.

For the patrol we inserted by vehicle. At that time 1 Squadron was using two LRPVs at the front as scout cars and protection, so one patrol was responsible for that. Then we'd have the Bushmasters, which were the big square four-wheel-drive troop-carrying vehicles – a truck basically – which was quite heavily armoured. The hull was shaped like a V so if there was a blast underneath it wouldn't go straight up; it would be deflected off to the sides. As it happened, this would save both lives and limbs in the days ahead.

Half the troop was dropped off south of the target village and the other half was deployed to the north. We did a few recces before all meeting up to roll on to the target. This work was all done at night and on the walk into where we were to meet the other half of the troop, our patrol bumped into some locals. They don't usually mill around at night and if they do they're usually farmers digging out waterways to irrigate their crops. But these guys were milling around excitedly for some reason and we became suspicious. As we walked up to them – tactically so that we were covering each other – they sensed something was wrong and ran off. We apprehended one guy, cuffed him and took him to the marry-up location.

We would have blindfolded him as well but he had to see where he was walking so we just kept his head down. Once we reached the other guys we covered his eyes to prevent him looking around.

The OC gave us a quick set of confirmation orders before we approached the designated compound. Half the troop went through one of the neighbouring compounds to make sure it would not be a threat during the task, and we made our way around the other side. On the way we apprehended two more men and took them with us. We then met up again outside the bigger target compound.

During the summer months the Afghans generally sleep outside where it is cooler, and some of the men sleep on the roofs. On this occasion as we reached the main door all the occupants seemed to be awake in the courtyard. One of the guys who had done a language course explained that we were Australian soldiers and we'd come to search the house. He politely asked the people inside to cooperate.

But when we tried to open the door leading to the compound we found it was locked and the occupants totally ignored repeated requests to open it. The compounds are built out of very tough mud brick, which will easily deflect small arms fire, but as it gets old it becomes brittle and will break up. One of the PCs called up the troop boss and asked permission to use an explosive charge to open the doors. 'Yep, no problem,' so we set a small charge and blew in the door, which allowed us to enter the inner compound.

All of a sudden everyone was wide awake, so we had to calm them down and keep the women and children separate from the men. In fact, there were only about four men in the group. We conducted a quick clearance of the compound; then my PC and I entered another small adjoining compound. It had a big vegetable patch but otherwise seemed deserted.

The other guys followed us in and again checked out the area. When they got round to the other side they said, 'Yeah it's clear as far as we can see,' so AS and I entered the building leading off the compound and found it was clear at the bottom level but there was a narrow stairwell leading up towards the roof. There was a whole heap of junk on the stairs – an old spring bed, half an old bike and parts of cars. We covered each other as we slipped past the junk as quietly as we could. It was really tight, especially because we had our body armour on, and as we got through the top doorway AS cleared his arc to the front. I was right on his arse so as he turned the corner I was a split second behind him.

There was a sentry on the roof and he must have heard us coming. He had quite a fancy set of webbing on, but all he had in it was two grenades. He was carrying an AK and strangely enough he wasn't looking our way; he was watching my PC and the others below. He had his back turned to us and as we got up there, AS said to him, in Pashto, 'Don't move. Don't move.'

But as he turned round we could see he was bringing his AK up to shoot. AS hit him three times in the chest very quickly, but because the 5.56 mm is only a small projectile it is very fast and more often than not misses the bone and cannot transfer its energy fully to the body, which meant the poor bugger was still raising his rifle to fire. 'Christ,' I thought and shot him in the head. He dropped instantly. This all happened in an instant and I was thankful for all the hours of bulk shooting we had done at the range, making snap shooting like this instinctive.

Basically at that range we've been trained to neutralise a threat in the head with what is generally called a double tap – two shots in quick succession to the head. If you shoot them in the right place they instantly drop, only requiring one round to be fired.

AS covered me while I searched the body. His fancy webbing was made out of leather and every millimetre was covered with studs – quite a setup. I removed the two grenades and took his arms out of the straps to get the webbing off him. We stayed on the roof because we had a good vantage point to cover the others and to look for more potential threats.

There were still a couple of locals milling around, so we covered the other guys searching the outer courtyard of this compound. We let them know when there was movement in certain places and told them where the bad guys were going and what they were doing. They checked them out and if they were suspect they apprehended them.

When we searched the two compounds we found quite a big cache of grenades, weapons, IED-making equipment and booster charges for RPGs – these are round sticks of explosive material about 5 centimetres in diameter and 30 centimetres long. There were 20 of those. I got tasked with rigging them up with a charge and once everyone was out of the way I blew the charge and destroyed all that materiel.

On the walk out we married up with the vehicles again, climbed in and headed away from the village. We'd been driving for only five minutes before the second LRPV in the line of march drove over an IED. It exploded under the rear wheels and badly injured the two guys travelling in the back – a reserve commando and an engineer. The reserve commando was an extra bod to provide security for the vehicles because the drop-off point was some distance from our area of operations. He busted his leg quite badly. We had to secure that area and call the Dutch recovery team in to drag the LRPV onto their trucks and get it out of there. They organised an AME for the two injured guys to get medical assistance as soon as possible. Our guys in the car didn't get hurt at all and were very lucky.

Then the OC of 1 Squadron organised a patrol to conduct a quick search of the immediate area. They had to clear some buildings to make sure we had a secure perimeter. The whole recovery process must have taken about eight hours. We'd been up all the previous day, worked all night and then had to deal with being IEDd in the blazing sun. It was about 44 degrees that day and we didn't get back to base until about 3 p.m. When we arrived back it was time for everyone to ask what had happened. I let the other guys answer the questions. At the time I was more interested in getting a good feed and some kip. I don't have any dramas sleeping after action like that. If I'm tired I'll sleep, but I probably won't sleep that long – maybe five hours – before I have to get up.

We had quite a big debrief the next day and came to the conclusion that over the winter the bad guys had dug in a lot of IEDs in key areas. The one that exploded had been there when we drove through but it hadn't yet been armed. After we had passed they had run up to the thing in a hurry and connected the battery. They could even have done it remotely, as they get smarter all the time.

The charge itself was 20 kilos of HME. They had put it in a 20-litre container and dug it in while the ground was soft. In summer the ground goes hard so all of a sudden you've got a rudimentary shaped charge, which means all the blast is getting forced into a small area and going straight up instead of in a wide V shape. This was probably quite fortunate for the blokes at the back because it just bored a big hole in the centre of the car and injured their legs. It could have been much worse.

We concluded that in this area the same guy was making all the IEDs and possibly laying them himself. He was using the same techniques and the same materials. In fact, right through that rotation we recognised his work in virtually every IED incident, even to the way the components were taped together and assembled. We gave him the code name Stiletto.

That was 1 Squadron's last job, and after watching C130 depart we waited for the rest of our troop to arrive. Our base at Tarin Kout was situated inside Kamp Holland, originally an American base, but then the Dutch took over in 2006. They turned it into a huge area easily a couple of kilometres long and the same wide. The whole place had completely changed since the first time I was there in 2005. It was now virtually unrecognisable. They had ripped down buildings and rebuilt it on a massive scale. We called our base Camp Russell after Andy Russell (an SAS sergeant who was killed on 16 February 2002). When 2 Squadron originally arrived there in 2005 the Americans allotted an area for the Australian contingent but it was bare so they lived in tents. Then they engaged some contactors and built wooden huts. In mid-2008 they ripped all the huts down and built brand new accommodation for us and by comparison it was very good indeed.

While Tarin Kowt was home, we often worked from forward operating bases. Part of our mandate was to provide protection to the engineer reconstruction team, which sometimes meant we had a few limitations placed on us and had to concentrate on the Taliban in and around Tarin Kowt. We needed to neutralise them before they hit soft targets like the engineers.

However, the more intelligence we got, the further afield we pushed, especially when we learnt that some of the bad guys in the Tarin Kowt area were moving out because we were starting to eliminate their command structure. This was no bad thing. It didn't mean that Tarin Kowt was safe either, but it was certainly better than it had been. However, you could still go 5 kilometres outside Tarin

Kowt and discover that the bad guys were planting IEDs; and you could still find weapon caches inside the area as well.

Our next job was a week-long vehicle-mounted patrol, and it was during this patrol Sean McCarthy was killed. We were very mindful of the IED threat, and did everything possible to avoid them, but still managed to drive onto one.

During the winter months, the Taliban had been busy digging IEDs into the soft ground on both well-used and secondary tracks, in preparation for the drier months when coalition vehicle movements would be more regular. So naturally we were all pretty pissed off when Sean was killed. Twenty kilos of HME was detonated right beneath Sean; the driver and vehicle commander were thrown from the car and injured also. The Afghan interpreter who was in the back lost both of his lower legs.

I was in a car that was a fair way behind, and when the explosion went off I knew exactly what it was and felt sick in the stomach. We were on the opposite side of a small feature that dulled the sounds of the blast. HME combusts a lot more slowly than military-grade explosive and is very identifiable after you've heard it a few times. It's not a sound you like to hear either.

We initially looked for a place to provide some security, but a call came through the radio asking for our patrol medic to assist Wal, a corps medic, who was treating Sean. We drove up and over the feature to drop TF off, then positioned ourselves on the high ground to provide overwatch. While we were waiting for the AME aircraft to arrive I pinpointed a well-constructed spotter location 1,700 metres away – an easy task for the .50-calibre Barrett sniper rifle.

I borrowed SG's rifle, as he was monitoring the channel for the AME. I tried not to make it obvious to onlookers that I was about to engage a certain spotter location, and concealed my location as best I could. I dialled in the range and made an adjustment for wind. No sooner had I done that, the AME informed us that they were five minutes out. SG then suggested that he could talk the Apache gunship onto my target, engaging it using their 30 mm canon. 'Good idea,' I said, then unloaded and packed away the Barrett.

I knew that whatever the Apache shot at with its canon wouldn't be around for too much longer. SG wheeled and dealed the aircraft and then gave, 'Clear hot!' to neutralise the spotter location, which then disappeared in dust.

Once Sean's body was on his way to Kandahar we organised the recovery of the damaged car. Again, we used the heavily protected Dutch recovery team to collect it, and once again they took forever to get to us. When we reached FOB Locke – named after Matt (Lockie) Locke MG (killed in action in Afghanistan in October 2007) – we licked our wounds and re-cocked for the rest of the task ahead. Driving anywhere after that made us extra nervous, almost expecting to be hit again at any time, so after the patrol we pretty much locked the LRPVs away to gather dust.

We eventually got the use of the Australian CH47s (Chinook helicopters) to insert us into jobs and then pick us up at the conclusion. On one of the first jobs using the Chinooks we inserted as a troop but at different locations around a small village in a narrow valley. The task was to complete a search of a suspected compound and apprehend any suspected Taliban fighters. As the patrol's scout I led the way into the village under cover of darkness and we began to explore it. My PC decided that he wanted to go static for a short time to conduct a listening stop. It wasn't long before I noticed a local man through my NVGs acting a bit suspiciously. I had a look into his small compound over a wall, but couldn't make out what he was doing. Just as I tried to check this guy out we got the call to continue so I had to leave him to it. What I didn't realise was that he was uncovering a rifle and 200 rounds.

We patrolled around a small feature 30 metres away and along an aqueduct. The patrol had become split in that short distance due to some thick foliage we had to pass through so we stopped for the other three to catch up. I scanned the high ground and then focused my attention to the front and the track we were travelling on towards our objective. I could sense something wasn't quite right and then I suddenly heard a faint noise above us. I quickly turned with my rifle in my shoulder pointing where I was looking with laser on. I immediately saw a bloke pointing a rifle at us and as soon as my laser illuminated a small dot on his forehead I released a shot from my M4 and he dropped instantly. He was the same bloke I was curious about earlier, but this time he was brandishing a .303 Winchester P14 bolt action rifle.

Because he was only 10 metres away the round was only just starting its trajectory and entered the corner of his left eye, just a little lower than where my laser touched him. We searched him and removed his weapon and rounds. We initially thought the shot would have alerted the Taliban in the village, but no-one seemed interested, so we continued on task to our objective. There was a lot of male activity at the compound, which made us a little nervous as we didn't know what to expect or how they would react to our presence. It was all a bit of an anticlimax, as we found very little in this compound and were picked up by Chinook shortly after daybreak.

A few days later we walked 16 kilometres to a job from an Australian FOB to target an IED facilitator. 3RAR were good enough to supply us with a section who were heavily tooled-up. A couple of their blokes carried the 7.62 mm MAG 58, an FN general-purpose machine gun identical to the British L7 GPMG. We dropped them off with our squadron sergeant-major at the 12-kilometre mark to act as cut off for any squirters trying to flee the area.

Our patrol led in the troop and upon reaching the objective we took up a cut-off position at the north-western end of the village. When the clearance began by the rest of the troop we noticed a few Taliban heading for the high ground, two of whom were openly carrying firearms. SG dropped a hellfire rocket onto one by a circling aircraft before he got away, and four of us followed up the others on foot, shooting one as he shouldered his AK. Although we didn't get the guy we were after, we killed a couple of his fighters and destroyed some IED-making equipment and weapons.

The threat of being involved in an IED incident was increasing. The whole task force, including the Dutch, who had recently lost a few lads, were running out of ideas on how to combat this hidden danger. We put a plan forward that would hopefully expose some of these IED facilitators, which got the green light. It involved driving down one of the most notorious roads in our AO and dropping off patrols at varying intervals to observe certain stretches of road. We were hoping to draw out the Taliban who would hear the vehicles drive by and then approach their previously laid IEDs to arm them. We would then engage them.

As darkness fell we occupied several Bushmasters and quietly slipped out of Camp Russell. My position in the Bushmaster was to man the front 7.62 mm machine gun; JB had the rear. The night temperature was warm and local activity was non-existent. All seemed to be going according to plan as we zigzagged our way through the dirt roads, stopping to clear suspected areas using the engineers and their metal detectors. Our patrol was dropped off first and when the Bushmasters disappeared from earshot we started to have a snoop around. A couple of local men who were sleeping in a field had been woken by our vehicle movement, and were desperately trying to see into the darkness to figure out what was going on. We went static and observed them through our NVGs for a while until they got their heads down again. Patrolling east we could make out movement of the second patrol that was dropped off and gave them a heads up of our location by radio. We continued to drift in the same direction when suddenly a radio message came through: 'Tango Oscar, this is T4, we've just been hit by an IED.'

Boom!

'Arr for fucks sake!' I said under my breath.

The lead patrol had driven onto an IED. The PC of that vehicle had started to give a quick situation report (sitrep) to the troop boss over the radio when the sound of the explosion reached us. We were approximately 5 kilometres away from the incident site. The PC then started a count-off of his guys over the radio and we were relieved to hear everyone answer. Our PC got on the net and advised the troop boss that we would remain static until needed. A US AME was organised without delay as Mark 'Donno' Donaldson and one other were blown from their positions behind the machine guns and were injured on impact with the road. No-one else was injured.

The road was being cleared by engineers at the time but this one was just missed. The Taliban sometimes do try to confuse road clearances by scattering metallic objects like washers or nuts onto the road. The Bushmaster rolled straight onto 20 kilos of HME, which tore the right rear wheel off, taking half its suspension with it, and vaporised the steel storage bins on the side.

'Tango three, this is Tango Oscar. Move to our location.'

'Tango three roger.'

The troop boss had just asked us to move to the incident site. We knew the AME was on its way and we would have to provide security for it. We made best speed to the area without dropping security, as by now every bad guy for kilometres had a pretty good idea of what had just occurred. About 1,500 metres out from the rest of the troop we heard the Blackhawk making its approach. The troop signaller made contact and one of the patrols marked the LS. As the helicopter flared to make its final descent the rotor wash disturbed a massive amount of very fine dust – a brownout – which clouded the pilot's and loadies' vision, causing them to lose sight of the ground and marker. They made a decision to get airborne again and make another attempt. We could hear what was going on as we patrolled to the noise, and initially we thought that the wounded were on board.

The Blackhawk circled above and then had another go at landing. *Whomp! Zing, zing, zing*, then silence.

'What the fuck was that?'

'The fuckin' aircraft has spudded in mate,' I answered. We all felt terrible. The Blackhawk crash of 2006 that I was involved in ran through my mind and I expected the worst. I couldn't help but think, 'Poor fellas, I hope they're okay.'

On arrival to the area we were given a heads up and the good news – everyone was okay but the Blackhawk had suffered a very heavy landing and was now irreparable. The frame was bent and all the rotor blades had sheared off, some of the debris narrowly missing some of our lads.

Another AME was organised, as was the recovery of the Blackhawk and Bushmaster. It was now starting to get light and we could make out the faint glow of fire from within the walls of nearby compounds caused by human activity. We were now looking at a situation that could go from bad to very much worse. Not only did we have the injured and two downed vehicles to look after, we also had the Blackhawk crew to protect. The Dutch recovery convoy had been alerted (they were probably thinking 'our favourite customers'), but we knew they would take at least eight hours to reach us. It was going to be a long day.

Obviously the scene attracted a lot of local attention from a distance, and we couldn't help but feel the culprits were amongst them checking out their handiwork. We did notice small pockets of middle-aged men taking a keen interest in us, which kept us awake in the baking 45-degree heat. The area around the IED was explored further by the engineers, who uncovered a secondary device buried in a wall just metres away from the first. This was also 20 kilos of HME, placed to hit the recovery team.

The sky became abuzz with several Apache helicopters as a Chinook secured the recovery of the Blackhawk, lifting it back to Tarin Kowt. The Chinook had a couple of goes at it before getting it right, but all the time it was manoeuvring into position it was covering a large area in dust. This would have created an excellent screen for the Taliban before attacking us. But fortunately this didn't happen. The Dutch recovery convoy turned up shortly after and proceeded to winch the busted Bushmaster onto a large truck. 'Thank fuck for that,' we said. 'Now we can get out of here!' Donno's injuries weren't serious and he stayed on; the other lad fractured a bone in his lower back and returned to Australia.

Another job that made the news back in Australia was when we apprehended a prominent Taliban leader. No shots were fired; the job just ran nice and smoothly. It was well planned and executed. The basic plan behind our activities was to get the Taliban leader, objective 'Spear'. We developed a heap of intelligence from several sources and in time we knew his routines and habits. We could almost pinpoint where he was going to be on a certain night. We would try to anticipate his moves and when credible intelligence arrived we'd be poised to react. It was similar to a police investigation tracking an offender's movements. We'd gather evidence and possible locations and then we had to figure out bit by bit how to track him down. We had to have locals working on our side and that was never easy. We were dealing with people who were at least 70 per cent against us. We were in a hostile environment the whole time, and wouldn't get any information out of anybody without greasing their palms.

Sometimes they would come forward with information to other agencies that would come back to us. This helped put the pieces of the puzzle together. We could see that he was known to frequent several compounds, and that his family lived elsewhere. The locals were saying, 'He sleeps there but goes back to his family in the morning.' Many times we just missed him.

Local hostility also prevented us getting a clear

idea of the enemy's strength on the ground. Numerous times we talked to locals and asked them how many bad guys were in the area. But still got that old chestnut: 'Taliban haven't been here for 12 months.' That had been their standard reply since 2005. But when we got the call to react to Spear there was a feeling we might be successful. We drove out of Tarin Kowt and within a short time we had reached our DOP. From there we patrolled the 3.5 kilometres to the target. The temperature was about 30 degrees at 2200 hours and quite humid. Each man carried at least 2 litres of water, a minimum of four magazines of 5.56 mm, one HE grenade, a pistol and other specialist equipment. As we reached the objective we saw a couple of local farmers diverting water from a creek onto their crops. We avoided them and the recce team married up with us and guided us onto the target.

Our patrol was the roof team, which meant I was always first to gain entry to the compound to start providing security and awareness for the rest of the troop. There was no-one sleeping on the roof this time, but we could see people sleeping outside within the compound walls. The boys then stealthily made their way into the compound and quietly woke the males. The Taliban leader, objective Spear, was one of them. We explored the compound and uncovered weapons and IED components and once the troop boss was happy the job was done he got us to patrol back to the vehicles taking Spear and a couple of others with us, who came quietly.

Shortly after this job those of our targets who were in close proximity to Tarin Kowt moved out to neighbouring Pakistan. We didn't know how long they'd be there so we began to focus our attention further afield. We learned that there was a target of ours not too far out of FOB Anaconda. We got in touch with the Americans who were having a few dramas of their own because they were down to almost a skeleton crew.

You could almost liken it to house arrest because they could barely leave their base. They were regularly getting fired upon by mortars, RPGs and heavy machine guns. They had the ANA working with them and they tried to develop a patrolling program but there were so many bad guys around that they could only leave their base for short periods for fear of being overrun.

So we thought we could try to kill two birds with one stone: we would primarily target our objective but if successful early, or if he disappeared, we would help the Americans out and try to give them a bit of freedom of movement. We'd see if we could push off the entrenched Taliban and perhaps neutralise some of their commanders.

In fact, the commanders were the key. I likened the situation to the organisational structure of a supermarket. I figured if we neutralised a shelf stacker they could easily get a new one in, but if we took out the general manager it would be much harder to find a replacement. And if he were taken out in really unpleasant circumstances they might find that no-one wanted the job. We found from experience that this tactic disrupted their activities.

We were also looking forward to the change of scenery and to say g'day to old acquaintances. The troop boss gave his orders and 'actions on' for the move, but we encountered problems with getting the two Chinooks to pick us up, which resulted in us gearing up and then being let down several times over a four-day period. The aircraft crews are subject to many restrictions and generally it took a little while for all the planets to align. This never really sat comfortably with us, and now and then we had to adjust insertion and extraction timings to daylight hours just to fit in with these restrictions. This was not a good idea to be alerting every Taliban member in the area to the massive signature dust cloud that the Chinooks leave. Darkness is our friend!

So, early afternoon on the fourth day we got word that the Army Chinooks were on a routine admin run and would pick up and deliver us to the US FOB.

It didn't take us long to organise our kit as it had already been packed and placed for a quick departure four days earlier; all we really had to do was blow the dust off. Unfortunately our patrol was down a member as one of the boys had rolled his ankle and couldn't walk. We were now five and JB picked up the extra responsibility of being the patrol medic along with his normal 2IC tasks.

Not long after arriving at Anaconda we conducted a few patrols trying to get this target of ours, and then found out through American intelligence sources that he was in Pakistan. Plan B: let's do some combined operations with the Americans to sort out some of these bad guys.

Our first combined operation was to try to create a bit of a stir and flush out the bad guys. The troop was split, half leaving just after dark, as we had a long way to walk to be in position by first light; the other half left very early in the morning but still under cover of darkness. The night sky as usual was very clear, there was no moon and the air was cool, almost perfect conditions for the walk. There was enough ambient light from the stars for our NVGs to capture and magnify, so we could see. Light pollution in Afghanistan isn't a problem, which means you can see thousands more stars than you've ever seen before.

It took some time but finally we started to climb a very steep and treacherous feature. We all had heavy packs as usual so the going was slow. It was a relief to reach the top and we went into all-round defence, then the two patrol commanders decided where each patrol would be positioned. From where we were we had very good OBs onto a very wide wadi, and a prominent vehicle track running from left to right.

Our patrol was responsible for the northern and the southern arcs; the other patrol, which had moved behind a feature to our flank, was responsible for the western arc but they still had observation down towards the south as well. Our other two patrols got into position on the high ground on the other side of the wadi, which was over 2 kilometres wide at the mouth. It was the end of August and the night air was freezing up in the mountains. We started observing long before daybreak with the hand-held TI, looking to pick up human movement.

That morning the Americans drove out in a different direction in their Humvees and came up behind us but on the other side of the green – about 2.5 kilometres from our position. On the way in they questioned a few local leaders to get a feel for the situation. Their presence was sure to be noted and this would help stir up the hornet's nest. However, by 11 a.m. we were still sitting in our position in the hot sun with nothing much happening. I was starting to think it might be a dud. As we sat there baking, JB suddenly said, 'Look at that!'

Three Taliban fighters were heading down the road in the direction of Americans. They were on our side of the wadi travelling east to west. Immediately we took up position behind our sniping rifles. Hoady and I had .338s, and SG had the 7.62 mm SR 25. There were two Taliban up front who looked like a protection party for the guy in the rear, about 10 metres behind them. This guy was on a mobile phone, possibly organising his fighters to hit the Americans. They were wearing chest rigs partially hidden under waistcoats but openly carrying AKs. They had no idea we were there.

We waited until they got into what is called 'the killing ground'. There was nowhere for them to go or any real cover to hide them. There was an old ruin about waist high on one side of the road but we made sure they moved past it before we engaged them. This was our first sniper ambush and we didn't want to screw it up. When they approached the ground of our choosing, we each checked the elevation and windage settings against each other and all came up with pretty much the same. Range – 550 metres, wind direction was left to right, wind strength appeared to be approx 12 km/h judging by the speed of the dust produced by their feet and the flapping of their clothes. We were also shooting from an elevated position and compensated for that also. The PC gave the call over the radio, 'Ready, ready! . . . ready, ready! . . . Ready! . . . Stand by . . . Fire.'

We all squeezed off a round at the same time. But all three rounds missed – we had misjudged just how strong the wind was. It could easily have gusted up to 18–20 km/h, and pushed the rounds slightly off to the right of the target. I was in the same boat as Hoady and hadn't shot moving targets with the .338 before. The muzzle velocity is a lot higher than a 7.62 mm, and trajectory is flatter. This would give you a different point of aim to the 7.62 mm. I shouldn't have aimed off as much.

The enemy darted towards a small creek line. As we fired a second shot I hit one guy in the chest; the round went straight through one of his AK magazines, which burst open. He was hurt bad but still managed to dive into the ditch with one of the others. The bloke to the rear who was on the mobile phone had turned and run towards the ruins. I focused my attention on him. When he stopped he was crouching on the western corner with his back to us. I realigned rapidly and adjusted my scope for the range; he was bobbing up and down with my crosshairs on his back. As I squeezed off a round he moved again slightly, and the 252-grain projectile went through his right shoulder. At first I thought I'd missed because I saw a dust cloud where the round hit the wall in front of him. 'Shit, he's still moving.' Then he got down and started crawling at the base of the wall. He was still in plain view. 'As I tracked him through my scope I started my breathing cycle, then squeezed off another round that entered the back of his head.

One of the other lads who was watching through his scope said, 'Targets down, mate.' I didn't see the round strike, due to the recoil, but as I continued with the shot follow-through and brought the crosshairs back onto the target, I could see he was motionless. By now all three fighters were down.

We stayed behind the rifles for a bit in case some others came along. A bloke came by on a motorbike and paused briefly when he saw the bodies. He then he took off like a bat out of hell.

It wasn't long before the Americans got back to us on radio: 'There's a vehicle coming towards the three dead guys. The vehicle's occupants are Taliban and they're coming to pick up the bodies.' The Americans had changed their position so they could observe up the valley. Sure enough, a Toyota Hilux with six guys in it came along the road. Through the windows we could see several weapons. They almost drove straight past the bodies but an older guy in the back started tapping the window and pointing. The car stopped and reversed with the Taliban looking out the windows. Right then the Americans sent a volley of 40 mm grenades, which burst all around the vehicle. By that stage I was lined up on the driver, Hoady was lined up on the rear passenger and SG had the guy in the back tray.

The Hilux driver planted his foot in an attempt to get out of there. Once again we all fired at the same time. I thought we'd missed because the car kept on going forward, but then slowly it drifted off the side of the road to a stop. There were still other targets inside the car so we neutralised those also.

In the other patrol to our flank one of the guys

had a 7.62 mm machine gun that he'd broken down to fit in his pack for the walk in. He started to engage the car as well. But by then they were all dead; apart from the guy in the back tray they had all been shot in the head – all from about 470 metres away. Our response was a sense of satisfaction that we'd done the job to the best of our ability. In fact, it was a great result because one of the guys killed was the eastern commander of the Taliban in that area.

Now there were nine bodies out there. So the silly buggers sent out another vehicle to bring them in. The Americans said, 'We've just heard there's a white van coming through. It's got Taliban in it also and they're coming to pick up the bodies.' This time there were only two guys, and when they stopped they both got out.

The Americans engaged again, which made these guys run for cover, so we engaged the fleeing targets but missed. They were running full pelt for the ruins and we had to get them before they got there. One guy jumped the wall of the ruins to get inside. He promptly showed himself again but was moving around. I fired and hit the target but I wasn't confident of a good hit as I saw a splash of dirt in front of him. The round actually went through his side, missing all his vital organs. He then found the only real bit of cover that the ruins gave him. Every time he showed his head we pinned him down. The other guy also found some cover but showed himself at the wrong time and paid the price. It was now getting late in the afternoon.

At this stage the Americans said it was time to go home and drove up towards the location of the bodies. We packed up our gear and came out of the hills to RV with the Humvees, as they were our ride home. We tried to get down the hill as fast as possible to get there first to conduct a tactical investigation but they beat us to it. The ANA, who were with the Americans, had gone through all the dead fighters and pilfered their AKs, ammunition and their webbing, and anything else they could find of importance.

We were not impressed, as this equipment could be used to build up an intelligence picture. The American medic was treating the guy who I'd shot and he was questioned shortly after and then released with a handful of antibiotics and a change of dressings. They thought it was best to let him go to see what would develop.

We cleaned the area up and got on the back of the cars to drive back to Anaconda. It was important for us to stay off the roads because of the imminent threat of IEDs. This was slow going and when we were about 1,500 metres outside the American FOB we got ambushed by a handful of fighters with small arms fire. We were broadside onto the enemy and the green, and to our right was a large steep feature. We only had one way to go. We expected the Americans to employ the usual vehicle-mounted drill to pepper-pot forward: one vehicle would fire while the other got into a position where he could engage, then the other would move. Instead they stopped, turned all their guns towards the enemy fire and threw everything they had at these fighters.

A couple of enemy rounds landed about 10 metres in front of our car so I instantly got out, presenting a smaller target. I jumped down behind my .338 and started observing to find a target to shoot. One of the boys was shouting at me but I didn't hear him. It wasn't until I got back into the car that he said to me, 'Don't ever do that again. You've got kids, mate.' I replied, 'What are you talking about?'

It turned out that one of the bad guys had pinged me and his rounds were kicking up all around me. I didn't see them. But there wasn't any other cover because we were on a slight slope and they could obviously see more than we could.

The American JTAC called in two F-18s and they did two 30 mm canon runs. I don't know whether that killed anyone, but we were still receiving single-shot fire as we got back into the cars and drove to the FOB.

Back at base we contacted a de-brief, and addressed a few issues. We had killed 11 that day. Our patrol was responsible for the majority and the other patrol that was close by engaged a couple of guys in the village. PF, their sniper, hit two; one crawled off wounded, the other was dead. However, we didn't spend much time congratulating ourselves. There was too much to do.

After an overnight rest we began to gear up for the next operation the following day. Little did we realise that it would turn into one of the biggest battles involving Australian troops since Vietnam.

16

AMBUSH! THE BATTLE
OF KHAZ ORUZGAN

Two days after engaging the fighters we were back out. We dropped off two of our patrols at night plus the troop HQ element at the base of a large ridgeline about 8 kilometres from Anaconda, and they inserted by foot. Our patrol plus one other drove out with the Americans and ANA during daylight. We had five armoured Humvees – three manned by Americans and two by the ANA – about 37 of us altogether, so the vehicles were choccas. Our patrol carried all the same weapons we had used a couple of days before, the .338 sniper rifle and 7.62 mm SR25, and TS, the patrol commander, and JB carried their M4s. As we moved out of Anaconda we passed through a village and drove up the valley we'd traversed on that earlier operation, all the time receiving chatter through a captured radio. This was being deciphered by an ANA terp (interpreter) and passed around the net to keep us informed about what the enemy were planning.

As we drove into the next valley the chatter became more excitable and we could see about 12 local men in the green rolling along with us watching what we were doing. This made me feel a little uneasy. As they paralleled us they were able to keep up because we were avoiding the roads as much as possible and had to negotiate obstacles in our path. We could see them getting a better idea of who and what we were.

At the end of the valley the Americans dropped us off. Tango 4, with Donno as their scout, led off towards a high feature and our patrol followed five minutes later. We were to occupy a couple of overwatch locations at either end of this feature. Basically, we were the bait to stir things up.

From the high ground we observed a fair amount of male activity in the village. One of the other patrols that had inserted that night was quite productive – they saw seven fighters trying to get into position to hit the Americans, so they engaged them and neutralised the lot at quite close range. By now the Americans had driven around the feature we were on and positioned themselves right on the edge of the village. This didn't seem to stir up too much activity, and looking back, we didn't realise it at the time, but all the fighters were probably concentrated in the valley behind us by then.

Once we closed that part of the operation down, our patrols walked down and met up with the Americans, who had driven back to pick us up. They said the interpreters had picked up a lot of intelligence suggesting we could get ambushed on the way out. We said, 'Okay, we'll just have to wait and see what happens.' It pains me to say it even now, but we had actually become quite complacent, probably because of previous failed Taliban actions and the ineffective ambush they had organised against us two days previously.

It was mid-afternoon, and one of the PCs contacted our troop boss and told him we should find a harbour position for now and move late at night. This was good planning but the Americans objected. They wanted to drive out right away, mainly because the ANA didn't have night vision goggles. You couldn't trust them with NVGs because you'd find they'd go missing or they'd sell them. So the American commander said, 'Look, we're going to have to drive out.'

The troop boss spoke to the American commander: 'Think seriously about staying in location as we can have a look around at night through Predator to pick up any activity.' Predator is an unmanned aerial vehicle (UAV) platform. But the Americans wouldn't agree; they wanted to get back, so we started driving into the valley.

That's where they were waiting for us – between 100 to 200 fighters, all armed to the teeth and determined to wipe us out. Their leader, the Taliban's area commander, must have been very switched on, very quick and very hard, because he obviously took the decision in the morning to ambush us on our way back. He organised his fighters very efficiently. As soon as we were out of view he must have sent his blokes climbing up into the hills to fortify their locations and position their guns for our return.

We had been driving about 20 minutes when the ANA guy in the back of our Humvee started to tell us what chatter he was picking up. 'They're coming towards the first ambush point.' At one stage he reported they said, 'Don't shoot yet, wait till they get past the house.'

I said, 'Where's the bloody house?' It could have been any number of compounds we were passing.

I got my answer almost immediately. They sprung the ambush with machine guns and mortars coming from the green to our left about 300 metres away. Our car was initially right in the centre of their fire, their killing ground. That first volley was a bit off target and no-one was hit. But with such a weight of fire coming at us we knew we were in for a good fight.

The Americans stopped the vehicles and put down quite a heavy weight of return fire but to no great effect. The bullets and mortars kept coming at us, heavy to start with but then more sporadic. Suddenly they began to engage the cars behind us. We were told what the Taliban leader had just said over the radio: 'Kill them, kill them all.' This did worry me as I could see that we had a long distance to move before we could escape the valley – and realised that this was very serious indeed.

We were approximately 80 metres back from the road to avoid IEDs, in front of us a steep-sided creek line about 10 metres deep ran from the road getting more severe the closer it got to the high feature to our right. We couldn't cross it so we had to head down towards the road and closer to the green where most of the fire was coming from. We found a crossing point 150 metres closer to the enemy, so the others increased their rate of fire to cover us across the road. Fortunately we didn't hit an IED; we would've really been screwed then. Once across we headed on an oblique angle up towards a higher point again and away from the green. But as we were doing this we started zigzagging up and down because every creek line that we came to was so washed away and so steep that we couldn't actually get the cars through it. And the higher up the slope we went, the worse the terrain got. We had no choice but to come back down towards the road again.

We could see the dust from where the Taliban were firing but we couldn't actually see any enemy. A few of the lads said they saw a bit of movement from left to right. But they were so well concealed the only thing I saw was further on down the valley when a fighter fired an RPG. I saw the dust cloud that was instantly produced from the back blast. I was straining, burning my eyes looking through my scope and the range finders trying to find a target but couldn't see a thing. They had dug themselves in really well. Some of the boys got off a fair number of 66 mm rockets using the shoulder-fired, one-shot rocket launcher. The Americans didn't seem to know what to do so we made some harsh suggestions about what we needed to do to get out of there and started to pepper-pot forward.

Suddenly we came under another heavy weight of fire. We put a lot of bullets and bombs into the air but there was not a lot of quietening down from the enemy. As we were thinking things were looking bad, it got worse and they engaged us from the high ground. We were in trouble!

The valley was about 3.5 kilometres long and we were right at the start of it when the ambush began. We couldn't turn back because they were dug in behind us. We had to press forward but we would be vulnerable throughout the whole length of the valley.

The single shots we were receiving from the high ground were getting more accurate and some of our guys started to get hit. Joe, one of the Americans in the car behind us who was firing the .50-calibre heavy machine gun, got a round through the forearm. This put him out of action so one of the ANA guys got up into the turret and made an absolute meal of it as he hadn't been trained in that weapon so he had difficulty operating it. JB, our 2IC, pulled him out of there and got behind the gun, putting down some pretty effective fire.

The cars bucked and leapt over the rough terrain but at least we were moving. However, we were now being hit from three sides – behind us at an oblique angle from where they had initiated the contact, from the left in the green and from the high ground to our right. What's more, it was a rolling ambush. As we went past and left their field of fire they would leapfrog each other, getting in front of us and setting up a position to have another crack.

It was about this time SG, the patrol JTAC, saw an Australian Chinook flying into the American FOB flanked by two Dutch Apaches. The Chinook would be no help to us as it was basically a transport vehicle, but the Apache gunships had hellfire rockets and 30 mm chain guns. They could be very effective so SG jumped on the radio and got hold of them. 'We're in an absolute doozy of a shitfight. We need your assistance as we're taking casualties!'

It wasn't long before they came over and began to circle high above the battleground. SG told them to neutralise the threat on the high ground, then to switch their attention to the green. He gave them a couple of target indications where he'd actually seen the enemy, but then, unbelievably, the Dutch Apaches refused to drop down to firing level. There they were at 15,000 feet while we were getting hammered; apparently, they wouldn't drop below that altitude unless they really had to.

We were very frustrated – to put it mildly. They wouldn't open up on the Taliban for fear they might draw some fire themselves. SG then said, 'We can use some of our weapons to mark where the bad guys are!' They replied, 'Yeah, okay do that.' SG got JB to mark the enemy position using the splash from the .50-calibre rounds, which struck the hillside creating large clouds of dust. But they still wouldn't engage. SG had had enough so he told them, 'If you're not going to engage then you might as well fuck off,' and so they did! Cheers, boys!

Fortunately the American JTAC, Evan was able to bring two F-18s on station. He was in my car and was frantically working with a laptop and a radio in each ear on different frequencies, talking to the pilots and calculating targets with a GPS and a laser range finder. The poor bugger was so wrapped up in what he was doing he had no awareness of what was going on around him. We got pinned down at one stage behind the car and I looked over and saw him out in the open, which exposed him to the enemy. I thought, 'Mate, what are you doing? You'll get pinged for sure.' I ran over to him and grabbed hold of him. 'Mate, you need to take cover.' He said, 'What?' Then he saw the rounds landing around us. 'Oh,' he said. 'Yeah, yeah.'

I decided since I wasn't doing any good with

the .338 sniper rifle I might as well stick with him and keep him out of trouble. He was controlling a lifeline that we desperately needed. If he was knocked over there was no-one else able to handle it. I thought, 'Let's get him out of the open and into cover.'

There were boys shouting target indications at Evan not really knowing how much he was trying to do all at once. So we ended up bouncing from car to car all the time being chased by small arms fire and RPGs. We were running up and down the line of these cars which was spread out close to 170 metres at one stage. Evan would get a target indication, and I had a quick chat with the blokes to get more targets and then we moved on. When we noticed the rounds getting too close, I grabbed hold of him and said, 'Let's move!' and we'd find a new position.

But there were times when Evan was relatively safe in cover, so that freed me slightly to work away from the car to try to identify a target to shoot . . . no luck! At one point I saw Donno doing the same. Evan organised a 500-pound airburst bomb to be dropped onto a mortar location. He gave the pilot a 'clear hot'. The pilot replied, 'Thirty seconds.' But because Evan was so wrapped up in what he was doing – talking to the other plane and lining it up for another run – he forgot the time and to warn us what was coming. Suddenly he shouted, 'Oh shit, incoming!' and as soon as he said it there was an almighty *boom* about 600 metres away. We heard the whiz of the shrapnel going over our heads and thought, 'Shit, that was bloody close.' But it neutralised the mortars and we were quite thankful for that.

He organised to drop another into the creek line in the green where some fighters were massing. I think one of the pilots had originally given him the heads up about them. Evan plotted the grid reference and relayed it to the pilot, and shortly another 500-pounder was sent steaming towards the ground. This time the bomb was set to explode on impact, neutralising the Taliban as they formed up to attack us. But we were still copping a flogging from the high ground, so Evan switched his focus.

By now we were about 90 minutes into the battle and as we reached SG's car one more time I saw a stretcher. PF had been shot through both legs and he was in a critical condition. Then I saw that SG had been shot. He was in a bad way; a round had entered his chest underneath his armpit as he surveyed the ground through his binoculars, and exited above his hip on the opposite side. His binoculars had copped a round also. The American medic – a champion of a guy – was frantically working on him. SG started developing breathing problems, which the medic diagnosed as a tension pneumothorax. This meant there was a lot of air inside his rib cage that was collapsing his right lung and pushing it to one side. So he relieved the pressure by pushing a 12-gauge canula – a very large needle – between the ribs above the lungs and into the top part of his chest cavity. Once that happened you could hear the whoosh of air escaping. SG could breathe a lot easier. They put a little tap on the canula so every now and again when the pressure built up they could release the tap, relieving the pressure.

One of the Afghan interpreters had been hit in the face, but the bullet travelled through his cheeks; it might have broken a tooth or two but otherwise he was bloody lucky.

We stopped off at the car where Donno was when suddenly a big burst of machine-gun fire came in from the high ground. It hit the car and small fragments of bullets peppered us. The PC of our other patrol got nicked on the wrist. He was holding it tightly with his right hand and screaming, I've been hit. I've been hit!'

I originally thought, 'Shit this bloke's in a bad way.' He screamed, 'Get me in that car.' So I moved out of the way and Donno opened the door for him. He got in and the car started to move again. I was walking hunched over beside the vehicle trying to present a smaller target when the left rear window wound down. The windows are nearly 5 centimetres thick, and the PC who had just got in cranked it down and put his hand out. 'Hey, Rob; put a field dressing on this will ya.'

I stopped for a bit as I was still unsure of how bad his wound was. 'Oh, okay,' I said, like a dumbass. I should have told him to put it on himself. I had a couple in my day sack, but that was in another car, so I went round the back of his vehicle and pulled one off someone else's pack. The car stopped, so I knelt down beside the door with my back to the enemy and ripped the packet open. The field dressing fell down and rolled towards the road. I ran down and picked it up but by the time I got it back to the car all the ribbons had come loose and were flapping around in the wind. The PC then said, 'Let me get out and I'll fix it,' but I had started to put it on as best I could. It was an absolute mess. And when I did the knot up on the ribbons I did it up right over his injury. His injury to me didn't look too bad, but the round could have hit a nerve, which made it feel worse than it was.

Rounds were still hitting the car as he wound the window up and reluctantly dragged himself out. He thanked me then started to bark a few orders at his guys.

The valley was now beginning to bottleneck. I figured it would be a good place for the Taliban to be waiting to start a ground assault. Had they done that they would've rolled us up because we were starting to run out of ammunition. I had 20 rounds in my pocket of 252-grain .338 and three rounds in my rifle.

Still shepherding Evan, I found my way back to the vehicle I'd been in initially. Several bullets had hit the windows creating a spider-web effect on the heavily armoured glass, but not penetrated. I moved around to the right side of the vehicle to talk to TS, who was trying his best to liaise between the American troop commander and our troop boss. I was amazed when the driver of the Humvee casually got out and came round to us. 'Hey, fellas, you guys get in the car. One of you drive and there's a spare seat in the back. I'll get out and start fighting.' We both said, 'No, mate, you get back in the car – you know it – so you drive.' And as rounds were hitting the car, he just casually walked around and got back into the driver's seat. What a champion.

We had to use the cars as cover because there wasn't anything else, and as they crept forward we had to continually change sides every time the weight of fire became too intense. Finding a depression in the ground was also good when the vehicles went static but as you got singled out the amount of rounds you began to attract increased, and it was time to leave.

The F18s did a couple of gun runs onto the high ground using their 30 mm canons. It was all very spectacular – a long stretch of dust suddenly appeared followed by the *Buurrpp* of the rounds hitting rock; a split-second later you heard the *whizz* from the gun as it expelled its rounds. But this action had minimal effect on the Taliban up in the hills. When the aircraft went off station, we had to wait for other planes that had already been activated and taken off from an aircraft carrier in the Gulf. At this point Evan came over and squatted down next to me during a lull and said, 'Hey, thanks for that, man.' He put his hand up for a high five but I was a bit distracted and just grabbed his hand and shook it. 'No worries, mate.' The cars started rolling again and we stood up.

Next thing, a volley of four RPGs from the high ground came in and straddled our car. One went long, one short, one landed underneath the car and the other one landed a metre beside me. It lifted us all off our feet. In an instant I felt the heat of the explosion from the RPG and couldn't see anything for dust. All seemed quite calm and quiet, and all motion slowed right down for a split second. I remember seeing two .338 sniper rifles falling to the ground slowly; one was mine and one was Hoady's. Then I hit the ground. It took me a second to work out what had just happened. 'Oh shit, I've been hit.' I was hesitant to look at the injuries because I didn't want to know how bad the wounds were. I still wanted to keep on fighting, even though I hadn't fired a shot. As I lay on the deck I could see the bomb dog Sabi through the dust. She was yelping and limping. Lucky for her I had been between her and the blast.

Donno said later when I got out of hospital that he saw the RPGs strike and watched us get blown about a metre off the ground. He thought we were dead.

The blast injured four of us. Evan got some shrapnel in his calf, Hoady got a bit of frag in his arse and TS took a piece in the calf. I took most of it. The shrapnel hit my foot, my calf, the back of my left leg, my arse and lower back. A couple of minutes after the RPGs hit I grabbed Hoady on the shoulder and shouted over the top of the battle, 'Mate, there's too many people around this car. It's a fucking bullet magnet.' I saw the ANA car up ahead all by itself. It wasn't really getting engaged and there was no-one standing around it, so I said pointing ahead. 'We've got to get to that car and get this fuckin' thing moving!' He nodded and said, 'Okay, I'm with you.'

The fire was beginning to intensify again, and an RPG that was fired from the green zoomed centimetres away from four of us. How no-one was hit I'll never know, but we all caught a glimpse of the dark, round object as it passed through. At that stage TS had just moved round to the right-hand side of the car to talk to the American captain again, and that's when a big burst of machine-gun fire hit the car and the immediate surroundings. I was okay, but Hoady copped one right across the arse. We didn't realise, but TS had been hit also. One round had struck his M4 on the bolt rendering it inoperable, the other drilled itself through his right buttock and came to rest directly in front of his coccyx.

Just as Hoady and I had begun our dash to the front car another volley of RPG fire came in. One burst above the back of the car, wounding an Australian engineer, Sabi's handler. His wounds weren't serious, but the explosion was close enough to injure the ANA interpreter in the face and blow him out the back of the car. He couldn't see due to the blood in his eyes and a few bits of steel. That's when Donno would have run out there to pick him up and carry him back to the car. I did see Donno on the odd occasion as Evan and I were moving between cars, but I didn't actually see the action for which he was awarded the Victoria Cross. Hoady and I were well on our way to the front car by that stage.

It was about a 40–50-metre stretch in front of us, and we got absolutely hammered by fire. I got clocked by a round on the elbow, which felt like I had been hit with a steel rod. Luckily as I was running the elbow was bent and it skimmed off. Had it been straight it would have gone right through the joint and I could have have lost my lower arm. I could see rounds striking in front of me creating small clouds of dust, and as I got to the car I saw several rounds strike the side of it. I decided to keep going as the car was now getting hammered by enemy fire, but as I moved off I was suddenly the magnet. Hoady was still behind me but had stopped at the car.

The driver of our original car was watching us and later said, 'Man, that was awesome. The bullets were chasing you everywhere; we thought you guys were history.'

I saw a ditch – a washout – about 20 metres in

front of the car, slightly off to the left flank and on the edge of the road. I ran down towards it and dived into it. It was probably about half a metre deep, just enough for my body to move around in. I still had my weapon so I got down behind it and started to observe for enemy targets.

We started to take rounds from a small knoll slightly right of us. It was almost 360-degree fire. I could tell that I'd been targeted. There were rounds cracking above me and hitting the edge of the washout from every side. It was at that point that I looked down at the ground and shook my head and wondered whether we were ever going to get out of this.

I was now hurting and covered in blood. As I was running between the cars I could really feel my wounds starting to stiffen up. Hoady was still taking cover beside the ANA car – six Afghans were in it. One guy was in the turret with the 7.62 mm machine gun. He was getting a few rounds off but it wasn't anything spectacular. Hoady saw how much fire was coming my way and did the right thing by me. He guided the Humvee to approximately 10 metres to my right, which protected me from the fire that was coming from the high ground. 'Rob, Rob, get up here!' I looked up and without hesitation ran for the car.

I looked in the window; five ANA soldiers were looking back at me with eyes like dinner plates.

Hoady banged on the windows and tried to open the door but they'd locked it. Finally, one of the blokes unlocked the doors, and that was it. Hoady pulled the driver out and jumped in his seat in an attempt to get the small convey moving. I pushed my way into the back seat of the Humvee with the help of an ANA guy, and made sure Hoady knew I was in. Hoady drove from then on.

'There's a compound about 200 metres in front of us,' I pointed out to Hoady. 'We need to use that as cover.' We also needed to get our wounded guys out of there. By now we didn't have any communications. Comms had shat itself, which is what usually happens. Hoady agreed, and said, 'Once we get to the compound and secure it at least we'll have a bit of a stronghold we can fight from, and then maybe at night we can get the injured away.'

The ANA driver who pushed me into the car was still holding onto the door as we took off. The car was so heavily armoured it made the doors extremely heavy and he was such a small bloke that he couldn't close it. And that's when he looked at his leg with a very worried expression on his face. He saw it had blood all over it. I looked at him and said, 'Don't worry mate, that's my blood; you're okay. Now close the fuckin' door!'

I tried to help him but it wasn't until the car was on the flat that we managed to close the door. We started to get some momentum going and the other cars followed. One of them came screaming past us followed by a second, and now the Americans were leading so we just followed on.

As we drove towards the compound we exited the valley and came up on the back end of the small knoll where we'd been copping a lot of fire from. Hoady turned the car slightly and stopped, hoping that our gunner would engage it. I don't think he understood what we were trying to do so I tugged on his leg trying to get him out of the turret. He was still attempting to rectify a stoppage and wouldn't budge. The Americans turned and stopped too and started firing up into the high ground. Still this fella wouldn't let his machine gun go, so I gave up and started handing up ammunition to him when he'd cleared the stoppage.

We were now quite close to the compound we saw as a stronghold, but we quickly realised that it was not suitable. At least we now had a chance to regroup, still under heavy fire. There was no way we could call in the medivac team. We'd have to head back to the FOB. Once we got out of the valley we had covered 3.5 kilometres, but we still had about 2.5 kilometres to negotiate over the home stretch. That took about 45 minutes. JB was doing a great job of wheeling and dealing the .50-calibre as we were still copping sporadic small arms fire, and remained in contact until we reached the FOB.

We were in contact for over four hours. Estimates vary about the number of Taliban fighters, but my guess is between 100 and 150. There were also foreign fighters – Chechen snipers – involved as well. This was confirmed by the Americans six weeks later. We had an indication of it the previous year in the same area when we received a bit of chatter from one of the Taliban on radio who said inadvertently, 'I've got some fighters here. What do you want me to do with them? I can't speak to them because they don't speak our language.' His commander then came on the radio and warned him not to ever speak of them again.

As we pulled in, the medics were waiting for us. Hoady and Donno helped me out of the vehicle. By that stage my legs had gone really stiff and sore, so Hoady helped me across to the front of the regimental aid post. He put me on the ground next to all the other wounded. I remember thinking to myself, 'Christ, how many blokes got hurt?'

Donno came over and cut my uniform off. That's when I saw holes in my clothes where I didn't have any injuries, except one on my upper leg where a round had come through my trousers and just grazed my thigh. He was telling me I had to get some morphine into me. I was saying, 'No, I'm all right, don't do it just yet. Save it for the other fellas.'

'Mate, you need morphine.'

'No, I'm good. I'm hurting but I'm still all there.'

As he was patching me up he said, 'Sorry, mate, I'm not a medic, I'm a signaller, I'm not doing too good at covering your wounds.'

'You're doing fine, mate; I'm a medic, and you're doing fine.'

He had blood all over his face. So I asked, 'What happened to you, mate?'

He said, 'Oh nothing, nothing.'

'Did you get hit?

'No, no. I'm all right. Don't worry about me, I'm good.'

'Then why is your head covered in blood? That's not dye running from your hair, mate, that's blood.' (Donno has ginger hair.)

'One of the Americans was shot in the head so I took his helmet because I didn't have one, and when I put it on it was full of blood and it leaked over my face.' The American had been killed instantly.

Then I remembered – my helmet was still strapped to the back of the Humvee. I didn't have the time to put it on. There were more important things to do.

One of our interpreters, who we rated highly, didn't come out with us that day, and when he saw the carnage and how many of his friends were injured he broke down in tears. He was asking people how he could help. He was a fantastic fella.

Nine out of 13 Australian soldiers had been wounded during that contact. Of the 11 SAS guys in the battle, seven were wounded; the other two casualties were engineers from the Incident Response Regiment (IRR). One of them got an armour piercing (AP) round through the kneecap, but all it did was make a neat 7.62 mm hole straight through his leg. He was very lucky. If it had been a ball round instead of AP the projectile would have spread on impact and he would have been in all sorts of trouble. The Taliban were using a lot of AP because they knew the Americans' cars were armoured. That's probably what saved SG's life, it was an AP round that hit him in the side which dived down under his heart then changed course slightly to exit above his hip.

I went out on the first casevac flight with SG and PF as I was classed as a priority two, as on examination Wal, the medic, noticed my stomach was sore in front of the holes in my back, he assumed the shrapnel may have penetrated deeper than it appeared. Thankfully that wasn't the case. The SSM met us at the helipad back in Tarin Kowt looking quite concerned. This was understandable: seven of his lads had just been hurt.

I was carried on a stretcher to a Dutch ambulance, which drove directly to the field hospital. As I reached the treatment room the doctors and nurses went into their drill conducting a thorough survey of my body and injuries, then inserted a canula into a vein on the back of my hand.

They asked me all the usual questions: 'Are you allergic to penicillin?' 'No.' 'Are you on any medication?' 'No,' and then pumped me full of morphine. They didn't operate until the early hours of the next morning.

TS, one of the engineers, PF and I were all in the

same room. PF was in a bad way. His legs were pretty messed up. After several operations they told him he would be looking at a 12-month recovery period. He's still not 100 per cent but he's improving all the time.

SG went to the big American hospital in Germany and underwent many hours of surgery. He came out of it well but I doubt whether he'll be able to parachute or dive again. But of course you can't tell him that. He's a tough little bastard!

There was a small American hospital at Kamp Holland as well, and a couple of their guys went there. A few more went to Kandahar.

I was in hospital for about five days because I had to keep going back into surgery to have my wounds debrided, cleaned and repacked. It wasn't until they were confident the wounds were free of bacteria that they would send me back to Camp Russell.

I was able to call George from Kamp Holland, which I did the following day. The day after, General Mike Hindmarsh, the Special Operations Commander, the Chief of the Army and a few other VIPs came through and spoke with us, which we appreciated.

I didn't see Evan again after that, and didn't get to speak to him about our experience. He had been taken to the American facility to treat his calf injury. Maybe one day.

I didn't see the bomb dog Sabi either. She went

missing after that RPG hit us; and then when her handler was wounded and put out of action she was lost in the confusion of the battlefield. It wasn't until 12 November 2009 – more than 14 months after the ambush – that the Americans were able to retrieve her through negotiation and return her to Australia.

17

THE FINAL DAYS

It was a pretty short rotation for most of the injured guys but I stayed on. I had about three weeks off work getting over my injuries and by that time I was itching to get back into it. But I was a bit concerned about the first job on my return because it took place during a full moon. We were always a bit reluctant to work when the illumination was too high as it meant we didn't have the advantage of our NVGs. The enemy could see clearly 600 metres on a full moon and at times a full kilometre.

On this occasion we were after a particular target when we got dropped off by vehicles about 4.5 kilometres from Tarin Kowt. Our target was approx 3.5 kilometres further and the plan was to walk the remainder of the distance to come up quietly onto his compound. As we approached the village we were contacted in the open. My first job back and suddenly we're getting shot at! I darted forward to take cover in a small aqueduct, hoping this wasn't going to be bad. No-one was hit but there were quite a few rounds coming our way and this split the troop.

TS had been repatriated back to Australia because of his wounds, which meant another sergeant took his place as our patrol commander. I remained as patrol scout. The PC and TF were behind me, slightly elevated on the hard-packed ground, which gently sloped towards me. I could hear *crack, crack, crack* over my head. I had a pretty good look around. *Crack, crack, crack*, again. I looked over my shoulder and up the rise and said to the PC, 'Hey, is that you?'

'Yeah, yeah, mate.' He then fired a couple of shots with his suppressor on, but this made a totally different noise. Someone else was doing the shooting.

Then both joined me in the aqueduct. There was a building ahead of us that could provide cover, so I said, 'Come on, let's go to that building.' We made a run for it while the other boys in the troop pepperpotted towards another. The rounds were falling between us and going over our heads.

When we reached the compound the first door we came to was locked. There was a family inside so one of the guys covered me and I remembered the Pashto words for 'Open the door'. A guy came up and indicated that he couldn't open the door, but pointed around the corner.

I looked around the corner. This would expose us to the guys shooting at us from the building 50 metres away, but sure enough there was a door. He opened it for us and we slipped inside. I cuffed his hands and feet and told him not to move, and told his family to stay inside the house. They were good. Then we made our way up to his roof.

On their roofs they generally have a parapet which is usually about half a metre high. We took cover behind the parapet and had a scout around. We heard a bit of a gunfight going on with the other half of the troop. We noticed fighters moving around on roofs opposite us. We decided to engage.

The patrol commander saw a bloke crawl through a gap between two walls on a roof; we were onto him straight away. Then suddenly we got information from a Predator that there was a vehicle heading towards us, possibly a police vehicle. We then saw about 12 guys appear from a corner 50 metres to our right flank. They were dressed in local civilian clothes but with chest rigs and AKs. We looked at each other and I said, 'This doesn't feel right.' So we shouted at them in Pashto to stop. 'Don't move! Don't move!' When the other half of the troop saw them they called them to stop as well. But they kept on coming. Eventually they too realised something wasn't right.

But it was too late, the police chief, and some of his guys were already dead. The situation quietened down and the troop boss organised a withdrawal. As we left the compound I removed the cuffs from the house owner and reassured them that everything was okay. We were all mindful of a 'blue on blue' (friendly fire casualities).

We aborted the operation. There were conflicting reports about how many others were dead – some said six, others said four plus a few injured. We covered each other as we moved to an unused compound behind us to reorganise ourselves before we patrolled back to our vehicles for a return to Tarin Kowt. That's when we discovered that the police chief had been killed. But it wasn't until a week or so later that we found out more about what had happened. The bloke who engaged us initially from his rooftop was getting death threats from the Taliban. They left a night letter on his door saying something like, 'If you don't join us or give us what we want, we're going to kill your family in front of you and then we're going to kill you.' So naturally he got scared and employed some family or friends to provide security on his compound. It is also highly likely that these guys had engaged the cops. No-one knows for sure.

This also could have been the night that the Taliban were going to pay him a visit. The guys on the roof of his compound would have seen us coming quite some distance away due to the quality of light, thinking we were Taliban, and it is possible that's when the police chief was alerted. There was a police compound about 1,500 metres down the road, so when they got the call they would've jumped into their cars all tooled up to join the other guys because they knew they were in for a fight. It seems as though everyone had turned up at the same time not knowing who was who, so the guys on the roof of the compound just started shooting.

When it all happened we were taking a fair amount of fire to our left, so naturally we all just tuned in on the muzzle flashes and went into the contact IA and engaged. Had we known the background of this trouble we would have given the place a really wide berth, or even taken a different route.

Actually, just before we withdrew someone had fired some mortars from our original direction of travel, which landed 300–400 metres away from us. We never did find out who fired them.

The Dutch and the Australians conducted an inquiry and found nothing untoward; it was just a bad accident. No-one knows who shot the fatal rounds.

After that we had a slack period of about a week and a half, so we decided to chase some targets further afield. The Chinooks were back on board to take us to a village that was about a 25-minute flight away. They dropped us 8–9 kilometres out and we walked towards the target compounds. As we got closer we took a couple of detainees who we found sleeping outside with AKs. They might have been farmers, or could even have been security as neighbouring villages do sometimes fight with each other. But we had to neutralise the threat so we took them with us. On the walk up to one compound of interest four blokes squirted – three headed towards the hills, and one bloke thought he'd take the lazy route and come back around. He walked straight into us. We got hold of him, cuffed his hands and took him with us also. Before we started the clearance of our second objective we dropped the detainees with troop HQ a little distance off the three buildings, which were joined to each other.

On the way up to the first building we saw a sentry outside with an old AK. He must have heard us coming in the darkness and was gingerly tip-toeing around trying to find out what it was. One of the other patrols got to him and shot him. Then we started clearing through the buildings.

Once the clearance was complete we sent some guys up onto the roof to maintain security. Not long after they got there two bad guys were seen hunched over their weapons and moving stealthily side by side to the back of the centre compound. The boys on the roof gave them the good news.

We didn't find the guys we were after – they'd squirted – but we got a few weapons and more IED-making equipment, which we took with us to our pick-up point.

We hit the same area the next night this time

using 4RAR. The size of the force required three Chinook drops, but we only had two Chinooks that night, so on the first run our troop was inserted at the southern end of the village while an element of 4RAR were dropped off to the north. The Chinooks then had to go back to pick up the other crew which dropped them 2.5 kilometres to the west of the village. The plan was to totally close down the village and apprehend anyone squirting.

Our patrol had brought two quad bikes out on the Chinooks and it wasn't long before we started chasing squirters with them. We had apprehended a couple of guys within minutes of rolling off the Chinook, but shortly afterwards we saw another making tracks for the high ground.

TF and JB secured the two we already had, and PC and I rode off towards this other guy. He could hear us coming but couldn't see as the night was dark. As we got closer we stopped the quads and pursued him on foot. He was doing his best to get away but we caught up. In Pashto I told him to stop and put his hands up. At first he didn't respond so I told him again.

This time he stopped but wouldn't put his hands up. He was on a slight oblique angle to me and I was trying to see what he was doing when I got a glimpse of what I thought was a chest rig. 'Has that guy got a chest rig, mate?' The patrol commander said, 'Yeah, mate,' and as he turned I could see part of an AK under his clothing. My laser was already on his head so I didn't take any chances and released a single 5.56 mm projectile that dropped him like a puppet with its strings cut.

We searched him and removed bucket loads of AK rounds, .303 rounds and 7.62 mm long, which would fit a Russian SVD sniper rifle. The cartridge case of this particular round is 3 mm longer than a standard NATO 7.62 mm and is slightly different in appearance. We couldn't figure out whether he was going to another location to pick up another weapon or going to meet up with someone who had a weapons cache to suit those rounds.

We questioned some goat-herders who were near the incident but let them go. Then we saw three squirters from the village running up a creek line parallel to us. Paul got our other two guys to link up so we could cover ourselves as we approached the squirters. In fact they were heading straight for us by now. When we reached them they were empty handed and one guy was only about 14, so we detained the father and another older bloke, letting the 14-year-old go.

The guys on the other side of the valley had killed a squirter and they also had a few detainees. We finished up with half-a-dozen detainees to go back in the Chinooks with us. We questioned them first then handed them on to the Dutch. If the Dutch believed they needed further questioning then they'd be sent to the Afghan Special Police or the Americans.

There was one final task before the tour ended. 2 Squadron had just arrived and we gave them a handover for the following year – 2009. We took them out on a job in the same way that 1 Squadron did for us to give them a good heads up of the way we were operating and to familiarise them to the ground. Nothing really came of the job. We found some opium and destroyed it, and uncovered a few weapons, which we took back together with a couple of detainees. We had already hit that compound earlier in the trip and found a good cache of IED-making equipment, a lot of weapons and a lot of opium. Once again we missed the bad guys – including Stiletto. I was disappointed we had missed objective Stiletto as he was causing the coalition forces in Oruzgan a huge headache with his IED-facilitating. But at the same time, these guys wake up to the war every day, and it was only a matter of time before the coalition forces caught up with them. During 2 Squadron's tour in 2009, they did!

I didn't realise it at the time but when we took off from Tarin Kowt for the flight home I would be leaving the fight in Afghanistan for the last time. When I arrived home to George and the girls I discovered just how hard it had been for them. Ash in particular was doing it tough. She is a lot closer to me than Lauren, who is more of an individual. Ash relies heavily on George and myself and the thought of me being injured or even worse, killed, frightened her to the point where she couldn't sleep. Even when I returned she had trouble sleeping, and when she did eventually convince herself to close her eyes, she had to make one last check, either verbally or visually, to make sure I was still at home. This really played on my mind a lot. It was the second scare my family had and I didn't think they could handle another. So shortly after Christmas I made the decision to leave the army and to pursue a career that wouldn't take me away from home for extended periods or place my life in danger.

I loved the work and the camaraderie of the regiment. It's not pretty at times but it is the cutting edge of the nation's defences. We are highly trained and good at what we do; everyone is focused on the job. And personally that can be very satisfying. But now I had to think of my family for a change and not just what I wanted.

On return home it took me a few days to readjust, as our sleep patterns were totally abnormal. Most of the time in Afghanistan we would try to run reverse cycle, which entailed sleeping during the day and getting up at 5 p.m. for breakfast. So it takes a while to get back into kilter. And at the same time you have to mentally unwind. While in hostile territory there is always something that you are thinking about to minimise the risks and maximise the effect of each operation, even if it's just about the kit that you need to take; or you might run a scenario through your head and part of that might help you decide what you're going to take on the job.

The Taliban are a tough enemy to deal with. They know the country and use it against us. Afghans have been fighting since the days of Alexander the Great, recruiting the kids when they're very young to fight the infidels. The Taliban still consider themselves the rightful power in Afghanistan, so there's a command structure that mirrors the actual system. If the government has a provincial governor, the Taliban has a shadow governor who runs the operations for the Taliban in the province. He then has district and city commanders under him and he answers to the equivalent of the federal government.

Mullah Omar was the top commander before he was captured by the Americans. He had a network of operational commanders under him but if you knock over one of the top ones, the others will move up the pyramid. Afghanistan is also tribal. They fight over who's going to move up and sometimes this works to our advantage. But in battle the Taliban soldier has all the advantages of playing on his home ground.

EPILOGUE

I've been accused over the years of being modest and quiet, but I have really had to come out of my shell to write this. I know you'll appreciate that I've had to maintain security and only refer to some blokes by either their nickname or initials, and also not mention some towns or villages in our Area of Operations in Afghanistan.

I've put my life on the line for other people now for the last 18 years with total disregard to my family. Now it's time to give something back, and give them the life they deserve. This has also prompted me to seek another career, one where I can spend a lot more time at home.

As I look back on my military career there's no doubt that my time with the SAS has been the highlight. The regiment has a well-deserved reputation.

It is full of characters who are hardened and very professional, as you'd expect them to be. It was a sad time to leave my mates. However, I rarely spent time with them outside of working hours as I really valued 'family time', which probably made my separation from the unit a little easier. But you do develop a very strong bond with the blokes, more so if they have been involved in the same incidents. But most SAS operators spend at least six months away from home a year, sometimes more. So when I'm home I like to put as much time in as possible with the family. My recreational activities like hunting and fishing trips have taken a back seat during my time in the regiment, but I've had to put my family first.

There is also a special place in my heart for the Royal Marine Corps. It was a place where I really felt at home and enjoyed myself while I learnt my trade. The bootneck (marines) attitude is very similar to that of the lads from SASR, and is a possible contribution as to why the regiment and SBS get on so well.

I picked up a book a little while ago about a bootneck called Mark Ormrod from my old unit, 40 Commando, who was horrifically injured in Afghanistan. This is a true account of sheer bootneck courage and determination to get his life back together and push his injuries aside; I was touched by his story. Sorry, Mark, bootnecks do cry!

I met the most memorable characters during my

time in the Royal Marines. Cheeky bastards always up for a laugh, but good hard soldiers also. Taff Cuddihey is one them and would have to be one of the top characters I've ever had the pleasure of knowing – a corps character not just a unit character. He is one of the toughest chefs you will ever come across. Standing in the breakfast queue one morning I noticed a bloke (or I should say 'fool'), complaining rather loudly about the state of the baked beans and the food in general. Taff was getting quite irate about his rudeness and we could all see what was about to happen as he had a fiery reputation. Taff moved to the front of the bain maries and grabbed this poor bloke's head and shoved it into the hot baked beans. His parting comment was, 'Now they're fuckin' ruined!'

Not many people messed around with Taff, least of all the bouncers at the Ivory Club, a nightclub in Taunton which 40 Commando used to patronise. He used to get very drunk, as we all did, and then fight with the bouncers for fun. A rumour going around at one stage was that Taff had knocked them all out over various nights. In fact, as Taff entered the club the bouncers always used to raise their hands and say, 'We don't want any trouble tonight, Taff.'

Taff is a part owner of a bar in Pataya, Thailand. I'm not sure of his arrangement with the Thai woman who runs it, but he used to spend every leave over there, generally taking some of the younger marines and leading them astray. He is a very likeable bloke and loyal to his mates. We used to take the piss out of him in Northern Ireland as he took his weight-lifting very seriously; he had a strict routine and even took protein and muscle-building powders. Unfortunately he never worked on his legs and he ended up looking like a toffee apple – big on top but with legs like a sparrow – and the subject of some good banter.

In 3RAR as I mentioned, I became very good mates with Lee, an ex-Grenadier guardsman from England. He is passionate about his hunting and is very good at it. We share the same values and have been great mates since day one of that reconnaissance course. We also both shared the same opinion of several blokes who were so-called instructors on that course.

Lee writes a lot of articles for hunting magazines and is a well-known for his stories of hunting with dogs. We had access to a hunting property outside Bathurst which produced a lot of game. We used it a lot during my time in Sydney. He passed selection for 4RAR and has also completed a couple of tours of Afghanistan.

I also became good friends with RS over the years, who was also at 3RAR. I met him when I was posted to support company after our first Timor trip; we played intercompany rugby together – fortunately on the same side since he is 6 ft 8 in (203 cm) and solid muscle. He is another who doesn't suffer fools but unlike Lee, RS can be very diplomatic about it when he needs to be. We did the same selection together and he is responsible for talking me out of throwing it all away. RS is very focused and completed the 13-week training program we were given as a guide for selection day by day, and activity after activity. He has excelled as an operator in the regiment, and is also an SAS sniper, but his main calling is as an as assaulter and he is exceptional. RS has also been in a few scrapes in Afghanistan and won the Medal of Gallantry there in 2006 with Matt Locke.

I have had some great experiences in the forces and have learnt some valuable life skills. I grew up fast in the marines and made some great friends. I could have had a full career in the regiment if I chose, but it would mean not being able to deliver my promise to my family of spending more time with them. It was time to give them a break. While I don't regret my time in the forces – in fact I'm truly proud of it – it's now time to be a father and a husband first.

THE ELEVEN RULES

These are my personal Standard Operating Procedures (SOPs) that I would try to implement if the situation or terrain allowed. Sticking to these SOPs will give you the best chance of success and survival.

1 Keep all movements slow, and always look before moving
   - Movement attracts the eye and will be the main thing that will compromise you.
   - Scan the ground to look for anything unnatural and to plan your next move.

2 Use the shadows
   - Shadows will conceal movement to a certain degree.
   - They will also soften your outline.

3 Never enter and exit a hide by the same route

- If you have been observed moving into an area it is likely that an op will be established to observe for more movement, or worse, an ambush.
- If you are being tracked it will prevent you coming face to face with the enemy.

4 Use natural foliage

- To be able to blend in to the surrounding area properly you need to use natural foliage. Man-made materials can be good but there's no substitute for the real thing.

5 Only fire 1 to 2 shots from the same location – if possible move after first shot

- Repeated shots from the same location will give your position away.

6 Whenever possible have a deception plan – false hides, false trails etc.

- If working in the same area for extended periods, having a deception strategy that you can observe will give you early warning that the enemy are on to you.

7 Marksmanship principles

- Position and hold must be firm enough to support the weapon.

- The weapon must point naturally at the target without any undue physical effort.
- Sight alignment or aiming must be correct.
- The shot must be released and followed through without disturbing the position of the weapon.

8 Eye on the crosshairs, target slightly blurred

- A reminder to focus on the crosshairs just before taking the shot and not on the target for correct aiming technique.

9 Shoot past a solid object

- This will give you cover from fire.
- It will also produce a sonic crack making an observer think the shot was fired from that object.

10 Always have an escape route

- If compromised you'll need to get out of your location undetected and unimpeded.
- Your escape route should have cover from fire but that is not always possible, at the very least, you should achieve cover from view.

11 Never sacrifice security

- A reminder not to be lazy or complacent. Good security will keep you alive.

BALLISTICS TERMINOLOGY

Action The breech mechanism of a rifle that loads, fires and unloads. This encompasses the trigger, magazine housing and bolt.

AP Armour piercing bullet. The projectile has a hardened steel or tungsten core designed to penetrate armour.

Ball Full metal jacket projectiles, a standard round which has a lead core enveloped in a copper jacket.

Ballistics Data concerning trajectory, velocity and energy (kinetic) of the bullet, or characteristics of a projectile before and after it leaves the muzzle of the weapon.

Bore The interior of a barrel.

Bullet drop The ballistic measurement of how far a bullet will drop after being fired. Bullets (projectiles) are affected by gravity, which gives it a trajectory – a curved flight path.

Calibre The diameter of the bore measured from the land surface. A rifled bore has grooves in it to cause the round to spin once fired; these are called 'land and grooves'. The projectile is slightly larger than the bore size so it will take up the space in the grooves giving it a gas seal.

Cartridge case The brass container that holds the propellant and projectile.

Chamber The enlarged part of a bore into which the round is placed. The round will fit snugly in the chamber, which is slightly larger than the round to allow for expansion of the cartridge case once fired.

Chronograph An electronic instrument used to measure the velocity of a projectile.

Culminating point The maximum height above a horizontal surface which a projectile rises to above the line of sight while in trajectory to a target. The maximum height a round will go before gravity starts to pull it back to earth. This will vary at different ranges.

Drift The amount of shift of a projectile to one side or the other due to its rotation in flight or air resistance. If a rifle bore is rifled with a right-hand twist (which is usually the case) the drift of that round will be slightly right. This is known as Magnus drift and is more noticeable at longer ranges.

Ejector A small spring-loaded post at the face of a bolt that will push the empty case out of the weapon.

Elevation The amount of adjustment needed to compensate for range.

Extractor Usually spring-loaded device at the face of the bolt that clips onto the rim of a cartridge case and then pulls it out of the chamber to be ejected.

Field of fire An area relatively free of obstruction into which a sniper can fire.

Field of view The angular measurement of how wide an area can be observed through an optical device. Spotting scopes generally have a narrow field of view, rifle scopes are wider, and binoculars wider still. During observation, you will look with the naked eye, if you see something, then use binoculars, and to clearly identify what you're looking at the spotting scope is used, adjusting the magnification.

Free-floating barrel A barrel that does not touch the stock or any other part of a rifle. The most accuracy you can get is from a barrel that is screwed into the action, but does not touch anything else.

Grain A unit of weight, there being 7,000 grains in a pound, and 437 grains in one ounce. The weight of a powder charge and the weight of a bullet are expressed in grains.

Group A number of shots, usually three to five, fired by a shooter at the one target using the same point of aim, position and hold.

Hide The temporary or permanent position a sniper occupies to engage a target. This should have excellent concealment and cover, good observation, and good entry and escape routes.

Hold off Aiming off to compensate for wind.

Lead The amount of allowance used by a sniper to lead in front of a moving target.

Line of sight (LOS) An imaginary straight line from the firer's eye through the sights to the point of aim.

Mil dot A tiny dot of very exact dimension in the scope's reticle pattern, used for range estimation, lead and hold off.

Minute of angle (MOA) A measurement that measures 1 inch at 100 yards (27mm at 100 metres). When a shooter says he can achieve a ½ MOA group at 100 metres, he means he placed three to five rounds on a target at 100 metres that measured 12–13 mm apart.

Mirage Heat waves. The image of the target will be slightly displaced due to the refraction of light through the heat waves; how much the target will be displacement depends on how fast the mirage is running. A sniper needs to be able to read a mirage accurately as it will help him an estimate on wind speed.

Mean point of impact (MPI) The centre of a group.

Muzzle brake A recoil reducing device attached to the end of a barrel that defects blast sideways or backwards to pull the rifle slightly forward. Unfortunately on the larger calibres like the .50 calibre, it will produce more of a signature, i.e. create more dust from the blast.

Point of aim The point where the sights are aimed.

Point of impact The point where the round strikes first.

Prone position Lying flat, head and shoulders raised and supported by the elbows leaving the hands free to hold and operate the weapon.

Rate of twist Term used to describe rifling by the distance in inches a bullet passes in the barrel during a single rotation. A .308 sniper rifle will typically have a 1:12 rate of twist, one complete turn in 12 inches.

Recoil The rearward movement of a rifle produced by its discharge. The severity depends on calibre, weight and velocity of the round. Other factors are the weight of the rifle (the lighter the rifle the more recoil), the design of the stock and the use of a suppressor (suppressors will reduce recoil).

Reticle Crosshair.

Rifling The helix formed in the bore of a barrel to give a spinning motion to a projectile passing through it. This spinning motion is what gives the projectile its accuracy and will keep it stable on its flight.

Range card A detailed sketch of a sector or arc of fire including all prominent terrain and man-made features, likely enemy routes and dead ground, also including ranges to key points. Can also include weather conditions and wind strengths for rapid adjustments to engage targets, can also include bearing to key points.

Sniper data A detailed record of ballistic data developed and periodically modified, on the performance of a particular sniper rifle and ammunition during varying weather conditions and ranges.

Spotter A sniper who helps another sniper detect and identify targets, then adjust his fire onto the target. He is also responsible for close range security. Usually called the No. 1 and No. 2, the No. 1 being the shooter and No. 2 the observer.

Suppressor A device that uses baffles and/or fine mesh to dissipate and slow the escape of gases from a weapon muzzle, reducing noise and signature. Usually affects trajectory, and can sometimes even increase accuracy.

Sear The lock or catch in a weapon that holds the firing pin back until released by the trigger.

Shooting platform Anything a sniper can use to

place himself or his weapon to accurately shoot from.

Swirl The disturbance in the air the observer can see through optics from a spinning projectile. This gives a good indication of where your round has struck the target, or missed.

Terminal velocity The remaining velocity or speed of a projectile at the point in its downward path where it is level with the muzzle of the weapon.

Trajectory The curved path the projectile follows on leaving the barrel until it strikes the target.

Trigger pull The resistance offered by a trigger when pressure is put on it. The force to overcome this is expressed in pounds or kilos. The average trigger pull is 3–6 pounds. The less trigger pull, the less you will anticipate the recoil and the shot will be release without any undue stress on the rifle.

Trigger squeeze The correct method of firing a weapon.

Tumble Used to describe a projectile that turns end over end.

Windage The amount of adjustment required to compensate or allow for the action of wind on the projectile in flight.

Zero The adjustment of an optical or open sight so that a bullet precisely hits a target at a given distance.

ABBREVIATIONS

AFP	Australian Federal Police
AME	air medical evacuation
ANA	Afghan National Army
AO	Area of Operations
AP	armour piercing
ATV	all-terrain vehicle
BPT	brigade patrol troop
CDF	Chief of the Defence Force
CO	commanding officer
CT	counter-terrorism
CTC	Commando Training Centre
DOP	drop-off point
DS	directing staff
FOB	forward operating base
GPMG	general purpose machine-gun
HE	high explosive

HME	home-made explosive
IA	immediate action
IED	improvised explosive device
IRA	Irish Republican Army
IRR	incident response regiment
JTAC	joint terminal attack controller
KIA	killed in action
LP	landing point
LRPV	long-range patrol vehicle
LSW	light support weapon
LUP	lay-up position
LZ	landing zone
MVT	medium-value target
NBC	nuclear, biological and chemical warfare
NVG	night vision goggles
OHP	overhead protection
OP	observation post
PLCE	personal load carrying equipment
PRC	potential recruits course
PSD	personal security detail
PT	physical training, 'phys'
PTI	physical training instructors
Q	quarter-master
QRF	quick reaction force
RPG	rocket-propelled grenade
RPs	restriction of privileges
RSM	regimental sergeant major
RUC	Royal Ulster Constabulary
RV	rendezvous
SAS	Special Air Service

SASR	Special Air Service Regiment
SF	sustained fire
SNCO	senior noncommissioned officer
SOP	standard operating procedure
SRO	special recovery operations
SSM	squadron sergeant major
STG	Special Tactics Group
TCL	tactical coordination line
TGT	target
TI	thermal imagers
TNI	Indonesian Army (Tentara Nasional Indonesia)
TOW	tube-launched, optically tracked, wire command, data link, guided missile
UFF	Ulster Freedom Fighters